D1348306

LEICESTER CITY

On This Day & Miscellany

Foxes Anecdotes, Legends, Stats & Facts

LEICESTER CITY
On This Day & Miscellany
Foxes Anecdotes, Legends, Stats & Facts

Matt Bozeat

LEICESTER CITY
On This Day & Miscellany
Foxes Anecdotes, Legends, Stats & Facts

All statistics, facts and figures are correct as of 1st October 2016

© Matt Bozeat

Matt Bozeat has asserted his rights in accordance with the Copyright, Designs and Patents Act 1988 to be identified as the author of this work.

Published By:
Pitch Publishing (Brighton) Ltd
A2 Yeoman Gate
Yeoman Way
Durrington
BN13 3QZ

Email: info@pitchpublishing.co.uk
Web: www.pitchpublishing.co.uk

First published 2008
Reprinted 2014, 2016

A catalogue record for this book is available from the British Library.

10-digit ISBN: 1-9054112-8-6
13-digit ISBN: 978-1-9054112-8-3

Printed and bound in Great Britain by TJ International

For Carla, Lydia, Mum and Dad

Always in my thoughts, Mum

INTRODUCTION

Long before they were the nation's favourite football team, Leicester City were my favourite football team. I waited 35 years – or thereabouts – to see them finish on top of the top division in English football.

Except, I hadn't.

I gave up on "Cit-eh" ever doing such a thing back in 1981. Then-manager Jock Wallace predicted Leicester would win Division One in the afterglow of victory over champions Liverpool at Filbert Street. We were relegated instead. Growing up, City were either fighting to stay in the top flight – or trying to get in it. And our best players always seemed to join Everton.

The Martin O'Neill era – four top ten finishes and a couple of League Cups – was surely as good as it was going to get...

Matt Bozeat – November 2016

LEICESTER CITY
On This Day & Miscellany

JANUARY

MONDAY 1ST JANUARY 1979

Gary Lineker made his Leicester City debut in a 2-0 win over Oldham Athletic at Filbert Street in a Division Two fixture. He didn't score, was dropped and had to wait more than three months for his first goal. Dave Buchanan grabbed the headlines against Oldham when he became City's youngest ever Football League debutant and youngest ever goalscorer at the age of 16 years 192 days.

SATURDAY 2ND JANUARY 1982

Jock Wallace's Leicester City started their FA Cup bid with a 3-1 win over Division One visitors Southampton at Filbert Street. A crowd of 20,598 saw Alan Young's powerful header send City on their way to victory. Young added another goal and Gary Lineker bagged the other for the Foxes with Kevin Keegan notching the Saints' reply.

FRIDAY 2ND JANUARY 1951

The television cameras came to Filbert Street for the first time to capture the action in an amateur international between England and Wales.

SATURDAY 3RD JANUARY 1987

Steve Moran bagged a hat-trick for Leicester City in a stunning 6-1 demolition of Sheffield Wednesday at Filbert Street. Alan Smith (2) and Paul Ramsey got the others.

SATURDAY 3RD JANUARY 1998

Leicester City took on Northampton Town in the third round of the FA Cup and there were those predicting an upset. Martin O'Neill's team were without a win in their previous five games and the Cobblers were going well in Division Two. But the visitors were never in the game. Ian Marshall, Garry Parker (penalty), Robbie Savage and Tony Cottee got the goals in a 4-0 romp and the visitors had defender Ian Clarkson sent off in the second half following a stamp on Muzzy Izzet.

SATURDAY 3RD JANUARY 2000

Matt Elliott's brace ensures Leicester City start the new Millennium with a 2-2 draw at Everton. The result ends a run of four successive defeats for the Foxes.

SATURDAY 4TH JANUARY 1992

Richard Smith volleyed in a last-gasp winner against top-flight visitors Crystal Palace at Filbert Street to send Leicester City into the draw for the fourth round of the FA Cup for the first time since 1985.

SATURDAY 5TH JANUARY 1985

Gary Lineker grabbed a hat-trick in the FA Cup third round clash with Burton Albion at Derby County's Baseball Ground, and then had it erased from the record books. The FA ordered the game to be replayed behind closed doors after Burton goalkeeper Paul Evans was struck by a missile thrown from the crowd. Alan Smith (2) and Steve Lynex also had goals wiped off after the FA's ruling.

SATURDAY 5TH JANUARY 1980

Neil Prosser popped up with an injury-time leveller for Isthmian League side Harlow Town at Filbert Street and Jock Wallace's Leicester City were heading for FA Cup humiliation. Martin Henderson had put Leicester ahead on 27 minutes and they should have had several more before the minnows secured a replay in the dying moments of the third round clash.

SATURDAY 5TH JANUARY 1991

David Pleat's Leicester City fell apart at Millwall in an FA Cup third round tie. They had both Paul Ramsey and Steve Walsh sent off and the lead given them by Tony James was wiped out by goals from the Lions in the 86th and 89th minutes.

SATURDAY 6TH JANUARY 1979

Keith Weller wore white tights while playing for Leicester City against Norwich City in the FA Cup third round at Filbert Street and scored a typically spectacular solo goal in a 3-0 win. He went on a run that took him past three challenges before firing home. It proved to be his last goal for the Foxes. Weller had earlier crossed for Larry May to put Leicester ahead. Martin Henderson bagged the third while Andy Peake also made his debut for the Foxes.

FRIDAY 7TH JANUARY 2000

Leicester City legend Ken Keyworth died in Rotherham, Yorkshire.

SUNDAY 8TH JANUARY 2006

Leicester City, struggling in the Championship under Craig Levein, took on Premier League Tottenham Hotspur at Filbert Street in the third round of the FA Cup. The game was going with the form book when the visitors took a 2-0 first-half lead in front of the BBC television cameras. Elvis Hammond gave Leicester hope, Stephen Hughes smashed in a second-half leveller and the Foxes snatched last-gasp glory when Mark De Vries made amends for an earlier miss by rolling home the winner in the dying seconds.

WEDNESDAY 8TH JANUARY 1992

Paul Fitzpatrick's diving header in the pouring rain in front of around 8,000 Leicester City fans at Meadow Lane sent Brian Little's team through to the northern final of the Zenith Data Systems Cup. His goal secured a 2-1 win for the Foxes after Tommy Wright had earlier cancelled out Craig Short's opener for the home side. The win set up a two-legged clash against Nottingham Forest with the winners going through to face the southern winners in the final at Wembley.

TUESDAY 8TH JANUARY 1980

Leicester City were beaten by non-league opposition in the FA Cup for the first time since 1914-15. John Mackenzie's goal secured a famous giant-killing for Harlow Town at their cramped Hammarskjold Road Sports Centre after a 1-1 draw.

SATURDAY 9TH JANUARY 1932

Ernie Hine bagged five goals as Leicester City romped to a 7-0 win at Crook Town in the FA Cup. Arthur Chandler and Walter Langford got the other goals for the Foxes.

SATURDAY 10TH JANUARY 1914

A cracking FA Cup fifth round tie against Tottenham Hotspur at Filbert Street saw Claude Stoodley's four goals haul Leicester City into a 5-3 lead with just ten minutes left. Spurs hit back to level and then won the replay 2-0.

WEDNESDAY 11TH JANUARY 1956

Arthur Rowley's hat-trick fired Leicester City to a 4-0 win at Luton Town in an FA Cup third round tie. Bill Gardiner got the other goal.

WEDNESDAY 11TH JANUARY 1978

Emile Heskey was born in Leicester.

SATURDAY 11TH JANUARY 1975

Mark Wallington started his spell of 331 consecutive games in goal for Leicester City in a 3-0 defeat at Everton in Division One.

WEDNESDAY 12TH JANUARY 2000

Leicester City went through to the quarter-finals of the League Cup after a thrilling clash against Fulham at Filbert Street. Geoff Horsfield, who went on to play for City, looked to have put the game beyond the home side when he netted after 75 minutes to make it 2-0 to the visitors. Steve Walsh's misdirected pass had led to Horsfield's goal and he set about making amends in stunning style with his rampaging run leading to Ian Marshall pulling a goal back. Walsh then sent the game into extra time with an equaliser. Fulham went ahead again, but Marshall made it 3-3 and Leicester held their nerve in the penalty shoot-out to go through 3-0.

SATURDAY 13TH JANUARY 1934

Leicester City started their bid for the FA Cup with a 3-0 win over Lincoln City at Filbert Street. The goals came from Arthur Maw, Arthur Lochhead and Jim Paterson.

SUNDAY 13TH JANUARY 1990

David Pleat's side self destructed on Tyneside. They led 4-2 at Newcastle United with just 16 minutes left and lost a nine-goal thriller with future Foxes boss Mark McGhee the last-gasp goal hero. David Oldfield made his Leicester City debut after joining in an exchange deal that took Wayne Clarke to Manchester City and the sides were level at 2-2 at the break. Tommy Wright and Steve Walsh were on target and Gary McAllister and Kevin Campbell put Leicester in charge at 4-2 before it all went wrong.

SATURDAY 14TH JANUARY 1984

Gary Lineker hit a hat-trick in a 5-2 win at Notts County in Division One. Kevin MacDonald and Andy Peake got the others.

SATURDAY 14TH JANUARY 1950

Willie Frame played his 459th and last game for Leicester City in the 3-0 defeat at Blackburn Rovers.

THURSDAY 16TH JANUARY 1997

Matt Elliott decided to join Leicester City, rather than Southampton, from Oxford United in a £1.6m deal.

SATURDAY 17TH JANUARY 2004

Micky Adams' Leicester City were stunned as Middlesbrough netted twice in injury time to snatch a point from their Premiership clash at the Riverside Stadium. Juninho put the home side ahead, latching on to a poor clearance from Leicester goalkeeper Ian Walker, who then made amends by keeping out Joseph Desire-Job's penalty. Leicester were level shortly after the restart, although Paul Dickov appeared to convert Steve Guppy's corner with his hand. Dickov put City ahead by converting Riccardo Scimeca's flick on after 65 minutes and the home side were in disarray when Marcus Bent's close-range finish made it 3-1. That was the way it stayed going into the last minute. Massimo Maccarone's goal appeared to be just a consolation for Middlesbrough, but they went on to snatch a point in the second minute of injury time through an own goal from Leicester defender John Curtis.

SATURDAY 18TH JANUARY 1997

Matt Elliott made his Leicester City debut in a 1-0 win at Wimbledon secured by Emile Heskey's goal.

TUESDAY 18TH JANUARY 2000

Joey Gudjonsson lashed home from 35 yards to secure a 1-0 win at Blackpool, and a trip to Championship rivals Reading in the fourth round of the FA Cup. The sides had battled to a 1-1 draw at the Walkers Stadium ten days earlier. Blackpool's line-up included former Leicester City skipper Simon Grayson.

WEDNESDAY 19TH JANUARY 2000

Leicester City went through to the fifth round of the FA Cup after a dramatic penalty shoot-out against Arsenal at Filbert Street. The Foxes hadn't won any of the previous ten meetings between the teams and it took several fine saves from goalkeeper Tim Flowers to keep the scoreline blank after 90 minutes to send the match into extra time. Flowers was replaced by Frenchman Pegguy Arphexad and he was City's hero in a shoot-out – that stretched to 14 kicks – saving Gilles Grimandi's kick to send City through 6-5 after Arnar Gunnlaugsson, Robbie Savage, Graham Fenton, Matt Elliott, Stuart Campbell and Emile Heskey had been on target for Martin O'Neill's team.

WEDNESDAY 19TH JANUARY 1972

Leicester City beat Wolverhampton Wanderers 2-0 in an FA Cup third round replay at Filbert Street and a crowd of 37,060 set a new record for gate receipts at the ground of £17,000. John Farrington and Len Glover got the goals.

WEDNESDAY 20TH JANUARY 1993

Julian Joachim scored a stunning solo goal at Barnsley in the FA Cup third round replay. He latched on to the ball just inside Barnsley's half, raced to the edge of the penalty area and then bent a right-footed shot into the top corner. It won the BBC's 'Goal of the Month' award, but Leicester City lost the match on penalties.

THURSDAY 20TH JANUARY 1938

Derek Dougan was born in Belfast.

SATURDAY 20TH JANUARY 2001

Roberto Mancini made his Leicester City debut in a 0-0 draw against Arsenal at Filbert Street to become the Foxes' oldest-ever debutant at the age of 36 years and 54 days old. City grabbed a point against the Gunners despite Matt Jones being sent off.

SATURDAY 20TH JANUARY 1962

Mike Stringfellow made his Leicester City debut in a 3-2 defeat at Everton. Jimmy Walsh and Howard Riley (penalty) were the Foxes' marksmen.

SATURDAY 21ST JANUARY 1961

Leicester City hammered Manchester United 6-0 in a Division One clash at Filbert Street. There were two goals apiece for Jimmy Walsh and Ken Keyworth in the romp in front of 31,308 fans. The other goals came from Gordon Wills and Howard Riley (penalty).

SATURDAY 21ST JANUARY 1989

Leicester-born goalkeeper Carl Muggleton made his Foxes debut in a 1-1 draw at West Bromwich Albion. Paul Reid grabbed City's goal in the Division Two clash.

SATURDAY 22ND JANUARY 1972

Keith Weller's stunning solo goal silenced the Trent End and sent Leicester City on their way to a 2-1 win at local rivals Nottingham Forest in Division One. Weller danced his way through several challenges before shooting home. Alan Birchenall got the other goal with Ian Storey-Moore grabbing Forest's reply.

SATURDAY 22ND JANUARY 1993

Leicester City and Notts County battled out a 1-1 draw at Filbert Street. Julian Joachim was on target for Brian Little's Leicester and the visitors' reply came from Mark Draper, who went on to play for the Foxes.

SATURDAY 22ND JANUARY 1999

Martin O'Neill's team suffered FA Cup embarrassment at Filbert Street. His Leicester City side were beaten 3-0 by Coventry City in a third round tie after two late goals.

SATURDAY 23RD JANUARY 1982

Jock Wallace's Leicester City went through to the fifth round of the FA Cup after coming away from Fourth Division Hereford United with a 1-0 win. Larry May headed home the only goal to ensure a tricky tie ended in victory and put City in to the hat for the last sixteen.

SATURDAY 23RD JANUARY 1937

Leicester City striker Jack Bowers continued his prolific form in front of goal. He scored for the sixth successive game in a 3-2 win over Plymouth Argyle that lifted the Foxes up to third in Division Two.

SATURDAY 24TH JANUARY 1920

Adam Black made the first of his 557 appearances for Leicester City in a 3-2 win over Hull City at Filbert Street. Jock Paterson (penalty), Ernie Walker and George Douglas got the City goals in a game that marked the start of a career that went on to span 15 years and 16 days.

TUESDAY 25TH JANUARY 2000

A goalless draw at Villa Park put Leicester in the driving seat in their League Cup semi-final. Aston Villa boss and former Foxes coach John Gregory suggested City had not attempted to cross the halfway line during the game, while City boss Martin O'Neill hailed a heroic performance from his side. Leicester had been hit hard by injuries and Tim Flowers made a couple of crucial saves.

WEDNESDAY 25TH JANUARY 2006

Craig Levein was sacked as Leicester City manager with the Foxes 22nd in the Championship.

WEDNESDAY 25TH JANUARY 1995

Mark Robins marked his debut for Leicester City after a £1m move from Norwich City with the only goal of the game at Premier League rivals Manchester City. The game was played in atrocious weather conditions and many supporters didn't reach Maine Road until 20 minutes before the final whistle while others didn't get there at all. Those that did make it saw Robins head home Jamie Lawrence's cross to boost Mark McGhee's team's chances of avoiding relegation. City printed a limited edition T-shirt for supporters who made it to Maine Road.

SATURDAY 25TH JANUARY 1975

A crowd of 32,090 at Filbert Street saw a classic FA Cup fourth round tie. Leicester City were 2-0 down at half-time against Isthmian League underdogs Leatherhead and only a goalline clearance prevented the Foxes falling further behind. Jon Sammels started City's second-half fightback, Steve Earle levelled the scores and Keith Weller spared the Foxes' blushes with the winning goal in a five-goal thriller.

TUESDAY 26TH JANUARY 2002

Martin O'Neill's team headed to Sunderland for the first leg of the League Cup semi-final after back-to-back drubbings at Filbert Street against Manchester United and Coventry City, by scores of 6-2 and 3-0, respectively. Sunderland were top of Division One, but Tony Cottee netted twice to hand Leicester City a 2-0 advantage going into the second leg.

SATURDAY 26TH JANUARY 1991

A 3-1 defeat at Filbert Street against Blackburn Rovers spelled the end of David Pleat's spell as manager of Leicester City. David Kelly scored City's goal and supporters protested as the Foxes crashed to a defeat that left them in deep trouble at the bottom of Division Two.

SATURDAY 27TH JANUARY 1968

Leicester City avoided being on the receiving end of an FA Cup third round upset at Colin Appleton's Barrow. Appleton was player-manager at the club in the Lake District and had inspired them to wins over Oldham Athletic and Altrincham in the previous rounds, but they were behind after three minutes against City. Frank Large's cross was turned into his own net by a Barrow defender and John Sjoberg headed home the second nine minutes after the restart before the home side pulled a goal back.

SATURDAY 27TH JANUARY 2001

Arnar Gunnlaugsson smacked home a spectacular winner to secure a 2-1 win at Aston Villa and send Leicester City through to the fifth round of the FA Cup. Ade Akinbiyi got City's opener and former Foxes striker Julian Joachim replied.

WEDNESDAY 27TH JANUARY 1943

Mike Stringfellow was born in Kirkby-in-Ashfield in Nottinghamshire.

SATURDAY 27TH JANUARY 1934

Leicester City booked their place in the fifth round of the FA Cup with a 6-3 win at Millwall. Arthur Chandler led the goal blitz with a double strike and the others came from Sep Smith, Arthur Maw, Arthur Lochhead and Danny Liddle.

SATURDAY 28TH JANUARY 1995

Iwan Roberts grabbed the only goal for Leicester City in an FA Cup fourth round tie at Portsmouth to send the Foxes through to the last sixteen.

MONDAY 28TH JANUARY 1991

David Pleat was sacked as Leicester manager with his side just above the relegation zone in Division Two.

SATURDAY 28TH JANUARY 1911

David Walker went down in the history books as the first Leicester Fosse player to ever be sent off at Filbert Street. He was dismissed in the Division Two game against Clapton Orient having earlier scored what turned out to be the winner in a 2-1 victory. Fred Shinton grabbed City's other goal.

SATURDAY 29TH JANUARY 2005

Leicester City came from behind to snatch a dramatic win at Reading in the fourth round of the FA Cup. The game was going with the form book when the Premier League Royals went ahead against their struggling visitors from the Championship with only ten minutes gone. Nicky Forster was on target and City should have fallen further behind 12 minutes later, but former Foxes striker Les Ferdinand shot wide when he had the goal at his mercy. Gareth Williams got the equaliser for the visitors on 32 minutes after smart work from David Connolly and James Scowcroft had carved open the Royals' defence. Scowcroft went on to be the Foxes' match winner in the last minute. He powered home a header from Jordan Stewart's cross to take his team through to the last 16.

SATURDAY 30TH JANUARY 1937

Leicester City suffered FA Cup embarrassment at Exeter City. The home side were locked in a battle at the bottom of Division Three (South) and sensed an upset after just ten minutes when an injury to Sep Smith meant City were left with only ten men. Exeter went on to claim a 3-1 victory with Danny Liddle on target for the Foxes.

SATURDAY 31ST JANUARY 1981

Jock Wallace's team inflicted the first home defeat on all-conquering Liverpool for 85 matches. They made the trip having lost their previous five games, but went on to topple the defending champions through goals from Pat Byrne and Jim Melrose in a 2-1 win at Anfield. Alan Young's own goal wasn't enough for the Reds to prevent City claiming a famous league double. City had been 2-0 victors when the sides clashed at Filbert Street five months earlier. The win lifted the Foxes off the bottom of the Division One table.

SATURDAY 31ST JANUARY 1998

Tony Cottee stunned Premiership leaders Manchester United with the goal that handed Leicester City their first win at Old Trafford in 17 visits. United had dropped just two Premier League points in front of their home fans that season before the game, and that all changed when Tony Cottee lifted home his first goal for the Foxes from a tight angle in the first half after latching on to Robbie Savage's pass. It was Cottee's first goal for City in just his third start for the club.

SATURDAY 31ST JANUARY 1976

Bob Lee grabbed the only goal for Leicester City in a 1-0 win over Manchester City in a Division One clash at Filbert Street. The result lifted them up to 13th in the table.

SATURDAY 31ST JANUARY 1970

Leicester City stayed ninth in Division One despite a 2-1 defeat at Watford. Len Glover was on target for the Foxes, but it wasn't enough to prevent them suffering back-to-back defeats. The result also made it four games without a win for City.

TUESDAY 31ST JANUARY 1961

Leicester City stormed through to the fifth round of the FA Cup with a 5-1 demolition of Bristol City at Filbert Street. There were two goals apiece for Ken Leek and Jimmy Walsh. Gordon Wills got the other goal.

LEICESTER CITY
On This Day & Miscellany

FEBRUARY

SATURDAY 1ST FEBRUARY 1986

Gordon Milne's team twice hit back after falling behind at Stamford Bridge to secure a point against Chelsea. The home side were chasing European qualification and the game was going with the form book when Duncan Shearer gave the home side the lead. Ali Mauchlen levelled for Leicester City and Steve Lynex secured a point with a 71st minute spot kick after Keith Jones had restored Chelsea's lead.

WEDNESDAY 2ND FEBRUARY 2000

Matt Elliott's header against Aston Villa at Filbert Street sent Leicester City back to Wembley for a third League Cup final in four years. Martin O'Neill's line-up included several players some way short of full fitness and they were fired up by Villa boss John Gregory's remarks about their lack of ambition in the first leg eight days earlier. Stef Oakes rattled the woodwork before Elliott headed home what proved to be the winner for the Foxes.

SATURDAY 3RD FEBRUARY 1962

David Gibson made his Leicester City debut and formed a partnership with fellow new signing Mike Stringfellow that helped inspire a 4-1 drubbing of Fulham in Division One. Fulham had been a bogey side for the Foxes in previous seasons and that looked set to continue when Johnny Haynes put the visitors ahead at Filbert Street. But Jimmy Walsh fired home the leveller for City and then a quick-fire double strike from Ken Keyworth and Howard Riley (penalty) put Leicester in charge at 3-1 ahead. Stringfellow then teed up Walsh's second to complete the scoring and end the jinx.

SATURDAY 3RD FEBRUARY 1968

Rodney Fern made his Leicester City debut in a 2-2 draw against Leeds United at Filbert Street. He was handed his chance in front of his home crowd by manager Bert Johnson, who was acting as caretaker manager during Matt Gillies' sick leave. City's scorers against Leeds were Mike Stringfellow and Frank Large.

SATURDAY 4TH FEBRUARY 1961

Leicester City became the first team to win at Tottenham Hotspur in a season that ended with the Londoners winning the Division One and FA Cup double. Jimmy Walsh was the two-goal hero for City in a 3-2 win. Ken Leek also scored.

SATURDAY 4TH FEBRUARY 1950

Leicester City stunned runaway Division Two leaders Tottenham Hotspur at White Hart Lane to give Norman Bullock's team a massive lift as they battled against the drop. There were 60,595 fans crammed inside White Hart Lane to watch the action and that remained the biggest crowd to watch Leicester until 2001. Most of them went home unhappy after goals from Charlie Adam and Bert Barlow secured maximum points for City.

SATURDAY 4TH FEBRUARY 1967

Bobby Roberts grabbed the only goal for Leicester City in a 1-0 win at Aston Villa that kept the Foxes eighth in Division One.

SATURDAY 4TH FEBRUARY 1984

Alan Smith's goal double couldn't save Leicester City from a 3-2 defeat at home to Birmingham City in Division One. Andy Peake's own goal proved to be the winner for the Blues.

SATURDAY 4TH FEBRUARY 1995

Leicester City were beaten 2-1 at home by West Ham United at Filbert Street. Mark Robins was on target for the Foxes making it two goals in as many games in the Premier League for the striker following his transfer to Filbert Street from Norwich City in a £1m deal. The defeat against the Hammers meant City stayed rooted to the foot of the table.

SATURDAY 4TH FEBRUARY 1956

Leicester City powered to a 5-1 win over Plymouth Argyle that lifted them up to third place in the Division Two table. Howard Riley and Arthur Rowley netted two goals apiece for the Foxes in the romp in front of 23,610 fans at Filbert Street and the other goal came from Jack Froggatt.

SATURDAY 5TH FEBRUARY 1972

Young goalkeeper Carl Jayes had a nightmare as Leicester City crashed out of the fourth round of the FA Cup against Jimmy Bloomfield's Leyton Orient at Filbert Street. Jayes was at fault for the second goal that took the game beyond the Foxes.

WEDNESDAY 5TH FEBRUARY 1964

Leicester City edged out West Ham United 4-3 in the first leg of the League Cup semi-final at Filbert Street. The Foxes were in charge at 4-1 through goals from Ken Keyworth, Bobby Roberts, Mike Stringfellow and Frank McLintock before the Hammers pulled two goals back with Geoff Hurst netting twice to give his side a lifeline going into the second leg the following month.

SATURDAY 5TH FEBRUARY 1983

Leicester City boss Gordon Milne had signed Gerry Daly on loan from Coventry City to boost his side's flagging hopes of gaining promotion from Division Two and he made his debut in the 1-0 win at Carlisle United. Kevin MacDonald got the only goal to spark City's promotion bid.

THURSDAY 5TH FEBRUARY 1931

Percy Richards made his Leicester City debut against Arsenal – and couldn't prevent the Gunners romping to a 7-2 win at Filbert Street. Jack Lambert bagged a hat-trick for the visitors and Cliff Bastin added a brace, while Ernie Hine grabbed both goals for the Foxes.

SATURDAY 6TH FEBRUARY 1909

Leicester Fosse bowed out of the FA Cup after a second round defeat against Derby County. The estimated crowd of 22,000 is believed to be the highest to have watched Fosse play at Filbert Street.

SUNDAY 6TH FEBRUARY 1955

Norman Bullock resigned as Leicester City manager with the Foxes in trouble near the bottom of Division One. His side had lost 2-0 at Newcastle United the previous day and an incident in a Whitley Bay hotel following the game resulted in his resignation. Johnny Morris, Bullock's main adversary, was suspended for 14 days.

SATURDAY 7TH FEBRUARY 1998

Theo Zagorakis made his Leicester City debut as a substitute against Leeds United at Filbert Street. Zagorakis was Greece's Player of the Year in 1997 and masterminded PAOK's victory over Arsenal in the Uefa Cup the following season to convince Leicester boss Martin O'Neill to sign him for £250,000 from PAOK. His debut ended with a 1-0 victory thanks to Garry Parker's penalty.

SATURDAY 8TH FEBRUARY 1964

George Best made his first visit to Filbert Street – and went home a loser. Leicester City had won five of their previous six league games and were fired up to avenge defeat against Manchester United in the FA Cup final nine months earlier. City still had nine of the cup final team in their line up, but it was Billy Hodgson, replacing the injured Howard Riley, who was the two-goal hero in a 3-2 win. Mike Stringfellow got the other and United's goals came from Denis Law and David Herd.

SATURDAY 9TH FEBRUARY 1957

David Halliday's Leicester City retained top spot in Division Two with a thrilling 3-2 win over promotion rivals Liverpool at Filbert Street. Billy Liddell and John Evans put the Merseysiders 2-0 ahead at the break and the City fightback was started by Derek Hines on 63 minutes. Arthur Rowley bagged the leveller and then buried a penalty with ten minutes left to secure a breathtaking come-from-behind victory.

FRIDAY 9TH FEBRUARY 1968

An unforgettable night at Filbert Street. Leicester City were 2-0 down inside half an hour against Manchester City in their FA Cup fourth round replay, but hit back to win 4-3 with Frank Large the two-goal hero. Rodney Fern and David Nish were the other scorers for the Foxes.

SATURDAY 9TH FEBRUARY 1935

Adam Black played the last game of a Leicester City career that included 557 appearances. But the occasion wasn't marked with a win as City were beaten 2-0 at Sunderland.

SATURDAY 10TH FEBRUARY 1973

Alan Birchenall will tell you all about his second goal against Leeds United at Filbert Street on this day if you ask him. In fact, you probably won't have to ask him! Leicester City hadn't beaten Leeds at home since 1959 and Birchenall got the breakthrough on 22 minutes when he stabbed home John Farrington's cross. His second came 11 minutes after the break and was a belter. He lashed home an unstoppable volley after Leeds goalkeeper David Harvey had saved from Frank Worthington. At the other end of the pitch, Malcolm Manley and Graham Cross performed heroics at the heart of Leicester's defence to keep out former Foxes striker Allan Clarke and Mick Jones.

SATURDAY 11TH FEBRUARY 1995

Leicester City, struggling at the bottom of the Premier League under Mark McGhee, clinched a surprise point at Arsenal. Mark Draper was on target for City and Paul Merson grabbed the Gunners' reply at Highbury.

WEDNESDAY 12TH FEBRUARY 1992

Leicester City and Nottingham Forest battled out a 1-1 draw in the first leg of the northern final of the Zenith Data Systems Cup. The prize at stake was a trip to Wembley for the final to face the winners of the southern final. Colin Gordon headed home in the second half to cancel out Scott Gemmill's opener and give Foxes' fans some cause for hope going into the second leg at the City Ground.

SATURDAY 13TH FEBRUARY 1988

Leicester City's revival under David Pleat continued with a 3-2 win over Leeds United at Filbert Street. Gary McAllister netted twice – including a penalty – and Nicky Cross got the other goal.

FRIDAY 14TH FEBRUARY 1896

Future Leicester City player and manager John Duncan was born in Lochgelly, Fife.

SATURDAY 14TH FEBRUARY 1981

Steve Lynex made his Leicester City debut in a 1-0 defeat at Sunderland after joining the Foxes from Birmingham City for £60,000.

SATURDAY 15TH FEBRUARY 1975

Leicester City held Arsenal to a goalless draw in an FA Cup fifth-round clash at Highbury. It was the fifth meeting between the sides during the season and City made the trip in confident mood having drawn previous games in North London in the league and League Cup. They had been boosted by the arrival of former Gunners defender Jeff Blockley since their last meeting and he played a major role in helping the Foxes secure a replay at Filbert Street.

SATURDAY 15TH FEBRUARY 1992

Kevin Russell was recalled to the starting line-up for the trip to Port Vale and was Leicester City's match-winner with both goals in a 2-1 win. He was on target after 11 and 68 minutes and City held on as the home side produced a grandstand finish.

SATURDAY 16TH FEBRUARY 1973

Leicester City were likened to Brazil by the national press after winning 4-0 at Luton in the fifth round of the FA Cup. Steve Earle got the first two, Frank Worthington added a third and Keith Weller completed the scoring in sensational style by dancing past several tackles on the muddy pitch and smacking an unstoppable left-foot shot into the top corner.

WEDNESDAY 17TH FEBRUARY 1999

Leicester City went into the second leg of their League Cup semi-final against Sunderland at Filbert Street leading 2-1, but were soon under pressure as Niall Quinn levelled the aggregate scores after 34 minutes. City still held the advantage on the away goals rule, but Tony Cottee eased the nerves with a 54th minute goal that followed his double strike in the first leg. Goalkeeper Kasey Keller ensured Leicester kept their advantage with a late save from Quinn.

SATURDAY 17TH FEBRUARY 1934

Arthur Chandler's two goals secured a 2-1 win at Birmingham City and sent Leicester City through to the quarter-finals of the FA Cup.

SATURDAY 18TH FEBRUARY 1898

Adam Black was born in Denny, Stirlingshire. He went on to make a club record 528 Football League appearances for Leicester City.

SATURDAY 18TH FEBRUARY 1995

Garry Parker made his Leicester City debut in an FA Cup fifth-round clash at Wolverhampton Wanderers. Parker arrived from Aston Villa and his signing helped smooth relations between the clubs following Brian Little's acrimonious departure from Filbert Street three months earlier. But his presence in midfield couldn't prevent City crashing to a 1-0 defeat at Molineux. Former Foxes striker David Kelly got the goal for the home team.

TUESDAY 18TH FEBRUARY 1997

Robert Ullathorne lasted just 11 minutes of his Leicester City debut as the Foxes battled out a goalless draw against Wimbledon in the first leg of the League Cup semi-final at Filbert Street. He was stretchered off with a broken ankle after twisting as he challenged for the ball. Emile Heskey went closest to breaking the deadlock in the game with a shot that came back off the post.

SATURDAY 18TH FEBRUARY 1928

An FA Cup fifth round clash against Tottenham Hotspur attracted a record crowd to Filbert Street. The majority of a crowd of 47,298 went home unhappy after Spurs went through to the sixth round with a 3-0 win.

SATURDAY 19TH FEBRUARY 2005

Dion Dublin's late header stunned Premiership Charlton Athletic at The Valley and sent Craig Levein's Leicester City through to the quarter-finals of the FA Cup. Leicester were on top early on and it was no surprise when Nikos Dabizas put them ahead with a 38th minute header from Danny Tiatto's cross. Charlton grabbed an equaliser in first half injury time through Shaun Bartlett. But City took the game to their hosts after the break and got their reward with just 13 seconds of normal time left when Dublin headed home to send the 4,000 travelling fans into ecstasy.

SATURDAY 20TH FEBRUARY 1999

Leicester City fielded the most cosmopolitan team in their history in the Premier League at Highbury. Martin O'Neill's starting 11 included nine different nationalities: Kasey Keller (USA), Pontus Kaamark (Sweden), Frank Sinclair (Jamaica), Matt Elliott (Scotland), Robbie Savage (Wales), Theo Zagorakis (Greece), Neil Lennon (Northern Ireland) and Arnar Gunnlaugsson (Iceland). The only Englishmen were Robert Ullathorne, Steve Guppy and Muzzy Izzet, who went on to represent Turkey. It didn't do them much good. Arsenal won 5-0.

SATURDAY 20TH FEBRUARY 1971

Goals from Rodney Fern and Malcolm Partridge secured a 2-1 win over Norwich City at Filbert Street in Division Two.

WEDNESDAY 21ST FEBRUARY 1996

Martin O'Neill took his Leicester City side to Wolverhampton Wanderers looking for his first win as Foxes manager after nine games at the helm. It proved to be worth the wait. City, fired up by playing against Mark McGhee's new team following his departure from Filbert Street two months earlier, stormed to a thrilling 3-2 win at Molineux. Emile Heskey was the two-goal hero for City – including the winner – and Iwan Roberts was also on target as Leicester kick-started their flagging promotion bid.

WEDNESDAY 21ST FEBRUARY 1934

Archie Gardiner made a stunning debut for Leicester City at Portsmouth. He bagged four goals and Danny Liddle grabbed the other in a 5-3 win at Fratton Park in the Division One clash.

SATURDAY 21ST FEBRUARY 1998

Emile Heskey got both goals for Leicester City in a 2-0 win over Chelsea at Filbert Street that lifted Martin O'Neill's team up to seventh in the Premier League. The result made it seven games unbeaten for City.

SATURDAY 21ST FEBRUARY 1981

Jock Wallace's Leicester City clinched a shock 2-1 win at Tottenham Hotspur to boost their hopes of avoiding an immediate return to Division Two. Steve Lynex and Pat Byrne were on target for the Foxes.

SATURDAY 22ND FEBRUARY 1958

Jimmy Walsh bagged four goals as Leicester City romped to an 8-4 win over Manchester City at Filbert Street. Howard Riley got two and the others came from Derek Hines and Derek Hogg.

SUNDAY 22ND FEBRUARY 2004

Leicester City and Tottenham Hotspur shared the points after an eight-goal thriller in the Premiership at White Hart Lane. The Sky Sports cameras were there to capture all the drama as ten-man Leicester battled back from 3-1 down to lead before Spurs snatched a point. Leicester fell behind when former Spurs goalkeeper Ian Walker let Michael Brown's free-kick slip through his grasp, but were level when Gary Doherty, once a transfer target for City, scooped the ball into his own net under pressure from Paul Dickov. Spurs were in charge at the break after Jermain Defoe and Robbie Keane netted to make it 3-1. The fightback started with Les Ferdinand's cool finish, but Leicester were handed a massive blow when James Scowcroft was sent off. The Foxes then stunned the home crowd by levelling. Steve Guppy's corner was powerfully headed home by former Spurs defender Ben Thatcher and incredibly, Leicester went on to snatch the lead. Dickov intercepted Doherty's back pass and Marcus Bent rolled the loose ball past former Leicester goalkeeper Kasey Keller and into the net. City couldn't hold on, however, and Defoe lashed home a late leveller via the underside of the bar.

SATURDAY 22ND FEBRUARY 2003

Leicester City fans voted against the proposal to revert to the club's original name of Leicester Fosse during the half-time interval of the 4-0 thrashing of Wimbledon. New Fox plc, the club's new owners, had made the proposal and fans were handed posters to register their vote. The overwhelming majority voted against change and City won the game 4-0 through Paul Dickov's hat-trick and Trevor Benjamin's goal to stay on course for promotion.

WEDNESDAY 22ND FEBRUARY 1995

It looked like being another miserable night in a miserable season. Leicester City fans had felt betrayed by Brian Little's departure for Aston Villa three months earlier and his new team piled on the misery at Villa Park. There appeared to be no way back for Leicester in the Premiership fixture as they trailed 4-1 with 13 minutes left. But the fightback started when Iwan Roberts headed home a Mike Galloway cross and David Lowe pulled another goal back to make it 4-3 and set up a thrilling climax. The game was deep into injury time when Lowe became the Foxes' hero by forcing home Colin Hill's header to snatch a point, giving City fans some cheer.

SATURDAY 22ND FEBRUARY 1997

Leicester City were without Muzzy Izzet, Neil Lennon and Emile Heskey for the visit of Midlands rivals Derby County to Filbert Street for a Premiership fixture. But it didn't matter. Ian Marshall scored a hat-trick in just 21 first-half minutes for the Foxes as Martin O'Neill's team hit back to win after going behind inside the opening two minutes to a goal from Dean Sturridge, who went on to play for the Foxes. Steve Claridge bagged a fourth for Leicester past former Fox Russell Hoult to complete the scoring. Derby's line-up included Gary Rowett and Jacob Laursen, who also went on to play for Leicester.

SATURDAY 23RD FEBRUARY 1963

Leicester City stayed second in Division One with a 3-0 hammering of defending champions Ipswich Town at Filbert Street. City had dumped Ipswich out of the FA Cup three weeks earlier and piled on the misery with goals from David Gibson, Mike Stringfellow and Howard Riley securing maximum points. Ken Keyworth missed out having scored in the previous six games, but it didn't matter as City boosted their title bid without his goals.

SATURDAY 24TH FEBRUARY 1996

Neil Lennon, who became Martin O'Neill's first signing when he made a £750,000 move from Crewe, made his debut in the 1-1 draw at Reading and it proved to be a memorable start for the highly-rated Northern Ireland international. He set up a goal for Neil Lewis and then conceded the penalty that enabled the Royals to earn a 1-1 draw in the Division One clash at Elm Park. Lewis never scored another goal for City.

WEDNESDAY 24TH FEBRUARY 1960

Frank McLintock, Albert Cheesebrough and Gordon Wills were the marksmen for Leicester City in a memorable 3-1 win over Manchester United at Filbert Street.

SATURDAY 24TH FEBRUARY 1934

Ken Keyworth, future City player, was born in Rotherham, Yorkshire.

MONDAY 24TH FEBRUARY 1975

The outcome of Leicester City's epic FA Cup fifth round clash against Arsenal was finally settled in extra time in the second replay at Filbert Street. John Radford rifled home a free-kick to send the Gunners through to the quarter-finals. The previous two games between the sides in the competition had ended in a goalless draw at Highbury and then a 1-1 draw at Filbert Street secured by Alan Birchenall's goal for the Foxes.

TUESDAY 24TH FEBRUARY 1981

Leicester City boss Jock Wallace revealed he had agreed terms to bring Dutch superstar Johan Cruyff to Filbert Street. Although now 33 years old, Cruyff had been rated the best player in the world and looked set to be paid between £4,000 and £5,000 per game for the remainder of the season as the Foxes battled against the drop from Division One. Wallace was convinced the payment would be recouped by an increase in attendances.

SATURDAY 25TH FEBRUARY 1984

Leicester City claimed a crucial 2-0 win over Ipswich Town at Filbert Street to boost their hopes of avoiding relegation from Division One. Alan Smith and John O'Neill got the goals.

WEDNESDAY 26TH FEBRUARY 1997

The decision to award a penalty against Leicester City in an FA Cup fifth round replay at Chelsea sparked a national outcry that prompted comment from Prime Minister and Blues fan John Major. The game was heading towards a penalty shoot-out when referee Mike Reed handed the home side a spot kick after Erland Johnsen took a tumble. Replays proved no contact had been made and Franck Leboeuf accepted the gift to put Chelsea through to the quarter-finals. The Blues went on to lift the cup at Wembley.

THURSDAY 26TH FEBRUARY 1981

Leicester City's ambitious bid to sign Johan Cruyff was called off. Foxes boss Jock Wallace got a call from Cruyff's agent saying the Dutchman was signing for Spanish club Levante after they reportedly offered him 50 per cent of gate receipts for their matches.

SATURDAY 26TH FEBRUARY 1983

Leicester City walloped Division Two promotion rivals Wolverhampton Wanderers 5-0. The game is remembered for an Alan Smith volley from 25 yards – rated by the club's programme editor as one of the most spectacular goals seen at Filbert Street for many years. Steve Lynex bagged two goals for Gordon Milne's side while Gary Lineker added another and Gerry Daly's sweetly struck shot from the edge of the penalty area completed the scoring.

WEDNESDAY 26TH FEBRUARY 1992

Leicester City were beaten 2-0 at Nottingham Forest's City Ground in the second leg of the Zenith Data Systems Cup northern final. Forest went through 3-1 on aggregate after the sides drew 1-1 at Filbert Street two weeks earlier and went on to lift the trophy at Wembley.

MONDAY 26TH FEBRUARY 1979

Leicester City crashed out of the FA Cup after defeat at Oldham Athletic in the fourth round. Future City hero Alan Young bagged a hat-trick for the Latics in a 3-1 win with Martin Henderson netting in reply for Jock Wallace's team.

SUNDAY 27TH FEBRUARY 2000

Leicester City skipper Matt Elliott lifted the League Cup at Wembley after his double strike secured a 2-1 win over Tranmere Rovers. Martin O'Neill's team were appearing in their third final in four years and went ahead against the underdogs from Division Two in the 29th minute when Elliott headed home Steve Guppy's corner. City were handed another boost on 63 minutes when Rovers defender Clint Hill was sent off for a second bookable offence after his challenge on Emile Heskey sent the Foxes striker crashing. Tranmere protested bitterly, but the ten men regrouped and stunned City by drawing level on 77 minutes through a well-taken goal from former Leicester striker David Kelly. Leicester were back in front four minutes later. Guppy supplied the cross again for Elliott to steer home his header and bring the cup back to Filbert Street for a second time in four years.

SATURDAY 28TH FEBRUARY 1925

Arthur Chandler crashed in five goals for Leicester City in a 6-0 thrashing of Barnsley in Division Two and John Duncan got the other.

SATURDAY 28TH FEBRUARY 1998

Leicester City's seven-match unbeaten run in the Premiership was ended by a 5-3 defeat at Blackburn Rovers. They gave Rovers a scare by coming back from 4-1 down to make it 4-3 before the home side added a fifth. City's goals came from Stuart Wilson, Muzzy Izzet and Robert Ullathorne.

SATURDAY 28TH FEBRUARY 1981

Steve Lynex was on target for Leicester City in a 1-1 draw against East Midlands rivals Nottingham Forest at Filbert Street, to boost the Foxes' relegation fight in Division One.

SATURDAY 28TH FEBRUARY 1953

Derek Hogg got the goal for Leicester City in a 1-1 draw against Nottingham Forest that took them up to fifth in Division Two.

SATURDAY 29TH FEBRUARY 1992

A 2-0 defeat at Millwall dented the play-off hopes of Brian Little's Leicester City.

LEICESTER CITY
On This Day & Miscellany

MARCH

SATURDAY 1ST MARCH 1997

Steve Guppy made his Leicester City debut in a 3-1 win at Wimbledon in the Premier League. He joined from Port Vale for a fee rising to £950,000 and moving to Filbert Street meant he was reunited with Martin O'Neill, who had worked with Guppy when he was manager of Wycombe Wanderers. Guppy's City career got off to the perfect start with three goals in the first half setting the Foxes on their way to victory. Matt Elliott netted twice for the visitors at Selhurst Park and Mark Robins added a spectacular bicycle kick.

SATURDAY 2ND MARCH 1963

Leicester City stayed second in Division One with a 2-0 win over Bill Shankly's Liverpool at Anfield. Foxes boss Matt Gillies saw goals from Ken Keyworth and David Gibson secure an eighth successive win in all competitions in front of a crowd of 54,842.

SUNDAY 3RD MARCH 1996

Steve Claridge took to the pitch at Ipswich for his Leicester City debut with his name misspelt on the back of his shirt. 'Clarridge', a £1m signing from Birmingham City, drew a blank in a game that was televised live. He must have been hoping the ink on his recently-signed contract wasn't dry as Ipswich netted three times in the opening 12 minutes of the Division One clash. Iwan Roberts gave Leicester hope with two goals – the second moments after Kevin Poole had saved a penalty at the other end – but Ian Marshall put the game beyond Martin O'Neill's team with a fourth in the dying minutes. Claridge didn't score a goal in his first six games for Leicester.

SATURDAY 3RD MARCH 1917

Leicester Fosse goalkeeper Herbert Bown got on the scoresheet in a 2-1 defeat at Hull City.

SATURDAY 3RD MARCH 1934

Arthur Chandler got the goal at Preston North End that sent Leicester City through to the semi-finals of the FA Cup.

SATURDAY 4TH MARCH 2006

An unforgettable goal from Joey Gudjonsson helped Leicester City to a 3-2 win over Hull City at the Walkers Stadium. The score was locked at 1-1 when Gudjonsson got the ball on the halfway line in the 64th minute. He looked up, spotted Hull goalkeeper Boaz Myhill off his line and launched a right-foot shot over him and into the net. Iain Hume had given the home side the lead against a team managed by former Foxes boss Peter Taylor before Hull levelled. Gudjonsson's wonder goal put Leicester back in front, but the game was heading for a draw after the Tigers levelled again. Gudjonsson grabbed the winner with seven minutes left.

SUNDAY 5TH MARCH 2000

Stan Collymore hit a terrific treble in Leicester City's 5-2 demolition of Sunderland at Filbert Street in the Premiership. Emile Heskey was also on the scoresheet and the prospect of them forming a partnership was mouth-watering for Foxes fans. It was not to be.

SATURDAY 6TH MARCH 1982

Legend has it that *Leicester Mercury* reporters in the office on the Saturday afternoon shift thought a bomb had gone off. Thankfully not. It was just the crowd cheering Leicester City's equaliser in the unforgettable FA Cup quarter-final against Shrewsbury Town. Larry May put Leicester ahead and then goalkeeper Mark Wallington was injured in a collision with Shrews striker Chic Bates. Two goals flew past Wallington while he was still groggy and Alan Young took over between the posts. Leicester were level when Shrewsbury defender Colin Griffin rolled the ball into his own net and Steve Lynex became the third Foxes players to wear the goalkeeper's jersey after Young was injured in a collision. Young returned between the posts when his head had cleared and Lynex set up Jim Melrose's goal that put Leicester ahead. Gary Lineker and Melrose added the fourth and fifth.

SATURDAY 7TH MARCH 1936

Colin Appleton was born in Scarborough. He went on to make 333 appearances for Leicester City.

SATURDAY 7TH MARCH 1981

Paul Ramsey made his Leicester City debut in a 1-0 win over Arsenal at Filbert Street. Tommy Williams got the only goal of the game in the Foxes' victory.

WEDNESDAY 8TH MARCH 1995

Emile Heskey, the promising teenage striker, made his debut in a 2-0 defeat at Queens Park Rangers in the Premiership. Heskey became the club's youngest top-flight debutant at the age of 17 years and 56 days. He was a pupil at The City of Leicester School in Evington, Leicester that was also attended by Gary Lineker.

SATURDAY 8TH MARCH 1919

Mal Griffiths was born in Merthyr Tydfil in Wales.

SATURDAY 9TH MARCH 1974

Joe Waters carved his name in Leicester City folklore with the second-half double at Queens Park Rangers that took the Foxes through to the last four of the FA Cup. Boss Jimmy Bloomfield handed the young Irishman his chance in the absence of Alan Birchenall and Alan Woollett and he put City ahead with a strike that was later voted 'Goal of the Month'. Waters added a second minutes later – coolly clipping his shot past the advancing goalkeeper – and Leicester were through to the semi-finals. But they had been under fire for much of the first half and were relieved to reach the half-time interval on level terms.

TUESDAY 9TH MARCH 1982

Mark Wallington's run of 331 consecutive appearances in goal for Leicester City came to an end. The injury suffered in the thrilling FA Cup quarter-final win over Shrewsbury Town at Filbert Street three days earlier ruled him out of the trip to Chelsea in Division Two. He was replaced between the posts by Nicky Walker and City were beaten 4-1. The Foxes goal came from Steve Lynex.

SATURDAY 10TH MARCH 2001

Leicester City were on the receiving end of an FA Cup upset as Second Division Wycombe Wanderers grabbed a dramatic 2-1 win at Filbert Street in their quarter-final clash. Wycombe had been so short of players in the countdown to the clash that they advertised on the internet and that led to striker Roy Essandoh being recruited on a two-week trial. He went on to head home the injury-time winner that stunned Filbert Street. Paul McCarthy had put Wycombe ahead in the second half before Muzzy Izzet equalised, but City's goalscorer and Robbie Savage were injured and Leicester unravelled. Wycombe boss Lawrie Sanchez was dismissed from the touchline after questioning the officials and he watched on a television monitor as Essandoh rose unchallenged to head home the winner. This defeat kick-started a club record spell of nine straight losses for Peter Taylor's team.

FRIDAY 10TH MARCH 2000

Emile Heskey left Leicester City to join Liverpool in an £11m deal – five days after joining forces with Stan Collymore to fire the Foxes to a 5-2 win over Sunderland.

TUESDAY 11TH MARCH 1997

Simon Grayson's header in the League Cup semi-final, second leg at Wimbledon sent Leicester City through to Wembley. He netted the equaliser after Marcus Gayle had put the Dons ahead at Selhurst Park. The game went into extra time and Garry Parker made two goal-line clearances to ensure Leicester won on the away goals rule.

SATURDAY 11TH MARCH 1972

Mark Wallington made his Leicester City debut and kept a clean sheet in the 2-0 win over West Ham United at Filbert Street.

WEDNESDAY 11TH MARCH 1992

Leicester City striker Paul Kitson joined Derby County in a £1.35m move that involved Phil Gee and Ian Ormondroyd making the move in the opposite direction.

TUESDAY 11TH MARCH 1958

John O'Neill was born in Derry, Northern Ireland.

SATURDAY 12TH MARCH 1960

Len Chalmers' own goal ended Leicester City's hopes of securing a place in the semi-finals of the FA Cup. He scored what proved to be the winner for Wolverhampton Wanderers in the sixth-round tie at Filbert Street. The visitors went through 2-1 with Tommy McDonald grabbing City's goal.

SATURDAY 12TH MARCH 1994

Brian Little's Leicester City climbed to second place in Division One with a 2-0 victory over Middlesbrough at Filbert Street. Julian Joachim and David Speedie were on target.

SATURDAY 12TH MARCH 1949

Leicester City grabbed a 3-3 draw at Bradford Park Avenue to make it 12 games without defeat. But the Foxes gleaned only eight league points from the unbeaten spell to remain in trouble at the bottom of Division Two. Don Revie netted twice at Bradford with Jack Lee also on target.

SUNDAY 13TH MARCH 2005

Former Leicester City striker Paul Dickov broke Foxes' hearts in the FA Cup quarter-final against Premiership Blackburn Rovers at Ewood Park. Dickov netted from the penalty spot with just eight minutes left after City defender Darren Kenton sent Morten Gamst Pedersen crashing in the box. City's protests were waved away and a run that had proved a welcome distraction from the struggles in the Championship came to a controversial end. David Thompson had rattled Leicester's woodwork with a third-minute free kick, but the visitors came back and Joey Gudjonsson and Mark De Vries went close before Dickov struck.

WEDNESDAY 13TH MARCH 1912

Septimus Smith, regarded as one of Leicester City's greatest-ever players, was born in Whitburn, County Durham.

SATURDAY 14TH MARCH 1992

Simon Grayson made his Leicester City debut in a 0-0 draw at Ipswich Town that is also remembered for Ian Ormondroyd having two goals ruled out in the first half.

MONDAY 15TH MARCH 1965

Leicester City ended the first leg of their League Cup Final against Chelsea trailing 3-2. Eddie McCreadie's spectacular goal gave the Pensioners the advantage at Stamford Bridge. Colin Appleton and Jimmy Goodfellow got the goals for City to give them a fighting chance going into the second leg.

MONDAY 15TH MARCH 1971

Leicester City were left fuming by defeat at Arsenal in an FA Cup sixth-round replay at Highbury. Rodney Fern had a header controversially chalked off for a push and then Charlie George grabbed the game's only goal to send the Gunners through to the semi-finals.

SATURDAY 15TH MARCH 1980

Paul Edmunds grabbed his first goal for Leicester City in a 2-0 win over Shrewsbury Town to keep the Foxes in the hunt for promotion from Division Two. Alan Young got the other goal for the Foxes.

SATURDAY 16TH MARCH 1957

Arthur Rowley blasted home the winner at Swansea Town to take Dave Halliday's Foxes eight points clear of Nottingham Forest at the top of Division Two. Derek Hines put Leicester City ahead after only four minutes, but Des Palmer's double put the home side ahead at the interval. Ian McNeil drew Leicester level six minutes after the restart and the winner came with 15 minutes left to keep City on course for promotion to the top flight.

SATURDAY 17TH MARCH 1934

Leicester City's FA Cup semi-final against Portsmouth attracted a crowd of 66,544 to Birmingham City's St Andrew's ground. They saw City's Sep Smith line up against brothers Jack and Willie, but it was Pompey striker John Weddle who took the headlines with a hat-trick that fired his side to a 4-1 win. Arthur Lochhead got City's goal in the first half, but the defence struggled to cope after Sandy Wood was left dazed following a collision with a touchline photographer that left him with a broken nose.

WEDNESDAY 18TH MARCH 1959

Leicester City's match against Birmingham City was the first midweek game to be played under floodlights at Filbert Street. City were beaten 4-2 in the Division Two fixture with Jimmy Walsh grabbing both goals for the Foxes.

SATURDAY 19TH MARCH 1975

Leicester City drew 1-1 with Liverpool at Filbert Street in Division One. Frank Worthington was on target for City and John Toshack replied for the Reds. Toshack had been on the brink of joining the Foxes four months earlier in a £160,000 deal. The Welsh striker trained with City before a medical query led to the deal falling through.

SATURDAY 19TH MARCH 1966

Mike Stringfellow got the only goal against Sheffield United at Filbert Street to lift Leicester City back into the top ten in Division One. The win took them to ninth in the table.

THURSDAY 20TH MARCH 1952

Steve Whitworth was born in Ellistown, Leicestershire

SUNDAY 21ST MARCH 1999

Leicester City suffered heartbreak in the League Cup Final against Tottenham Hotspur at Wembley. Allan Nielsen headed home from close range in injury time to take the trophy back to White Hart Lane. Leicester were playing against ten men from the 63rd minute following the dismissal of Spurs midfielder Justin Edinburgh who was sent off after a clash with Robbie Savage. There were few chances in the game and City came closest to breaking the deadlock before the late drama when Spurs defender Ramon Vega denied Emile Heskey a shot at goal with a last-ditch challenge.

WEDNESDAY 21ST MARCH 1979

Steve Whitworth made his 400th and last appearance for Leicester City. They beat Fulham 1-0 at Filbert Street through a Dave Buchanan goal and Whitworth went on to join Sunderland later in the month.

SATURDAY 22ND MARCH 1975

Chris Garland grabbed all the goals for Leicester City in their 3-2 win over Wolverhampton Wanderers at Filbert Street that secured two priceless points in the battle against relegation from Division One.

SATURDAY 23RD MARCH 1957

Jimmy Walsh made his debut in a 3-1 defeat at home to Fulham after joining from Celtic.

SATURDAY 23RD MARCH 1963

A club-record run of ten straight wins in all competitions had taken Matt Gillies' Leicester City up to second place in Division One and set up a top-of-the-table clash against leaders Tottenham Hotspur at Filbert Street. Fans started queuing hours before kick-off and the gates were shut with 41,622 fans crammed inside to watch a match billed as a possible championship decider. Mike Stringfellow put Leicester ahead, but Bobby Smith and Jimmy Greaves replied. City were relieved when the referee blew his whistle for half-time seconds before Greaves put the ball in the net for what would have been a crucial third goal. They made the most of the reprieve with Ken Keyworth grabbing a second-half equaliser.

THURSDAY 23RD MARCH 1961

The FA Cup semi-final replay between Leicester City and Sheffield United at the City Ground ended goalless after extra time. That meant the two sides had failed to produce a goal in three and a half hours of forgettable football.

MONDAY 23RD MARCH 1964

Leicester City went to West Ham United for the second leg of the League Cup semi-final with a 4-3 lead and goals from Frank McLintock and Bobby Roberts secured a 2-0 win at Upton Park that took the Foxes through to the final.

TUESDAY 23RD MARCH 1993

Leicester City made it six successive wins in Division One (second tier) with a 3-1 victory at Cambridge United's Abbey Stadium. David Lowe was on target twice for the Foxes after Julian Joachim had opened the scoring for the Foxes.

SATURDAY 24TH MARCH 1956

Leicester City stayed second in Division Two despite a 6-1 defeat at promotion rivals Swansea Town. Jack Froggatt grabbed the consolation goal for the Foxes. Incredibly, City had won by the same margin when the sides had clashed at Filbert Street four months earlier in the season.

SATURDAY 24TH MARCH 1990

David Pleat's Leicester City had received a double boost two days before the Division Two clash against Plymouth Argyle at Filbert Street. Gary McAllister turned down a deadline day move to Nottingham Forest and Republic of Ireland striker David Kelly joined from West Ham United for £300,000. Kelly impressed on his debut and McAllister gave City the lead with a penalty after 27 minutes. Plymouth secured a point in their battle against the drop when Nicky Marker equalised 12 minutes after the restart.

FRIDAY 24TH MARCH 1967

Leicester City ended a run of three games without a win at Manchester City. They ran out 3-1 winners to claim their first win at Maine Road since 1930 and climb to seventh in Division One and boost their chances of securing qualification for Europe. The first three goals all came from the penalty spot with the home side going ahead after Richie Norman's handball. City were level three minutes after the restart. Jackie Sinclair netted from the penalty spot after he had been up-ended and scored another spot kick on 61 minutes to put the Foxes ahead after a foul on Paul Matthews. Mike Stringfellow put the game beyond the home side by turning home City's third from a David Gibson free kick.

SATURDAY 25TH MARCH 1989

Ali Mauchlen bagged both goals for Leicester City in a 2-0 win over Birmingham City in Division Two in front of 9,564 fans at Filbert Street. The result made it three games unbeaten for David Pleat's team and kept them 15th in the table.

TUESDAY 26TH MARCH 1985

Gary Lineker grabbed the first of his 48 goals for England in a friendly against the Republic of Ireland at Wembley. His goal proved to be the winner in a 2-1 victory. Trevor Steven put England ahead on the stroke of half-time and then Lineker struck on 76 minutes after being set up by substitute Peter Davenport. Liam Brady pulled a goal back for the visitors in the 87th minute.

SATURDAY 26TH MARCH 1977

Larry May made his Leicester City debut in a 0-0 draw against Bristol City in Division One as an 18-year-old.

MONDAY 27TH MARCH 1961

Goals from Jimmy Walsh and Ken Leek secured victory over Sheffield United in their second FA Cup semi-final replay at St Andrew's and took Leicester City through to face Division One champions Tottenham Hotspur at Wembley. The previous two meetings had failed to produce a goal, but there was more drama this time. Ian King had a penalty saved after 11 minutes before Walsh headed Leicester into the lead to end a run of 451 minutes without a goal. Leek added a second just after the interval and the Blades were handed a lifeline on 65 minutes when they were awarded a spot kick. But Graham Shaw shot wide and City were on their way to Wembley.

FRIDAY 27TH MARCH 1992

Northern Ireland international Colin Hill made his Leicester City debut after arriving on loan from Sheffield United in a 2-1 win at Tranmere Rovers in Division One. Ian Ormondroyd got City's opener and Phil Gee thumped home a spectacular winner.

SATURDAY 27TH MARCH 1993

Leicester City's 3-1 win over Charlton Athletic at Filbert Street set a club record of seven successive league wins. Steve Walsh bagged two goals and Julian Joachim the other in a win that kept Brian Little's team on course for promotion to the Premier League.

SATURDAY 28TH MARCH 1953

Tom Dryburgh netted for Leicester City after just ten seconds of their Division Two clash against Swansea Town and Johnny Morris got the Foxes' other goal in a 2-1 victory.

SATURDAY 29TH MARCH 1969

Steve Guppy was born in Winchester, Hampshire.

SATURDAY 30TH MARCH 1996

I'll keep this brief. A section of Leicester City fans protested and some called for manager Martin O'Neill to be sacked after a 2-0 defeat at home to Sheffield United in Division One. Muzzy Izzet made his debut in midfield after joining on loan from Chelsea and Julian Watts also made his first start for the Foxes. Watts' partner at the heart of defence was Brian Carey, who never played for Leicester again.

SATURDAY 30TH MARCH 1974

Leicester City took on Liverpool in the FA Cup semi-final at Old Trafford. Jimmy Bloomfield's team had set pulses racing with wins at Luton Town and Queens Park Rangers in the previous rounds and might have hoped to draw either Newcastle United or Burnley in the last four. Instead, they faced Liverpool in what turned out to be a disappointing spectacle. The Reds had more possession, but hard work from Leicester defenders Malcolm Munro and Graham Cross kept clear-cut chances to a minimum in front of a crowd of 60,000 in Manchester. The best chance of the match fell to Liverpool striker Kevin Keegan in the dying minutes and he shot against the post when it looked easier to score to ensure the game went to a replay.

SATURDAY 30TH MARCH 1957

Ian McNeill scored after just ten seconds of Leicester City's Division Two clash at local rivals Nottingham Forest. Derek Hines got the other goal in a 2-1 win for the Foxes. The win kept City on top of the table and was the perfect response to the 3-1 defeat at home to Fulham seven days earlier.

TUESDAY 31ST MARCH 1981

Jock Wallace's City battled to a 3-3 draw at Manchester City in Division One., with goals from Tommy Williams, Alan Young and Jim Melrose.

LEICESTER CITY
On This Day & Miscellany

APRIL

MONDAY 1ST APRIL 1969

April Fools' Day – and the joke was on Leicester City. They travelled to local rivals Coventry City for a crucial relegation battle and were on course for a point with seven minutes left with the score goalless. City looked set to make the breakthrough when they were awarded a penalty after Brian Greenhalgh was scythed down, but the referee changed his mind after consulting his linesman and the Sky Blues made the most of the reprieve. They raced away to the other end of the pitch and Neil Martin scored what proved to be the winner.

TUESDAY 2ND APRIL 1996

Steve Claridge grabbed his first goal for Leicester City in a 1-0 win at Charlton Athletic that launched Martin O'Neill's team's charge for the Division One play-off places.

SATURDAY 2ND APRIL 1949

Leicester City battled to a 1-1 draw against Grimsby Town in Division Two and there was heartbreak for Foxes goalkeeper Ian McGraw. He suffered a hand injury that kept him out of the FA Cup Final against Wolverhampton Wanderers at Wembley four weeks later. Ken Chisholm got the goal for City against the Mariners.

SATURDAY 3RD APRIL 1982

Leicester City suffered FA Cup semi-final heartbreak against Tottenham Hotspur at Villa Park. Jock Wallace's Second Division underdogs were beaten by a Garth Crooks strike and midfielder Ian Wilson's own goal. City defender Tommy Williams suffered a broken leg.

SATURDAY 3RD APRIL 1954

Leicester City climbed back up to second in Division Two with a 1-0 win over Bristol Rovers at Filbert Street. Jack Froggatt got the winner for the Foxes in front of 27,369 fans.

SATURDAY 4TH APRIL 1959

Jimmy Walsh was Leicester City's two-goal hero in front of 40,795 fans at Filbert Street. Walsh grabbed both the Foxes' goals in a 2-1 win over Aston Villa that secured two precious points in the battle against relegation from Division One.

TUESDAY 5TH APRIL 1998

Leicester City and Derby County fought out a thrilling 3-3 draw at Filbert Street – and all six goals came in a 29-minute spell. Iwan Roberts bagged a hat-trick for Leicester and former Foxes striker Paul Kitson got two for the visitors.

SATURDAY 5TH APRIL 2003

Micky Adams' Leicester City team took another step towards promotion from Division One with a 2-0 win over Grimsby Town at the Walkers Stadium. Trevor Benjamin and Callum Davidson were the marksmen for the Foxes.

MONDAY 5TH APRIL 1965

There was League Cup Final heartbreak for Leicester City at Filbert Street. They went into the second leg against Chelsea trailing 3-2 to a side that boasted stars such as Bonetti, Harris, McCreadie, Tambling, Bridges and Venables. Bobby Roberts had an early effort for the home side smothered and Leicester were well on top throughout. But they couldn't find a way through and the trophy that they had won 12 months earlier was held aloft by Terry Venables in front of the directors' box.

WEDNESDAY 5TH APRIL 1978

Frank McLintock was sacked as Leicester City manager with the Foxes heading for relegation from Division One.

SATURDAY 5TH APRIL 1958

Arthur Rowley and Howard Riley bagged two goals apiece in a 5-3 win over Aston Villa at Filbert Street that handed Leicester City a boost in their battle against relegation from Division One.

SUNDAY 5TH APRIL 2004

Leicester City's hopes of staying in the Premier League were handed a hammer blow at Leeds United in front of the Sky Sports cameras. They battled back from 2-0 down to level through goals from Paul Dickov and Muzzy Izzet, but a late winner from Alan Smith handed victory to Leeds and left the Foxes in deep trouble.

SUNDAY 6TH APRIL 1997

Emile Heskey bundled home a late equaliser against Middlesbrough to force a replay in the League Cup Final. The sides had met at Filbert Street three weeks earlier and Brazilian Juninho inspired the visitors to a 3-1 win. Fearing a repeat, Leicester City boss Martin O'Neill handed Swedish international Pontus Kaamark the job of shackling Middlesbrough's little playmaker. He did just that, but nobody could stop Italian striker Fabrizio Ravanelli firing 'Boro into the lead in extra time. Heskey came to Leicester's rescue with three minutes left.

SATURDAY 6TH APRIL 1957

Leicester City took a step towards clinching promotion to Division One with a 5-3 win over West Ham United. Arthur Rowley was the goal hero with his fourth hat-trick of the season and the others came from Billy Wright.

SATURDAY 6TH APRIL 2002

Leicester City were beaten 1-0 at home by Manchester United and relegated from the Premier League in what proved to be Dave Bassett's last game in charge. The Foxes had been booked for the drop for several weeks and it was confirmed by Ole Gunnar Solskjaer's 62nd minute goal. It ended the Foxes' six-year stay in the top flight.

SATURDAY 7TH APRIL 1993

Steve Walsh was the last-gasp goal hero in a 2-1 win over Oxford United at Filbert Street that made it nine games unbeaten for Brian Little's team and Richard Smith took the plaudits at the other end of the pitch. Smith went between the posts after Carl Muggleton was injured in the second half and he kept out Oxford. City's other goal came from Steve Thompson's first-half penalty that opened the scoring. Muggleton never played for Leicester again.

TUESDAY 7TH APRIL 1953

Arthur Rowley bagged his 100th goal for Leicester City in his 122nd appearance for the club. He got two goals in a 3-2 win over Rotherham United in Division Two.

MONDAY 8TH APRIL 1963

Leicester City drew 1-1 at Blackpool and went top of Division One for the first time since September 1927. Ken Keyworth got City's goal.

MONDAY 8TH APRIL 2002

Micky Adams took over as Leicester City manager having been assistant to Dave Bassett. The Foxes were already relegated from the Premier League when Adams was appointed.

SATURDAY 9TH APRIL 1966

Mike Stringfellow got both goals for Leicester City in a memorable 2-1 win at Manchester United in Division One. The result took the Foxes up to seventh in the top flight.

WEDNESDAY 9TH APRIL 1975

Leicester City's relegation fears in Division One were eased by a 1-0 win over Middlesbrough at Filbert Street. Frank Worthington got the goal.

SATURDAY 9TH APRIL 1994

Brian Little's Leicester City team kept the pressure on the top two teams in Division One with a 3-2 win over Sunderland at Roker Park. Julian Joachim netted twice and on-loan midfielder Paul Kerr got the other from the penalty spot.

SATURDAY 10TH APRIL 1897

Willie Freebairn became the first Leicester Fosse player to ever be sent off. Freebairn got his marching orders in the 2-1 defeat at Lincoln City having earlier scored Fosse's goal.

SATURDAY 10TH APRIL 1937

Leicester City's clash with Aston Villa attracted a then-record crowd of 39,127 to Filbert Street and they saw Foxes striker Jack Bowers grab the game's only goal. The result kept the Foxes second in Division Two with three games of the season left.

SATURDAY 11TH APRIL 1987

Leicester City and relegation rivals Aston Villa battled out a 1-1 draw at Filbert Street in Division One. Steve Moran was the marksman for City.

SATURDAY 12TH APRIL 1980

Jock Wallace's team struck a crucial blow in the battle for promotion from Division Two with a 2-1 win over Birmingham City at Filbert Street that took them up to second place. Wallace raised a few eyebrows with his decision to leave out Gary Lineker, bring in Geoff Scott at full-back and move Bobby Smith forward, but he was vindicated by two goals inside the opening half-hour. Ian Wilson lashed home from 30 yards after just ten minutes and Scott crossed for Alan Young to double the lead with a header on 28 minutes. Leicester City stayed on top, but had to endure a tense final 11 minutes after John O'Neill's handball gifted the visitors the chance to halve the arrears from the penalty spot.

SATURDAY 12TH APRIL 1969

Leicester City's Division One survival hopes were dealt a massive blow by a 2-1 defeat against Liverpool at Filbert Street. Peter Rodrigues got City's goal in front of 28,671, but the visitors went away with both points courtesy of goals from Emlyn Hughes and Ian Callaghan.

MONDAY 12TH APRIL 1971

Rodney Fern masterminded a 3-1 win at Luton Town that extended Leicester City's unbeaten run to 11 games, kept them on top of Division Two and dented the Hatters' promotion ambitions. Leicester went into the game having not conceded a goal for four games and that run was ended just two minutes into the game when John Sjoberg turned the ball into his own net. City stormed back with Fern the architect. Malcolm Manley headed an equaliser just before the break, John Farrington fired home a free-kick on the hour and Ally Brown added a third.

TUESDAY 12TH APRIL 1966

Goals from Tom Sweenie and Jackie Sinclair lifted Leicester City up to sixth in the Division One table. It was a third straight victory for Matt Gillies' team.

SATURDAY 13TH APRIL 1991

Leicester City's hopes of avoiding what would have been a first-ever drop into the third tier of English football looked bleak after a 2-1 defeat at relegation rivals West Bromwich Albion. Don Goodman grabbed the winner in the last minute for the Baggies. The game had started well for Leicester with Kevin Russell putting them ahead after just two minutes. Former Foxes striker Winston White levelled just before the break and then Goodman had the final word with the winning goal.

SATURDAY 13TH APRIL 2002

Micky Adams started his spell in charge of Leicester City with a 2-2 draw at Everton in the Premier League. The Foxes were on course for maximum points when Brian Deane netted twice in the first half to put them 2-0 ahead at the interval. They were denied victory by Darren Ferguson's 86th minute equaliser after Nick Chadwick had halved the arrears for the Toffeemen.

TUESDAY 14TH APRIL 2001

Leicester City and Southampton shared the points and six goals after a thriller at The Dell. The home side led 2-1 at the break with Egil Ostenstad netting twice and Neil Lennon rifling home from 25 yards in reply. David Hirst put the Saints two goals clear four minutes after the interval, but Matt Elliott handed Leicester a lifeline three minutes later. The leveller came deep into injury time. There was a handball in Southampton's penalty area and Garry Parker crashed home the resulting spot kick.

SATURDAY 14TH APRIL 1956

Mal Griffiths made his last appearance for Leicester City against West Ham United at Filbert Street. He was on target in the 2-1 win with Willie Gardiner grabbing City's other goal. Griffiths made a total of 420 appearances for the Foxes and was the first Leicester player to score at Wembley. He got City's goal in the 1949 FA Cup final defeat against Wolverhampton Wanderers.

WEDNESDAY 15TH APRIL 1964

Davie Gibson's chip from 20 yards meant honours were even after the first leg of the League Cup Final with Stoke City going into the second leg at Filbert Street seven days later.

SATURDAY 15TH APRIL 1989

On the same day as the Hillsborough tragedy when 96 fans died at the FA Cup semi-final between Liverpool and Nottingham Forest, Leicester City ended Chelsea's 27-match unbeaten record with a 2-0 Division Two win at Filbert Street. Paul Reid put David Pleat's team in front and Nicky Cross forced home the second from close range.

SATURDAY 15TH APRIL 1995

A 4-0 defeat against Manchester United meant Leicester City were relegated from the Premiership. Andy Cole got two goals for the Reds.

TUESDAY 16TH APRIL 1997

Martin O'Neill's heroes brought major silverware back to Filbert Street for the first time since 1964 after a 1-0 win over Middlesbrough at Hillsborough in their League Cup Final replay. Steve Claridge was the Foxes' hero again. He hooked home the only goal in extra time after Steve Walsh had headed down Garry Parker's free-kick and goalkeeper Kasey Keller came to Leicester City's rescue moments later with a crucial save. The win secured the Foxes' place in the following season's Uefa Cup.

SATURDAY 16TH APRIL 1983

Gary Lineker was on target twice in a 3-1 win over Rotherham United at Filbert Street and that meant he became the first Leicester City player since Arthur Rowley in 1957 to score 25 goals in a season.

SATURDAY 16TH APRIL 1892

Leicester Fosse were hammered 11-0 at Rotherham Town in the Midland League. Horace Bailey was Fosse's under-fire goalkeeper.

SATURDAY 16TH APRIL 1963

Ken Keyworth bagged a hat-trick in just six minutes in Leicester City's thrilling 4-3 win over Manchester United in Division One. Terry Heath got the other goal and Denis Law grabbed a treble for the visitors.

SATURDAY 17TH APRIL 1971

Leicester City stayed top of Division Two with a goalless draw at Sunderland. The result stretched their unbeaten run to 14 games.

SATURDAY 18TH APRIL 1970

A 2-1 win over Queens Park Rangers at Filbert Street wasn't enough to secure promotion for Leicester City to Division One. They finished third in the table after goals from David Nish and Ally Brown ensured victory over Rangers.

FRIDAY 19TH APRIL 1957

A 5-1 win at Leyton Orient secured the Division Two title. Debutant Jimmy Moran got on the scoresheet as Leicester City enjoyed a goal romp in the spring sunshine with Arthur Rowley and Derek Hines also on target. Orient defender Facey is credited with two own goals by some sources, but Leicester gave the opening goal to Billy Wright.

SATURDAY 19TH APRIL 2003

A crowd of 31,909 at the Walkers Stadium saw Micky Adams' Leicester City secure promotion to the Premier League with a 2-0 win over Brighton & Hove Albion. Muzzy Izzet put the Foxes on course for victory with a glancing header from Paul Dickov's cross after just ten minutes and the lead was doubled just before the break. Izzet was the provider with a cross that Jordan Stewart powerfully headed into the roof of the net. That was enough to clinch maximum points and spark scenes of wild celebration at the final whistle.

SATURDAY 19TH APRIL 1975

Mike Stringfellow played his last game for Leicester City in the 0-0 draw against East Midlands rivals Derby County at Filbert Street in Division One. Stringfellow made a total of 370 appearances for the Foxes and bagged 97 goals.

MONDAY 19TH APRIL 1954

Leicester City's 4-0 win over Blackburn Rovers took the Foxes to the brink of promotion to Division One. Arthur Rowley and Johnny Morris shared the goals at Filbert Street in front of a new record crowd of 40,047.

SATURDAY 20TH APRIL 1981

Leicester City were left in deep trouble at the bottom of Division One after a 2-1 defeat at relegation rivals Brighton & Hove Albion. An ill-tempered game burst into life in the 40th minute when Jim Melrose had a goal disallowed. Two minutes later Alan Young was sent off following a second bookable offence. Leicester still went ahead before the break courtesy of Kevin MacDonald's header, but two goals in the space of four second-half minutes powered the Seagulls to victory. The result proved to be crucial at the end of the season with Brighton staying up and Leicester being relegated.

SATURDAY 20TH APRIL 1935

There was controversy as Leicester City slipped deeper into relegation trouble in Division One following a 1-1 draw at Sheffield Wednesday. Sandy Wood broke his collarbone and City were left fuming after the referee ruled that Tony Carroll's shot had not crossed the line when the scores were locked at 1-1. Gene O'Callaghan netted the goal for the Foxes.

WEDNESDAY 21ST APRIL 1909

Leicester Fosse were humiliated 12-0 at Nottingham Forest and an investigation revealed that the players may have been suffering after spending the previous day celebrating the marriage of former team mate 'Leggy' Turner. The *Leicester Chronicle* reported: "Fosse have taken a good many beatings in their time, but they have never before participated in such a farcically absurd game."

WEDNESDAY 21ST APRIL 1999

Emile Heskey was ruled out of the game at Liverpool through illness, Ian Marshall stepped in and was the last-gasp goal hero. He was on target in injury time to ensure Leicester City stretched their unbeaten run to seven games.

SATURDAY 21ST APRIL 1926

A bad day for goalkeepers. Arthur Rowley was born in Wolverhampton and he went on to become the Football League's record goalscorer and is second only to Arthur Chandler in City's goalscoring charts.

MONDAY 22ND APRIL 1957

A 4-1 defeat at home to Leyton Orient didn't spoil the celebrations at Filbert Street as Leicester City were crowned Division Two champions in front of 27,582 fans. Billy Wright got the goal for City. Arthur Rowley finished the season with 44 goals and that haul included four hat-tricks.

SATURDAY 22ND APRIL 1967

Alan Woollett made his Leicester City debut as a substitute in the 2-2 draw against Sheffield United in Division One that was secured by goals from Mike Stringfellow and Bobby Roberts. He went on to make a total of 260 appearances for his home-town club.

WEDNESDAY 22ND APRIL 1964

Leicester City got their hands on their first major trophy after beating Stoke City in the second leg of the League Cup Final at Filbert Street in front of a crowd of 25,372. The scores were locked at 1-1 after the first leg seven days earlier and Mike Stringfellow put Leicester ahead in the return with just six minutes on the clock. David Gibson's header restored the lead after the visitors levelled and Leicester had one hand on the trophy when Howard Riley put them 3-1 ahead on the night and 4-2 in front on aggregate. Stoke pulled one back in injury time to set up a tense climax, but Leicester hung on and jubilant skipper Colin Appleton lifted the trophy.

MONDAY 22ND APRIL 1935

Arthur Chandler played the last game of his record-breaking Leicester City career in the 2-2 draw against Grimsby Town at Filbert Street. Danny Liddle got both goals for City. Chandler remains City's record goalscorer. He found the target an astonishing 273 times in 419 appearances.

SATURDAY 23RD APRIL 1983

Ian Wilson's shot bobbled its way into Fulham's net and Leicester City folklore at Craven Cottage to strike a crucial blow in the battle for promotion to Division One.

TUESDAY 24TH APRIL 1979

Gary Lineker's first goal for Leicester City gave Jock Wallace's team a 1-0 win at Notts County in Division Two. He went on to score 102 more goals for his home-town club.

SATURDAY 24TH APRIL 1954

A 3-1 win at Brentford took Norman Bullock's team to the Second Division championship. Mal Griffiths, John Morris and an own goal powered Leicester City to victory.

SATURDAY 24TH APRIL 1937

Leicester City secured promotion to Division One with a 2-1 win against East Midlands rivals Nottingham Forest at Filbert Street. Jack Bowers and Arthur Maw got the goals for City in front of a crowd of 24,267 and their hopes of securing the championship were boosted by promotion rivals Blackpool being held to a 1-1 draw by bottom team Doncaster Rovers. That meant the battle for top spot went into the final day of the season.

SATURDAY 24TH APRIL 2004

Paul Dickov's missed penalty against former club Manchester City at the Walkers Stadium left Leicester City in deep trouble at the bottom of the Premier League. Both sides were desperate for points and the visitors went ahead in front of a sell-out crowd of 31,457 late in the first half through Michael Trabant's goal. James Scowcroft drew the Foxes level and they looked set to claim maximum points after being awarded an 81st minute spot kick after Trabant sent Muzzy Izzet crashing. Dickov's shot from 12 yards was kept out by David James to strike a massive blow to Micky Adams' team's hopes of avoiding an instant return to the Championship following the previous campaign's promotion.

SATURDAY 25TH APRIL 1925

George Carr got the only goal for Leicester City against Bradford City at Filbert Street to secure promotion from Division Two in front of 25,000 fans. Reg Osborne had earlier missed a penalty – City's fifth miss in nine attempts during the season – but it didn't matter.

SATURDAY 26TH APRIL 1969

A third FA Cup Final in the 1960s – and fourth in total – ended in more heartbreak. Leicester City were led by David Nish – at 21-years-old the youngest ever FA Cup Final captain – and his team were beaten by Neil Young's 23rd minute goal. Peter Rodrigues, Allan Clarke and Andy Lochhead went close to a leveller, but it never came and an eight-year-old Gary Lineker cried all the way back home to Leicester.

SUNDAY 26TH APRIL 1998

Leicester City stunned Derby at Pride Park with a four-goal blitz inside the opening 15 minutes. Emile Heskey and Muzzy Izzet put City in charge inside three minutes and Heskey and Ian Marshall added the others.

SATURDAY 26TH APRIL 2008

Leicester City were on the brink of relegation to the third tier of English football for the first time in their history after relegation rivals Sheffield Wednesday left the Walkers Stadium with a 3-1 win. Ian Holloway's team knew victory would secure survival and Iain Hume gave them an early lead. There were more celebrations when City goalkeeper Paul Henderson kept out Deon Burton's spot kick. But a goal late in the first half from Bartosz Slusarski drew Wednesday level and Leicester fell apart after the break. Steve Watson put the visitors ahead, Hume missed a penalty and Leon Clarke bagged a late third.

SATURDAY 26TH APRIL 1958

Leicester City travelled to Birmingham City needing a point to avoid relegation from Division One. Foxes boss David Halliday took a gamble by handing Len Chalmers his debut and bringing in Ian McNeill for Arthur Rowley. His gamble paid off. McNeill was the hero with the 50th minute goal that secured survival.

SATURDAY 26TH APRIL 1980

Leicester City were on the brink of promotion to Division One after a 2-1 win over Charlton Athletic at Filbert Street. Alan Young and Bobby Smith were on target.

MONDAY 27TH APRIL 1908

Tommy Shanks got the goal at Stoke City that secured second place in Division Two for Leicester Fosse and a first ever top-flight campaign. Fosse made the trip to the Potteries knowing they needed a point to clinch promotion and Shanks ensured they claimed maximum points with a close-range finish after Fred Shinton's shot had been saved. Horace Bailey, who had recently been capped by England, was in fine form between the posts to deny Stoke a leveller. The team arrived back at Leicester station at 10.25 in the evening and were met by thousands of celebrating fans.

SATURDAY 27TH APRIL 1963

There were 65,000 fans at Hillsborough for the FA Cup semi-final against Liverpool and they saw Mike Stringfellow's 18th minute header send Leicester City through to their third FA Cup final, and second in three years.

TUESDAY 27TH APRIL 1971

Leicester City knew a point at Bristol City would be enough to secure promotion to Division One and they were in no mood to miss their chance. Frank O'Farrell's team dominated from the start at Ashton Gate and Ally Brown grabbed the only goal of the game with three minutes left. Sheffield United's 5-1 win over Cardiff City on the same night clinched the title for City.

SATURDAY 27TH APRIL 1929

Leicester City travelled to Huddersfield Town with hopes of winning Division One for the first time in their history. They were second behind leaders Sheffield Wednesday with two games to play. The Owls led by three points and clinched the title after late drama in both games involving the title challengers. John Duncan put City ahead at Huddersfield and they were denied victory by George Brown's equaliser with nine minutes left following a rare mistake by Foxes goalkeeper Jim McLaren. Sheffield Wednesday grabbed a late leveller against Burnley at Hillsborough and City's chance of championship glory was gone.

SATURDAY 28TH APRIL 1973

Leicester City headed to Anfield aiming to wreck Liverpool's party. The Reds needed only a point to be crowned Division One champions – and Jimmy Bloomfield's battlers made them work for it. The majority of the crowd of 56, 202 breathed a sigh of relief when Mike Stringfellow's goal was ruled out and the Reds got the point they needed from a goalless draw. The Foxes ended the season in 16th place.

SATURDAY 28TH APRIL 2001

Leicester City's 1-0 loss at Newcastle United in the Premier League was a club-record ninth successive defeat. Carl Cort, ironically a target for Foxes boss Peter Taylor the previous summer, got the only goal of the game at St James' Park.

SATURDAY 28TH APRIL 1962

Frank McLintock's goal double ensured Leicester City ended the season with a 2-1 victory over local rivals Nottingham Forest. The result meant that Matt Gillies' team finished 14th in Division One. They fell behind against Forest to Les Julians' first-half opener, but a reshuffled City team with Len Chalmers on the right wing, McLintock at inside-right and Graham Cross leading the line, turned the game after the interval. McLintock netted twice to give Foxes fans plenty to celebrate going into the summer break.

SATURDAY 29TH APRIL 1961

Leicester City handed a debut to 17-year-old Graham Cross and he scored against Birmingham City in a 3-2 win for his home-town club in Division One. Howard Riley and Ken Leek got the other goals for the Foxes. Cross also scored on his debut for City reserves when he was just 15-years-old.

SATURDAY 29TH APRIL 1978

Leicester City's 3-0 win over Newcastle United on the final day of the season came too late to save them from relegation to Division Two. Goals from Mark Goodwin, Roger Davies and Geoff Salmons at least gave Foxes fans an enjoyable end to the season.

SATURDAY 30TH APRIL 1949

Leicester City's first FA Cup final ended in a 3-1 defeat against Wolverhampton Wanderers at Wembley. City were the underdogs – they were battling against relegation from Division Two – and played like it in the first half. Jesse Pye's goals put Wolves 2-0 ahead at the break before Mal Griffiths gave City hope by pulling one back after the goalkeeper spilled Ken Chisholm's shot. The game was decided in the space of a few seconds. Chisholm sparked celebrations among Leicester fans when he found the target from a tight angle on 64 minutes. But the 'goal' was ruled out and within a minute it was 3-1 as Sammy Smyth netted at the other end.

SATURDAY 30TH APRIL 1966

Graham Cross got all the goals in Leicester City's 2-1 win over Nottingham Forest at Filbert Street. His own goal put Forest ahead after 20 minutes. He levelled at the other end a minute later and got the match winner on 33 minutes.

WEDNESDAY 30TH APRIL 1986

Leicester City were left on the brink of relegation to Division Two by a 2-0 defeat against Liverpool at Filbert Street. A crowd of 25,779 saw goals from Ian Rush and Ronnie Whelan send the battle for survival at the bottom into a nerve-wracking final day of the season.

SATURDAY 30TH APRIL 1983

Gordon Milne's Leicester City made it 12 games unbeaten at home with a 0-0 draw against Bolton Wanderers at Filbert Street. City had been expected to beat the side bottom of the Division Two table just seven days after the sensational win at Fulham and the result meant City stayed just outside the top-three promotion places.

MONDAY 30TH APRIL 1962

David Thompson marked his Leicester City debut with a goal against Tottenham Hotspur in the Division One clash at Filbert Street. Graham Cross was the other marksman for City in a 3-2 defeat.

LEICESTER CITY
On This Day & Miscellany

MAY

SATURDAY 1ST MAY 1971

A 2-1 win at Portsmouth capped a 17-match unbeaten run that powered Frank O'Farrell's team to the Second Division championship. John Farrington and Ally Brown were the marksmen.

SATURDAY 1ST MAY 2004

Leicester City drew 2-2 at Charlton Athletic and were relegated from the Premier League. Micky Adams' team went ahead in the fifth minute through a spectacular strike from Marcus Bent before the Addicks hit back through goals from Jonathan Fortune and Paolo Di Canio. Les Ferdinand belted home an unstoppable free-kick with two minutes left, but it wasn't enough to save City from the drop just a year after they had been promoted to the top flight as Championship runners-up.

SATURDAY 1ST MAY 1937

Leicester City clinched the Division Two championship with a 4-1 thumping of Tottenham Hotspur at Filbert Street. Jack Bowers got two goals for City and the others came from Arthur Maw and Tony Carrol.

SATURDAY 2ND MAY 1925

John Duncan's two goals in the 4-0 drubbing of Stockport County at Filbert Street took his tally for the season to 30 and secured the Division Two championship for Leicester City. Arthur Chandler completed an ever-present season with a goal and George Carr added the other. The result completed an astonishing end to the season for Peter Hodge's team. The results from December 6 were as follows: 16 wins, eight draws and only one defeat.

SATURDAY 2ND MAY 1988

Paul Groves became the first Leicester City substitute to score on his debut in the 3-0 win over Huddersfield Town at Filbert Street. Groves, signed by Foxes boss David Pleat from Burton Albion, scored a second-half header after Nicky Cross had earlier netted twice.

SATURDAY 2ND MAY 1981

Jim Melrose got all Leicester City's goals as they ended a relegation season with a 3-2 win at Norwich City that also condemned the Canaries to the drop to Division Two.

MONDAY 2ND MAY 2016

9.56pm to be precise... The moment Leicester City, 5,000/1 outsiders at the start of the season, became Premier League champions. Tottenham Hotspur had to beat Chelsea at Stamford Bridge to have any chance of catching City at the top of the Premier League table. Harry Kane and Hueng-Min Son kept their hopes alive with goals that put them 2-0 up, but Gary Cahill halved the arrears and with six minutes left, Eden Hazard struck a spectacular equaliser for Chelsea. Spurs couldn't find a response and at the final whistle, Leicester, Leicestershire and anyone with Leicester or Leicestershire in their blood celebrated. This was better than the day David Pleat was sacked, beating Manchester United from 3-1 down, winning at Wembley or even the time Ian Ormondroyd tripping over his own feet at Ipswich Town when he was clean through on goal. All rolled into one. Leicester City – forgive me for repeating myself, but it makes me feel good – were the Premier League champions. And yes, Nottingham was watching.

SATURDAY 3RD MAY 1980

Larry May headed the only goal at Jimmy Bloomfield-managed Leyton Orient to secure the Division Two title for Jock Wallace's Leicester City team. The result meant the Foxes finished the season with a seven-game unbeaten run that included six wins.

SATURDAY 3RD MAY 1986

Leicester City avoided the drop from Division One on a nail-biting final day of the season thanks to a 2-0 win over Newcastle United at Filbert Street. The result, and a defeat for relegation rivals Ipswich Town at Sheffield Wednesday, meant Gordon Milne's team escaped a relegation that had looked certain for much of a disappointing season. City had lost their previous three games and shipped ten goals before the visit of Newcastle. But the nerves were eased by Ali Mauchlen's first-half strike and Ian Banks netted the second from the penalty spot to prompt celebrations at the final whistle from the majority of a 13,171 crowd.

WEDNESDAY 3RD MAY 2000

Goals from Tony Cottee and Phil Gilchrist clinched a 2-0 win for Martin O'Neill's Leicester City at Liverpool in the Premiership and maintained the Foxes' tremendous record at Anfield. Pegguy Arphexad was the visitors' other hero. The French goalkeeper was in superb form between the posts and Liverpool remembered his performance and ended up signing him.

SATURDAY 3RD MAY 1997

Leicester City and Premier League champions Manchester United battled out a thrilling 2-2 draw in the sunshine at Filbert Street. Steve Walsh and Ian Marshall were the goalscorers for City with Ole Gunnar Solskjaer grabbing both replies for the table toppers.

MONDAY 3RD MAY 1994

Leicester City stayed fourth in Division One with a 1-1 draw against Bolton Wanderers at Filbert Street. Phil Gee got the goal for Brian Little's team in the penultimate game of the regular season before the play-off semi-finals. City had already secured their place in the play-offs.

SUNDAY 4TH MAY 2008

Gary Lineker described this as "the worst day in the club's history". He was right. Leicester City were relegated to the third tier of English football for the first time following a 0-0 draw at Stoke City, who were promoted to the Premier League. Ian Holloway's team made the trip to the Britannia Stadium knowing their superior goal difference would keep them up if they emulated or bettered Southampton's result in their home date with Sheffield United. Southampton fell behind, but went on to snatch a 3-2 win and Leicester could only manage a draw at Stoke.

SATURDAY 4TH MAY 1954

Teenager Bernie Thomas bagged a hat-trick in a 4-0 thrashing of Bolton Wanderers at Filbert Street that came too late to prevent Leicester City finishing bottom of Division One. Thomas became the youngest-ever player to score a hat-trick for the Foxes. He was only 17 years and 350 days old. Derek Hogg scored the other goal.

WEDNESDAY 4TH MAY 1966

Peter Shilton made his debut for Leicester City. He kept a clean sheet in a 3-0 win over Everton at Filbert Street. Jackie Sinclair, Derek Dougan and Paul Matthews got City's goals.

SATURDAY 4TH MAY 1985

Gary Lineker's two goals in a 4-3 defeat at Queens Park Rangers took him to a century of goals for Leicester City in his 214th game. Ian Wilson got the other.

SATURDAY 4TH MAY 1935

Leicester City went into the last game of the season at Portsmouth knowing they needed a victory and Middlesbrough to lose at Chelsea to stay in Division One. City went behind after just six minutes, Gene O'Callaghan levelled, but Middlesbrough's draw at Chelsea meant it wasn't enough.

SATURDAY 4TH MAY 1939

Frank Womack resigned as Leicester City manager before the 2-0 defeat against Wolverhampton Wanderers that was the final game in a season that ended in relegation from Division One.

SATURDAY 5TH MAY 2001

Peter Taylor's Leicester City ended a club-record run of nine successive defeats with a 4-2 thrashing of Tottenham Hotspur at Filbert Street. Gary Rowett, Dean Sturridge, Steve Guppy and Robbie Savage got the goals for City.

MONDAY 6TH MAY 1985

Gary Lineker scored both Leicester City's goals in a 2-0 win over Sunderland in what proved to be his final appearance at Filbert Street.

SATURDAY 6TH MAY 1961

Leicester City were back at Wembley for the FA Cup Final against Tottenham Hotspur. Boss Matt Gillies sprang a surprise before kick-off when he picked Hugh McIlmoyle instead of top scorer Ken Leek and disaster struck when an injury to Len Chalmers meant City had to play with effectively ten men for 70 minutes. Bobby Smith and Terry Dyson got the second-half goals that took the cup back to White Hart Lane.

SATURDAY 7TH MAY 1987

David Pleat's Leicester City denied Middlesbrough promotion to Division One with a shock 2-1 win at Ayresome Park. Middlesbrough knew victory would secure their place in the top flight, but goals from Peter Weir and Gary McAllister secured victory for the visitors and spoiled the party.

SATURDAY 7TH MAY 1949

The end of an era. Septimus Smith, regarded as one of Leicester City's greatest-ever players, made his final appearance for the Foxes. Leicester, beaten in the FA Cup Final by Wolverhampton Wanderers seven days earlier, ended the Division Two season with a 1-1 draw at Cardiff City secured by Jack Lee's goal. In total, Smith played 586 games for the Foxes – including 213 during World War II.

SATURDAY 7TH MAY 1983

Robbie Jones marked his Leicester City debut with a goal in a priceless 2-1 win at Oldham Athletic that took Gordon Milne's team to the brink of promotion to the First Division. Paul Ramsey got the winner for the Foxes to keep them third.

SATURDAY 7TH MAY 2016

Leicester City were presented with the Premier League trophy – designed by a Birstall jeweller! – after a 3-1 win over Everton at the King Power Stadium. Scorers were Jamie Vardy (two) and Andy King and the crowd, with a few exceptions, chanted: "Champions of England, we know what they are."

SATURDAY 8TH MAY 1999

A 2-0 win over Newcastle United at Filbert Street lifted Martin O'Neill's Leicester City up to 10th place in the Premiership. Muzzy Izzet and Tony Cottee got the goals for the Foxes.

SUNDAY 8TH MAY 1994

Leicester City's 1-1 draw at Wolverhampton Wanderers ensured they finished the Division One season with a nine-game unbeaten run. Gary Coatsworth got the goal for Brian Little's team that meant they finished fourth in the table and secured a trip to Tranmere Rovers in the first leg of the play-off semi-final.

SUNDAY 9TH MAY 1992

Hide behind the sofa time. Leicester City lost 7-1 at Newcastle United in front of the television cameras. They trailed 6-0 at the break and former Leicester striker David Kelly scored a hat-trick. So did Andy Cole. Fortunately, Brian Little's team had already booked their place in the play-offs. Steve Walsh's goal did give the visiting fans something to cheer. "We drew the second half," he said afterwards.

SATURDAY 9TH MAY 1987

A 0-0 draw at Oxford United meant Bryan Hamilton's Leicester City were relegated from Division One in Alan Smith's last game for the club before he joined Arsenal. At least the draw meant Leicester ended a run of 17 successive defeats away from home. Smith had agreed to join the Gunners two months earlier for an £800,000 fee and was then loaned back to City for the rest of the campaign to help the battle against the drop.

SUNDAY 10TH MAY 1992

Thrashed 5-1 at Cambridge United eight months earlier, Brian Little's team returned to the Abbey Stadium for the Division One play-off semi-final first leg and came away with a 1-1 draw to take into the second leg three days later. Kevin Russell put the Foxes ahead with a sweetly-struck shot from the edge of the penalty area and Leicester-born Dion Dublin levelled for Cambridge.

SATURDAY 11TH MAY 2002

It's what the old place would have wanted. Leicester-born Matt Piper grabbed the last ever goal at Filbert Street – and it was a stunner. His diving header secured a 2-1 win over Tottenham Hotspur, but Leicester City still went down from the Premiership with their relegation having already been confirmed. There wasn't a dry eye in the place.

SATURDAY 11TH MAY 1985

Gary Lineker made his last appearance for Leicester City in a 4-0 defeat at Luton Town in Division One. Lineker ended the season with 24 goals and that made him the joint top scorer in Division One with Chelsea striker Kerry Dixon. He went on to join Everton during the summer.

SUNDAY 12TH MAY 1996

Leicester City were held to a goalless draw in the first leg of the semi-final against Stoke City at Filbert Street. Goalkeeper Kevin Poole pulled off an astonishing double save early in the game and Brian Little's team were glad to go into the second leg in the Potteries on level terms.

WEDNESDAY 13TH MAY 1992

Leicester City secured a return to Wembley after 23 years with a 5-0 crushing of Cambridge United in the second leg of the Division One play-off semi-final. The score was tied at 1-1 after the first leg and Tommy Wright (2), Steve Thompson, Kevin Russell and Ian Ormondroyd found the target as Cambridge fell apart.

SATURDAY 14TH MAY 1983

Gordon Milne's team drew 0-0 with Burnley at Filbert Street and that was enough to secure promotion to Division One at Fulham's expense. The result stretched Leicester City's unbeaten run to 15 games. But the promotion celebrations had to wait. The Football League held an enquiry after Fulham complained that their last game at Derby should be replayed because a pitch invasion meant it finished 75 seconds early. The appeal was rejected and Leicester were promoted.

SUNDAY 14TH MAY 1995

A 2-2 draw at Southampton came too late to save City from relegation from the Premiership. They finished the season unbeaten in their last three games, but won only six times throughout the campaign.

SUNDAY 14TH MAY 2000

Leicester City's 4-0 defeat at Sheffield Wednesday on the final day of the season didn't prevent them securing their best-ever finish in the Premier League. Martin O'Neill's team finished the season eighth.

SUNDAY 15TH MAY 1994

Brian Little's team drew 0-0 at Tranmere Rovers in the first leg of the Division One play-off semi-final. Gavin Ward made several crucial saves for Leicester City and Simon Grayson may have used his hand to keep out another goal-bound effort, but the only people that noticed were the crowd and the players.

TUESDAY 15TH MAY 1996

Garry Parker hit a second-half winner at Stoke City to take Leicester City through to the Division One play-off final at Wembley for the fourth time in five seasons.

SATURDAY 15TH MAY 2004

Leicester City bowed out of the Premiership after a 2-1 defeat at Arsenal. The result meant the Gunners ended the season unbeaten, but they had to come from behind to beat Micky Adams' team. Paul Dickov put the Foxes ahead with a 26th minute header following good work from Frank Sinclair. Thierry Henry levelled from the spot and Patrick Vieira grabbed the winner.

SUNDAY 16TH MAY 1993

Redevelopment work on Filbert Street's Main Stand meant the first leg of the Division One play-off semi-final against Portsmouth had to be played at Nottingham Forest's City Ground. Substitute Julian Joachim was Leicester City's second-half goal hero with a stunning solo goal that delighted a Trent End packed with Foxes' fans. He got the ball just inside his own half, sped away from his marker and then accelerated past another couple of challenges before poking home the only goal of the game through the goalkeeper's legs.

MONDAY 16TH MAY 1977

Leicester City were beaten 1-0 at home by Leeds United in Division One in what proved to be Jimmy Bloomfield's final match in charge.

SATURDAY 16TH MAY 2015

With a goalless draw at Sunderland, Nigel Pearson's Leicester City completed the greatest of great escapes. For 130 days, including Christmas Day, City had been bottom of the Premier League table –

and with eight games remaining, their situation was desperate. They were seven points adrift of safety. Somehow, City gave themselves a chance by winning five out of their next six games – a loss at home to champions Chelsea was the only hiccup in the run – to take them out of the drop zone and with results elsewhere going their way, a point at the Stadium of Light, that owed much to the acrobatics of goalkeeper Kasper Schmeichel, was enough to keep Leicester in the top flight for another season.

SATURDAY 17TH MAY 1969

Leicester City, beaten in the FA Cup Final by Manchester City three weeks earlier, headed to Manchester United knowing they needed a victory to stay in Division One. The Reds were fired up because it was Sir Matt Busby's last game in charge, but the Foxes got off to the perfect start with David Nish giving them a first-minute lead at Old Trafford. The Foxes were behind by the fourth minute, however, with George Best weaving his magic to put United on level terms before the home side snatched another moments later to take the lead. Rodney Fern grabbed a second for City, but they were beaten 3-2 and suffered the drop to Division Two.

SUNDAY 17TH MAY 1992

Gary Lineker missed the chance to draw level with Bobby Charlton's record haul of 49 goals for England in a 1-1 draw against Brazil in a friendly at Wembley. Leicester City legend Lineker had a first-half penalty saved by goalkeeper Carlos Gallo and David Platt scored four minutes after the break to secure a 1-1 draw for Graham Taylor's team as they prepared for the start of the forthcoming European Championships in Sweden.

SATURDAY 18TH MAY 1974

Leicester City players Peter Shilton, Keith Weller and Frank Worthington were in the England side beaten 2-0 by Scotland at Hampden Park.

TUESDAY 19TH MAY 1993

Brian Little's team booked their return to Wembley for a second successive Division One play-off final by holding Portsmouth to a 2-2 draw at a highly-charged Fratton Park. Leicester City went through

3-2 on aggregate. They trailed at Pompey and then Ian Ormondroyd stabbed home the leveller and Steve Thompson's strike put them ahead. Portsmouth made it 2-2 on the night, but Julian Joachim's first leg cracker proved to be the difference between the sides. On the same night, Chris Pyatt became the first boxer from Leicester to win a world title. He outpointed Sumbu Kalambay for the vacant WBO middleweight championship at the Granby Halls in his home city.

MONDAY 20TH MAY 1940

Leicester City battled to a goalless draw at Birmingham City in the Regional League Midland Division.

WEDNESDAY 20TH MAY 1998

Martin O'Neill's Leicester City drew 0-0 at Tampa Bay Mutiny on their American tour.

WEDNESDAY 22ND MAY 1974

Frank Worthington got his first goal for England in a 1-1 draw against Argentina at Wembley.

MONDAY 23RD MAY 1977

Jimmy Bloomfield resigned as Leicester City manager. The Foxes finished 11th in Division One despite winning only one of their last ten games. That represented a failure to a club who had ambitions of European qualification, at least, going into the season.

FRIDAY 23RD MAY 2008

Ian Holloway was sacked as Leicester City manager. He had failed to prevent the club being relegated to the third tier of English football for the first time in their history.

WEDNESDAY 24TH MAY 1978

Jock Wallace was named Leicester City's new manager. He had previously been in charge at Scottish giants Rangers and inherited a team that had just been relegated to Division Two.

SATURDAY 25TH MAY 1963

Leicester City were beaten 3-1 by Manchester United in the FA Cup Final. City were favourites going into the game. They had been chasing the league and cup double before suffering a slump in form, while United had been battling against the drop. Denis Law and David Herd put United 2-0 ahead before Ken Keyworth's diving header with nine minutes remaining handed Leicester a lifeline. Herd's second goal put the game beyond the Foxes.

FRIDAY 25TH MAY 2007

Martin Allen was appointed Leicester City manager having previously been at MK Dons and Brentford. He didn't last long.

MONDAY 25TH MAY 1992

Leicester City missed out on a place in the newly-formed Premier League after a controversial penalty sent them crashing to defeat in the Division One play-off final at Wembley. The decisive moment in the clash with Blackburn Rovers came in the dying minutes of the first half. David Speedie took a tumble under Steve Walsh's challenge and former Leicester striker Mike Newell stepped up to net from the penalty spot. City were denied a leveller after the break by several goal-line clearances and Muggleton kept out Newell's second spot kick late in the game.

SATURDAY 26TH MAY 1984

Leicester City striker Gary Lineker made his England debut. He came on in the second half of a 1-1 draw against Scotland at Hampden Park. He had ended the previous season with 22 goals in Division One to earn his call-up.

SATURDAY 26TH MAY 1973

Leicester City beat Ipswich Town 3-2 in a pre-season match in Barbados as part of a post-season tournament. Frank Worthington netted twice for the Foxes while Len Glover bagged the other goal.

MONDAY 27TH MAY 1999

The clock was ticking towards a penalty shoot-out in the Division One play-off final at Wembley between Leicester City and Crystal Palace when a free-kick dropped to Steve Claridge just outside the penalty area. He swung a boot at the ball and sent it sailing into the top corner of the net past stunned goalkeeper Nigel Martyn. There was barely time for Palace to restart the game before the referee blew the whistle to herald the end to one of the most dramatic games held at Wembley. Claridge admitted afterwards that he mishit his shot and that the ball went in off his shin. Nobody in Leicester cared. Leicester had earlier fallen behind to Andy Roberts' first-half opener and Garry Parker levelled from the penalty spot with 14 minutes left after Muzzy Izzet had been sent crashing in the box.

WEDNESDAY 27TH MAY 1964

Gordon Banks had one of his less demanding games. He was in goal for England in their 10-0 thumping of the USA in a friendly in New York.

WEDNESDAY 28TH MAY 1969

Leicester City teammates Peter Shilton and David Nish played for England under-23s in the 1-1 draw against their Portugal counterparts in Funchal.

WEDNESDAY 29TH MAY 1996

Leicester City defender Colin Hill was part of the Northern Ireland team that upset the odds by holding Germany to a 1-1 draw in a friendly.

MONDAY 30TH MAY 1994

Leicester City finally won at Wembley and not before time. This was their seventh game at the grand old stadium. Steve Walsh was the Foxes hero in the 2-1 win over Derby County. He had spent most of the previous eight months on the sidelines following a cruciate ligament injury, but came to City's rescue after they fell behind to Tommy Johnson's opener. Walsh levelled with a header from Gary Coatsworth's cross and got the winner with four minutes left. Simon Grayson swung over a cross that Ian Ormondroyd headed goalwards. Rams keeper Martin Taylor got a hand to the ball, but Walsh was there to slot home the winner and send City back into the top flight.

MONDAY 31ST MAY 1993

In the space of 12 breathless minutes Leicester City wiped out Swindon Town's 3-0 lead in the Division One play-off final at Wembley to draw level. Julian Joachim belted home the first, Steve Walsh headed home Lee Philpott's cross and Steve Thompson kept his cool to slide home the leveller after Mike Whitlow had made the break and pulled the ball into his path. But with seven minutes left, Swindon striker Steve White went down under Colin Hill's challenge and Paul Bodin netted the penalty to break Leicester hearts at Wembley. Again. That made it six defeats at Wembley for City and followed the previous season's controversial defeat against Blackburn Rovers in the play-off final.

LEICESTER CITY
On This Day & Miscellany

JUNE

THURSDAY 1ST JUNE 2000

Martin O'Neill was announced as Celtic's new manager after four and a half years at Leicester City. In his time at Filbert Street, O'Neill took the Foxes to four successive top-ten finishes in the Premiership – and two League Cups – and will be remembered as one of the best managers in the club's history.

TUESDAY 1ST JUNE 1971

Leicester City started their challenge for the Anglo-Italian Cup with a 1-0 defeat at Cagliari.

MONDAY 2ND JUNE 2003

England played Serbia and Montenegro in a friendly at the Walkers Stadium. Leicester City goalkeeper Ian Walker was named in Sven-Goran Eriksson's squad, but didn't get the chance to play in front of his home crowd. Joe Cole blasted home England's winner after Steven Gerrard had earlier put them ahead and Serbia and Montenegro levelled on the stroke of half-time.

TUESDAY 3RD JUNE 1969

Allan Clarke got two goals for the English FA XI in a 4-0 win over Guadalajara. Clarke's Leicester City teammate Peter Shilton was in goal and he saw the Foxes striker open the scoring with a header before adding another strike.

TUESDAY 4TH JUNE 1971

Jon Sammels netted a goal double and Keith Weller was also on target for Leicester City, but it wasn't enough to prevent a 5-3 defeat against Atalanta in their second game in the Anglo-Italian Cup.

SATURDAY 5TH JUNE 1999

Leicester City defender Matt Elliott was sent off playing for Scotland against the Faroe Islands in a European Championship qualifier. The game ended in a 1-1 draw.

WEDNESDAY 6TH JUNE 1962

Mark Bright, future Leicester City striker, was born in Stoke-on-Trent, Staffordshire.

MONDAY 7TH JUNE 1971

Leicester City grabbed their first win in the Anglo-Italian Cup in their third match with a 2-1 win over Cagliari at Filbert Street. David Nish and Keith Weller were the marksmen.

SATURDAY 7TH JUNE 1947

Leicester City's Division Two season came to a late end with a 2-0 win over Fulham at Filbert Street that was secured by goals from Charlie Adam and Don Revie. The result meant the Foxes finished ninth in Division Two.

SATURDAY 7TH JUNE 1986

John O'Neill became the most capped Leicester City player in the club's history. O'Neill earned his 38th cap for Northern Ireland in the 2-1 World Cup defeat against Spain in Guadalajara. The game took him past Gordon Banks' tally of 37 caps for England.

SATURDAY 8TH JUNE 1940

Goals from Logan and Houghton meant Leicester City finished their Regional League Midlands Division campaign with a 2-0 win over Northampton Town at Filbert Street.

TUESDAY 9TH JUNE 1998

Leicester City goalkeeper Kasey Keller came on as a second-half substitute for the USA in a 4-0 friendly win over FC Gueugnon in France.

THURSDAY 10TH JUNE 1971

Leicester City ended their Anglo-Italian Cup campaign with a 6-0 walloping of Atalanta at Filbert Street. Keith Weller scored twice in the romp and the others came from David Nish, Jon Sammels, Len Glover and John Farrington.

TUESDAY 11TH JUNE 1968

Leicester City completed the signing of Allan Clarke from Fulham for a British record transfer fee of £150,000. Frank Large went to Craven Cottage in exchange. Clarke was an England under-23 international and in two seasons at Fulham had scored 29 and 26 goals, respectively, for the Cottagers to demand the record fee.

MONDAY 12TH JUNE 2000

Peter Taylor became Leicester City boss following Martin O'Neill's departure to Celtic. Taylor had previously been in charge at Gillingham.

FRIDAY 12TH JUNE 1986

Leicester City defender John O'Neill made his 39th and last appearance for Northern Ireland in a 3-0 defeat against Brazil in Guadalajara in the World Cup. He had previously surpassed Gordon Banks' record of international appearances while at Leicester.

SATURDAY 13TH JUNE 1908

Leicester Fosse goalkeeper Horace Bailey earned his fifth and last cap for England in a 4-0 win over Bohemia in Prague. In his five appearances for his country, Bailey conceded only three goals and England netted 35 times at the other end.

SUNDAY 14TH JUNE 1959

Bob Hazell, future City defender, was born in Kingston, Jamaica.

THURSDAY 15TH JUNE 2000

Leicester City midfielder Muzzy Izzet made his debut for Turkey in a 0-0 draw against Sweden in the European Championships.

MONDAY 16TH JUNE 1913

Leicester Fosse set off on a 46-hour, sea and sail journey to Gothenburg for a whirlwind five-match tour paid for by the Swedish FA.

SUNDAY 16TH JUNE 1985

Gary Lineker made his last England appearance as a Leicester City player. He got two goals in a 5-0 win over the USA in a friendly in Los Angeles.

WEDNESDAY 17TH JUNE 1992

Gary Lineker made his final appearance for England. He was substituted after 61 minutes of a vital Euro 92 clash against Sweden in Stockholm. Ironically, he was replaced by former Foxes strike partner Alan Smith. England went on to lose 2-1 and crash out of the tournament with boss Graham Taylor criticised for his decision to withdraw Lineker, who finished with 48 goals from 80 appearances.

WEDNESDAY 18TH JUNE 1913

Leicester Fosse started their five-match pre-season competition in Sweden with a 3-2 win over an Orgryte/IFK Goteburg Combined XI. Fred Mortimer got two goals for Fosse.

THURSDAY 19TH JUNE 1958

Trevor Hebberd, who went on to play for Leicester City, was born in New Alresford in Hampshire.

FRIDAY 20TH JUNE 2008

Nigel Pearson was appointed Leicester City's manager following the dismissal of Ian Holloway. Ironically, Pearson had been in charge the previous season at Southampton, who had stayed in the Championship at City's expense and sent the Foxes crashing out of the top two divisions in English football for the first time in their history.

SATURDAY 21ST JUNE 1913

Fred Mortimer bagged a hat-trick for Leicester Fosse in a 4-0 drubbing of a Stockholm Select XI as part of their five matches in Sweden.

SUNDAY 22ND JUNE 1913

Leicester Fosse made it three straight wins on their tour of Sweden with a 4-2 thumping of the Swedish national team that was inspired by Tommy Benfield's goal double.

WEDNESDAY 23RD JUNE 1971

Jimmy Bloomfield was unveiled as Leicester City's new manager following the departure of Frank O'Farrell to Manchester United. Bloomfield had impressed in taking Leyton Orient to the Third Division championship the previous season.

MONDAY 23RD JUNE 1969

Leicester City striker Allan Clarke was put on the transfer list. City boss Frank O'Farrell said: "Clarke has told me several times that he was not anxious to play in Second Division football. So, it has been decided that it would be in the best interests of the club and player if we put him on the open-to-offers list."

TUESDAY 24TH JUNE 1913

Tommy Benfield netted twice as Leicester Fosse cruised to a crushing 5-1 win over Gefle IF in their pre-season tour of Sweden. Fosse's other marksmen in the victory were Teddy King, Tom Waterall and Fred Mortimer. The result made it four straight wins on the tour with just one game remaining.

TUESDAY 24TH JUNE 1969

Allan Clarke left Leicester City for Leeds United in a £165,000 deal that broke the British transfer record set 12 months earlier when he joined the Foxes from Fulham. In his only season with City, Clarke finished with 16 goals in all competitions. He was man of the match in the FA Cup Final. His 12 goals in the league couldn't keep City in Division One.

TUESDAY 24TH JUNE 1986

Steve Walsh joined Leicester City from Wigan Athletic for a fee of £100,000. He was brought to Filbert Street by boss Bryan Hamilton having helped his Wigan team win the Freight Rover Trophy in 1985.

FRIDAY 25TH JUNE 1971

Neil Lennon was born in Lurgan, Northern Ireland.

WEDNESDAY 26TH JUNE 2002

Leicester City midfielder Muzzy Izzet came on as a second-half substitute for Turkey in the World Cup semi-final against Brazil in Japan. Izzet came on in the 73rd minute for Umit Davala and couldn't help Turkey overhaul the lead given to Brazil by Ronaldo's strike four minutes into the second half. Brazil went on to win the World Cup with a 2-0 victory over Germany in the final. Playing in the semi-final capped a sensational rise for Izzet. He was plucked from Chelsea reserves by then Leicester boss Martin O'Neill in March 1996 and the midfield playmaker went on to become a Foxes legend by helping the team to promotion, four successive Premier League top-ten finishes and two League Cup victories.

WEDNESDAY 26TH JUNE 1968

Future Leicester City striker Iwan Roberts was born in Bangor, Caernarvonshire.

TUESDAY 27TH JUNE 1967

Tony James, future Leicester City defender, was born in Sheffield. He will forever be remembered by Foxes fans for the goal against Oxford United at Filbert Street on the last day of the 1990-1991 season that saved City from what would have been a first-ever relegation to the third tier of English football.

FRIDAY 27TH JUNE 1913

Leicester Fosse ended their five-match Swedish trip in stunning style. They beat the Swedish national team for the second time with a 4-2 win and that made it five straight victories for Fosse on the club's first-ever pre-season tour. Prince Eugene was in the crowd and saw Fred Mortimer bag a hat-trick for Fosse. That took his tally for the historic five-match trip to ten goals. Fosse ended the tour having scored 20 goals and conceded just five at the other end.

FRIDAY 28TH JUNE 1974

Neil Lewis was born in Wolverhampton.

WEDNESDAY 29TH JUNE 1960

Ali Mauchlen was born in Kilwinning, Ayrshire. Mauchlen went on to join Leicester City, along with Motherwell teammate Gary McAllister, in August 1985 and became a hero to Foxes fans.

MONDAY 30TH JUNE 1982

The *Leicester Mercury* reported that Scottish Premier League side Motherwell were hoping to recruit Foxes boss Jock Wallace. Leicester City stated that there had been no contact from Motherwell, but newspaper reports in Scotland suggested a move was imminent. The previous season, Wallace had steered City to the semi-finals of the FA Cup where they were beaten 2-0 by eventual winners Tottenham Hotspur at Villa Park. He also guided the Foxes to the Second Division championship in 1979-1980, although he was unable to keep them in the top flight the following season despite predicting his team could win the title. Wallace had arrived at Filbert Street from Scottish giants Glasgow Rangers in the summer of 1978 and rebuilt the club's fortunes.

LEICESTER CITY
On This Day & Miscellany

JULY

TUESDAY 1ST JULY 1986

Leicester City received a welcome £250,000 windfall when Gary Lineker completed his move to Barcelona from Everton for £2.75m. Lineker had scooped the Golden Boot at the World Cup in Mexico during the summer. He scored six times as England reached the quarter-finals.

TUESDAY 2ND JULY 1985

Goalkeeper Mark Wallington left Leicester City for Derby County for a fee of £25,000. He made 460 appearances for the Foxes – including a club-record 331 consecutive games.

SUNDAY 3RD JULY 1881

Horace Bailey, Leicester Fosse's first England keeper, was born in Derby.

TUESDAY 4TH JULY 2000

Gary Rowett became Peter Taylor's first signing as Leicester City manager when he joined from Birmingham City for £3m. Taylor had taken charge at Filbert Street following Martin O'Neill's decision to join Celtic and was preparing the team for their fifth successive season in the top flight.

TUESDAY 5TH JULY 1898

Pat Carrigan, who went on to be a key member of Leicester City's defence for more than six years, was born in Lanarkshire, Scotland.

TUESDAY 6TH JULY 1971

Former Leicester City striker Hugh McIlmoyle quit football to become a van driver – much to the surprise of Preston North End! He had been on the brink of joining them from Middlesbrough.

FRIDAY 7TH JULY 2000

Callum Davidson joined Leicester City from Premiership rivals Blackburn Rovers for a fee of £1.75m as Foxes boss Peter Taylor continued his summer spending spree.

MONDAY 8TH JULY 1996

Muzzy Izzet completed a £650,000 move from Chelsea to Leicester City. He had been on loan for the last two months of the previous season.

MONDAY 9TH JULY 2001

Leicester City boss Peter Taylor completed the signing of former England goalkeeper Ian Walker from Tottenham Hotspur for £1.75m. Walker, who had made four appearances for his country, was brought in to compete with Tim Flowers for the goalkeeping jersey in the forthcoming Premiership campaign.

SUNDAY 10TH JULY 1927

Don Revie, future Leicester City player, was born in Middlesbrough.

SUNDAY 11TH JULY 1965

Tony Cottee was born in West Ham, London. He went on to become one of the success stories of Martin O'Neill's spell as Leicester City manager.

MONDAY 12TH JULY 1982

Jock Wallace resigned as Leicester City manager having led the Foxes into the semi-finals of the FA Cup the previous season. He was strongly linked with a move to Scottish Premier Division side Motherwell and City threatened to take them to court if Wallace joined them following his departure from Filbert Street after four years in charge.

MONDAY 13TH JULY 2015

Claudio Ranieri was appointed Leicester manager – and Leicester legend Gary Lineker was underwhelmed. It was, Tweeted the national treasure and crisp thief, an "uninspired choice".

FRIDAY 14TH JULY 1972

Leicester City announced their intention to abandon their traditional blue and white and wear an all white kit for the forthcoming season.

THURSDAY 15TH JULY 1982

Leicester City fans and board were left fuming as Jock Wallace was unveiled as Motherwell's new manager at a press conference at the Scottish Premier League club.

WEDNESDAY 16TH JULY 1997

Foxes striker Emile Heskey netted twice as Martin O'Neill's Leicester City ran out 7-1 winners at Penzance in a pre-season friendly.

FRIDAY 17TH JULY 1971

Ipswich Town agreed a fee of £100,000 for Arsenal forward Jon Sammels, who had also attracted interest from Leicester City and asked for a few days to think over the offer.

FRIDAY 18TH JULY 1997

Leicester City were 3-1 winners at Torpoint in a friendly. The goals came from Sam McMahon, Steve Guppy and Emile Heskey.

MONDAY 19TH JULY 1982

Alan Smith joined Leicester City from non-league Alvechurch. He was signed by acting boss Ian McFarlane after Jock Wallace's departure to Scottish Premier League side Motherwell.

SATURDAY 20TH JULY 2002

Dennis Wise was sent home from the pre-season tour of Finland and suspended after teammate Callum Davidson suffered a double fracture of his cheekbone following a dispute during a game of cards. The incident led to Wise being sacked by Leicester City.

WEDNESDAY 21ST JULY 1971

Jon Sammels became Jimmy Bloomfield's first signing as Leicester City boss when he joined from Arsenal in a £100,000 deal.

THURSDAY 22ND JULY 1982

Former Coventry City boss Gordon Milne was appointed Leicester City manager following the departure of Jock Wallace to Motherwell.

TUESDAY 23RD JULY 2002

Gary Lineker officially opened the Walkers Stadium as Micky Adams' team prepared for the new season after relegation from the Premier League in the previous campaign under previous boss Dave Bassett.

MONDAY 24TH JULY 1950

Leicester City reported back for pre-season without striker Jack Lee. There had been outrage among fans when news broke that Foxes boss Norman Bullock was selling him to local rivals Derby County for £16,000. Arthur Rowley joined from Fulham as a replacement for Lee.

TUESDAY 25TH JULY 2000

Ade Akinbiyi joined Leicester City from Wolverhampton Wanderers for a club record fee of £5m. Foxes boss Peter Taylor hoped Akinbiyi would fire his team into Europe.

FRIDAY 26TH JULY 1935

Ken Leek was born in Ynysybwl, near Pontypridd in Wales.

THURSDAY 27TH JULY 1989

Wayne Clarke joined Leicester City from Everton more than two decades after brother Allan came to Filbert Street in a record-breaking transfer. As part of the deal, Mike Newell left Leicester for Everton.

FRIDAY 28TH JULY 2000

Darren Eadie was on target as Leicester City won 1-0 against Finn Harps in Ireland.

SATURDAY 29TH JULY 1989

Wayne Clarke bagged his first goals for Leicester City, after joining from Everton, in a 6-1 pre-season win against Swedish side Solleftea. David Puttnam added two and Steve Wilkinson and Paul Groves also scored.

SATURDAY 30TH JULY 1966

Leicester City goalkeeper Gordon Banks was between the posts as England lifted the World Cup at Wembley. England beat West Germany 4-2 with Geoff Hurst scoring a hat-trick. Banks earned his 33rd cap on the greatest day in English football history.

FRIDAY 30TH JULY 1999

Former England goalkeeper Tim Flowers joined Martin O'Neill's team from Blackburn Rovers for a fee of £1.1m. Flowers had helped Blackburn win the Premiership crown in 1994-95 as Jack Walker's millions funded the title charge.

WEDNESDAY 31ST JULY 1946

Allan Clarke, future Leicester City striker, was born in Willenhall, Staffordshire. Clarke's moves to and from Filbert Street two decades later set records for British transfer fees.

LEICESTER CITY
On This Day & Miscellany

AUGUST

FRIDAY 1ST AUGUST 1997

Robbie Savage joined Leicester City from Crewe Alexandra. He was left out of the Railwaymen's team for the previous season's play-offs after refusing to sign a new contract and came to join Martin O'Neill's Premiership team in a deal rising to £650,000.

THURSDAY 1ST AUGUST 1993

David Speedie joined Brian Little's Leicester City from Blackburn Rovers and Foxes fans were divided. Speedie had been a target for City fans since the play-off final in 1992 when he took a tumble under a challenge for Steve Walsh and Mike Newell netted from the penalty spot to end Leicester's Premier League dream.

TUESDAY 1ST AUGUST 1989

Tommy Wright, a cousin of former City favourite Jackie Sinclair, made a £350,000 switch from Oldham Athletic to join David Pleat's team.

FRIDAY 2ND AUGUST 2002

Dennis Wise was sacked by Leicester City after he was found guilty of serious misconduct following an incident on the pre-season tour of Finland that left teammate Callum Davidson with a double fracture of his cheekbone. The dispute followed a game of cards.

SATURDAY 2ND AUGUST 1975

Leicester City started the Anglo-Scottish Cup tournament with a 1-1 draw against Hull City, and without Graham Cross. The club's directors suspended him for continuing to play cricket for Leicestershire in July instead of reporting back for pre-season training. Cross helped Leicestershire win their first ever County Championship trophy in their history, but this incident spelled the beginning of the end for his record-breaking career at Filbert Street that included 599 senior games including appearances in two FA Cup finals and two League Cup finals.

SUNDAY 3RD AUGUST 1997

Martin O'Neill's Leicester City warmed up for their return to the Premiership with a 2-1 win at Northampton Town in a game to mark the Cobblers' centenary. Emile Heskey and Stuart Campbell got the goals for the Foxes at Sixfields Stadium.

SUNDAY 4TH AUGUST 2002

Leicester City's first-ever game at their new Walkers Stadium ground ended in a 1-1 draw with Athletic Bilbao. Tiko put the Spaniards ahead and Jordan Stewart put his name in the history books by bagging the leveller for Micky Adams' team in front of around 24,000 fans.

SATURDAY 5TH AUGUST 2000

Ade Akinbiyi got his first goal in a Leicester City shirt following his club record £5m transfer from Wolverhampton Wanderers. Akinbiyi grabbed City's goal in a 3-1 defeat at Tranmere Rovers in a pre-season friendly.

THURSDAY 6TH AUGUST 1992

David Lowe, a £200,000 signing from Ipswich Town, suffered a shattered cheekbone in the 3-1 pre-season friendly defeat against Borussia Monchengladbach at Filbert Street. Richard Smith grabbed the goal for Brian Little's team against the German visitors.

SATURDAY 7TH AUGUST 1971

Leicester City lifted the Charity Shield at Filbert Street. The match pitted the previous season's Second Division champions against First Division champions Liverpool and Steve Whitworth got the only goal to give Jimmy Bloomfield the perfect start to his spell as Foxes manager. Remarkably, Whitworth never found the target in 400 Football League, FA Cup and League Cup appearances for Leicester.

WEDNESDAY 8TH AUGUST 1984

Leicester City fought out a 2-2 draw with Scottish giants Rangers in a pre-season friendly at Ibrox. John O'Neill and Gary Lineker were on target for the Foxes.

SATURDAY 9TH AUGUST 1997

Robbie Savage made his Leicester City debut as a substitute in a 1-0 win over Aston Villa at Filbert Street on the opening day of the Premier League season. Ian Marshall got the only goal for Martin O'Neill's team.

SATURDAY 10TH AUGUST 1968

Allan Clarke marked his Leicester City debut after his £150,000 British record transfer from Fulham with a goal in the 1-1 draw against Queens Park Rangers. Rangers were making their debut in the top flight after back-to-back promotions and included Clarke's brother Frank in the line-up. Allan put City ahead and Les Allen grabbed an equaliser.

SATURDAY 10TH AUGUST 2002

Brian Deane was the two-goal hero in Leicester City's first league game at the Walkers Stadium, a 2-0 win over Watford in the Championship.

SATURDAY 11TH AUGUST 1979

Alan Young marked his Leicester City debut after a £250,000 transfer from Oldham Athletic with a goal in the 2-1 defeat at home to Rotherham United in the first round of the League Cup.

FRIDAY 12TH AUGUST 1921

Matt Gillies was born in Loganlea, West Lothian.

MONDAY 13TH AUGUST 1984

Leicester City's Centenary Match ended in a 1-1 draw against Aberdeen at Filbert Street. Steve Lynex scored from the penalty spot to ensure honours were even at the end.

SATURDAY 14TH AUGUST 1971

Jon Sammels made his debut for Leicester City in a 2-2 draw against Huddersfield Town. He went on to make 271 appearances for the Foxes. Ally Brown got the opening goal for City with just 45 seconds on the clock and David Nish added Leicester's second goal.

SATURDAY 14TH AUGUST 1993

David Speedie made his Leicester City debut in a 2-1 win over Peterborough United at Filbert Street that was secured by a late goal from Tony James. Steve Thompson grabbed the opener from the penalty spot.

FRIDAY 14TH AUGUST 1998

Frank Sinclair completed a move from Chelsea to Leicester City for a club record fee of £2.55m.

SATURDAY 15TH AUGUST 1987

Leicester City central defender Steve Walsh grabbed the headlines for the wrong reasons after being sent off in the opening-day defeat against Shrewsbury Town at Filbert Street. He was dismissed for breaking the jaw of striker David Geddis, who had earlier grabbed what proved to be the only goal of the game in the Division Two fixture. Walsh was later handed an 11-match suspension by the Football League.

SATURDAY 15TH AUGUST 1998

Martin O'Neill's Leicester City were denied maximum points at Manchester United on the opening day of the Premiership season by David Beckham's last-gasp free-kick. The Foxes opened up a 2-0 lead at Old Trafford through goals from Emile Heskey and Tony Cottee before Teddy Sheringham pulled a goal back to give the Reds hope. The game was in its dying moments when Beckham curled home the goal that broke Leicester's hearts and denied them the perfect start to the campaign. Frank Sinclair made his City debut the day after joining from Premiership rivals Chelsea in a club-record deal.

SATURDAY 16TH AUGUST 1975

An incredible start to the season at Filbert Street. Leicester City and Birmingham City battled out a 3-3 draw in Division One. The Foxes were left with only nine men following the sending-off of Chris Garland, and Jeff Blockley being replaced through injury after City's substitute had been used. City equalised twice to earn a point with Jon Sammels (penalty) and Brian Alderson finding the target for the home side before an own goal by a Blues player secured a draw in front of a crowd of 25,547.

SATURDAY 16TH AUGUST 1980

Jim Melrose made his Leicester City debut in a 1-0 defeat at home to Ipswich Town in Division One. Melrose was brought to Filbert Street by Foxes boss Jock Wallace in a deal worth £250,000 from Scottish Premier League side Partick Thistle.

SATURDAY 17TH AUGUST 1985

Gary Lineker made a swift return to Filbert Street with Everton after joining the Division One champions during the summer in an £800,000 deal. He was upstaged by Mark Bright, whose spectacular double fired Leicester City to a 3-1 win after Bobby Smith had opened the scoring. Russell Osman made his debut for the Foxes after a £240,000 transfer from Ipswich Town.

SATURDAY 17TH AUGUST 1991

Brian Little's first game in charge of Leicester City ended in a goalless draw at Swindon Town in Division Two.

SATURDAY 18TH AUGUST 2001

Peter Taylor's Leicester City suffered humiliation on the opening day of the Premiership season. They were walloped 5-0 at Filbert Street by newly-promoted Bolton Wanderers.

SATURDAY 19TH AUGUST 1950

Arthur Rowley made his Leicester City debut at Bury and his late winner was the first of 265 goals for the club. Rowley went on to become the most prolific scorer in the history of the Football League, but fans were reportedly unhappy when he arrived from Fulham. They felt Rowley was a cheap replacement for popular striker Jack Lee.

SATURDAY 19TH AUGUST 1978

Leicester City boss Jock Wallace handed John O'Neill his debut at Burnley on the opening day of the Division Two season. O'Neill was still a 20-year-old student at Loughborough University at the time, but made an assured debut in a 2-2 draw secured by goals from Billy Hughes (penalty) and Trevor Christie. O'Neill went on to become City's most capped player. He represented Northern Ireland 39 times and appeared in two World Cups.

SATURDAY 19TH AUGUST 2000

Steve Walsh made his 449th and final appearance for Leicester City in the goalless draw against Aston Villa in the Premiership at Filbert Street. The game marked Peter Taylor's first game in charge of the Foxes.

MONDAY 20TH AUGUST 1974

Dennis Rofe was Leicester City's unlikely last-gasp goal hero in a 4-3 win at Birmingham City. He bagged the winner after goals from Frank Worthington (2) and Keith Weller.

SUNDAY 21ST AUGUST 1994

Leicester City made their debut on satellite television and were beaten 3-1 by Newcastle United in front of the Sky Sports cameras. Brian Little's team were making their bow in the Premier League after securing promotion via the play-offs and Julian Joachim grabbed City's goal.

WEDNESDAY 22ND AUGUST 1945

Alan Birchenall was born in East Ham, London.

SATURDAY 23RD AUGUST 1986

Steve Walsh made his debut for Leicester City in the 1-1 draw against Luton Town at Filbert Street after joining from Wigan Athletic. Bobby Smith got the goal for the Foxes in the Division One fixture.

WEDNESDAY 23RD AUGUST 1972

Frank Worthington marked his Leicester City debut with a goal at Old Trafford. George Best got the hosts' reply in a 1-1 draw.

SATURDAY 23RD AUGUST 1980

Division One champions Liverpool were stunned at Filbert Street. Andy Peake lashed home an unstoppable opener from 25 yards and Martin Henderson added a second after the break. Boss Jock Wallace predicted his team would go on to win the Division One title.

SATURDAY 23RD AUGUST 1958

Ken Keyworth made his Leicester City debut in a 2-0 win over Everton at Filbert Street secured by goals from Ken Leek and Howard Riley, watched by a crowd of 34,446.

SATURDAY 23RD AUGUST 1975

A 3-0 defeat at Newcastle United marked the final game of Graham Cross's career with his home-town club. Cross made a club record total of 599 appearances for Leicester City in his 16 years at Filbert Street.

SATURDAY 24TH AUGUST 1974

Leicester City went into the record books for all the wrong reasons. Mark Wallington – in goal against Liverpool at Anfield because Peter Shilton was in a contract dispute – conceded the quickest-ever penalty. He brought down Steve Heighway after he had intercepted Malcolm Munro's stray pass and Alec Lindsay netted the spot kick. There were just 19 seconds on the clock in the Division One clash. Lindsay netted a second penalty after Keith Weller handled and the Leicester midfielder pulled a goal back for the visitors with 15 minutes left. But the Foxes couldn't conjure up an equaliser.

SATURDAY 24TH AUGUST 1985

Ali Mauchlen made his Leicester City debut as a second-half substitute in a crushing 5-0 defeat at Oxford United in Division One. Mauchlen had arrived earlier in the month from Motherwell, along with Gary McAllister, in a deal worth £250,000.

SATURDAY 25TH AUGUST 1923

Arthur Chandler made his Leicester City debut in a 1-1 draw at Hull City after joining from Queens Park Rangers, where he was a fringe player. He drew a blank at Hull, but didn't have many more. Chandler finished his first season with 24 goals, and his City career with an impressive haul of 273 goals in 419 appearances.

SATURDAY 25TH AUGUST 1990

David Pleat's Leicester City team started the season with a 3-2 win over Bristol Rovers at Filbert Street. David Kelly got the Division Two season off to the perfect start with the opener after just two minutes, Pirates defender Ian Alexander obligingly lobbed into his own net from 30 yards and Tommy Wright almost burst the net with a second-half thunderbolt. They also had two efforts disallowed, but let Rovers back into the game with two goals. The early season optimism didn't last long. The Foxes went on to lose their next seven games and spent the campaign battling against the drop.

SATURDAY 26TH AUGUST 1967

Leicester City snatched an unlikely point at Manchester United after goalkeeper Peter Shilton was injured. Bobby Roberts took over from Shilton between the posts and Mike Stringfellow's goal stunned Old Trafford and secured a 1-1 draw in the Division One clash.

SATURDAY 26TH AUGUST 1933

Arthur Maw was on target after just four minutes on the opening day of the season to set Leicester City on their way to a 3-2 win at Aston Villa. He added another goal and Arthur Lochhead was also on target for the Foxes. On the same day, City's reserve-team striker Jack Gurry was even quicker out of the blocks. He scored just 30 seconds into the second string's game against Charlton Athletic reserves at Filbert Street and went on to get a hat-trick in a 5-1 win that meant the club started with a win double.

WEDNESDAY 27TH AUGUST 1997

Steve Walsh popped up in the sixth minute of injury time to snatch a 3-3 draw against Arsenal at Filbert Street and spark a confrontation with Ian Wright that the Leicester City legend says he's always asked about by City fans. Dennis Bergkamp put the Gunners 2-0 ahead, Emile Heskey pulled one back and Matt Elliott made it 2-2 in the second minute of injury time. Bergkamp put Arsenal back in front a minute later with a stunning goal to complete his hat-trick... then Walsh came to the rescue.

SATURDAY 27TH AUGUST 1988

Goalkeeper Martin Hodge made his Leicester City debut in a 1-1 draw against West Bromwich Albion at Filbert Street. Hodge joined David Pleat's team from Sheffield Wednesday for £200,000 and suffered a stomach muscle injury on his debut that ruled him out for several months. Ali Mauchlen was City's marksman in a game that also marked the City debut of Tony Spearing after his summer move from Norwich City.

TUESDAY 28TH AUGUST 2007

Leicester City's Carling Cup second round tie at Nottingham Forest was abandoned at half-time after City defender Clive Clarke had a suspected heart attack and was rushed to hospital. Leicester were trailing 1-0 at the time.

SATURDAY 28TH AUGUST 1982

Alan Smith made his City debut and Charlton Athletic left Filbert Street with maximum points after a 2-1 win. Bobby Smith got City's goal.

WEDNESDAY 29TH AUGUST 2007

Martin Allen was sacked as Leicester City manager after just four games in charge. He left after a falling out with owner Milan Mandaric. Ironically, his last game in charge was a 4-1 drubbing of Watford that was the best performance of a wretched season that ended in relegation.

SATURDAY 30TH AUGUST 1972

Keith Weller's hat-trick fired Leicester City to a thrilling 3-2 win over Liverpool at Filbert Street. John Toshack grabbed both replies for the Reds. It was 11 years before another player hit a hat-trick against Liverpool with Terry Gibson finding the target three times for Coventry City in Division One.

SATURDAY 31ST AUGUST 1963

Leicester City powered to the top of Division One with a 7-2 demolition of Arsenal at Filbert Street. The goal glut owed much to an injury to Gunners keeper John McClelland. He suffered a fractured collarbone and England striker Joe Baker replaced him between the posts. Leicester led 2-1 when McClelland was injured with Howard Riley's seventh-minute opener being added to by Ken Keyworth. Keyworth added another and David Gibson bagged a brace with the others coming from Mike Stringfellow and Frank McLintock.

WEDNESDAY 31ST AUGUST 2016

With the transfer deadline fast approaching, Leicester signed striker Islam Slimani for a club-record fee. Claudio Ranieri upped his bid to a whopping £29.7 million to land the Algerian international from Portuguese side Sporting Lisbon.

LEICESTER CITY
On This Day & Miscellany

SEPTEMBER

SATURDAY 1ST SEPTEMBER 1908

Leicester Fosse's first ever game in Division One ended in a 1-1 draw against Sheffield Wednesday and Jimmy Donnelly had the distinction of scoring their first ever top-flight goal.

SATURDAY 1ST SEPTEMBER 1973

Division One champions Liverpool were held to a 1-1 draw at Filbert Street. Jimmy Bloomfield's Leicester City had started the season with a pair of 1-1 draws away from home and fell behind on 50 minutes. Peter McCormack pulled the ball back and John Toshack powered his header into the City net. Peter Shilton pulled off several fine saves and then the equaliser came on 70 minutes. Alan Birchenall's header from a Len Glover corner flew into the net and City had another point.

SATURDAY 1ST SEPTEMBER 1962

Leicester City stormed to a fourth successive victory that took them up to fourth place in Division One. Bolton Wanderers were the visitors to Filbert Street and they trailed at the break to Jimmy Walsh's goal. The scores were level when Richie Norman put through his own goal, but Matt Gillies' team responded with strikes from Walsh, Graham Cross and David Gibson to claim maximum points. Mike Stringfellow drew a blank having found the target in the opening four games of the season.

SATURDAY 2ND SEPTEMBER 1961

A 5-1 win at Birmingham City lifted Leicester City into the top half of Division One. Ken Keyworth opened the scoring after 11 minutes and the home side fell apart after the break. Gordon Wills pounced twice in as many minutes to open up a 3-0 lead and Jimmy Walsh piled on the misery for the Blues with a brace. Jimmy Bloomfield was on target for Birmingham.

WEDNESDAY 2ND SEPTEMBER 1970

Steve Whitworth made his Leicester City debut in the 4-0 thumping of Bristol City at Filbert Street in Division Two. John Farrington, Bobby Kellard, Ally Brown and David Nish (penalty) scored.

WEDNESDAY 3RD SEPTEMBER 1986

Leicester City grabbed their first win of the Division One season at the third attempt and it proved to be worth the wait. Defending champions Liverpool were toppled 2-1 at Filbert Street in front of a crowd of 16,344 fans. Gary McAllister and Russell Osman got the goals that handed Bryan Hamilton his first win as Foxes manager with the reply coming from Kenny Dalglish.

FRIDAY 4TH SEPTEMBER 1936

Len Chalmers was born in Corby, Northamptonshire.

WEDNESDAY 4TH SEPTEMBER 1957

Derek Hines grabbed his 100th goal for Leicester City in a 3-2 defeat at Sunderland. Tommy McDonald got the other goal for the Foxes.

MONDAY 5TH SEPTEMBER 1927

Leicester City went top of Division One after a 1-1 draw against Sheffield United stretched their unbeaten start to the season to four games. Arthur Chandler got City's goal, but their stay at the top was brief. City were knocked out of the top two days later.

TUESDAY 6TH SEPTEMBER 1994

Leicester City striker Julian Joachim played for England under-21s in a goalless draw against Portugal under-21s at Filbert Street.

SATURDAY 7TH SEPTEMBER 1991

Leicester City's unbeaten start to the Division One season under new manager Brian Little continued with a 2-1 win over Bristol City at Filbert Street that made it five games without defeat. Colin Gibson's unstoppable 25-yard thunderbolt put City on their way to victory and Paul Fitzpatrick bagged what proved to be the winner. The unbeaten start to the season came to an end seven days later with a 3-0 defeat at Middlesbrough.

WEDNESDAY 7TH SEPTEMBER 1960

A 3-2 loss at Wolverhampton Wanderers made it four straight defeats for Leicester City in Division One. Their goals at Molineux came from Jimmy Walsh and Gordon Wills.

TUESDAY 8TH SEPTEMBER 1981

Stewart Hamill got the only goal for Leicester City against Barnsley at Filbert Street – and never played for Jock Wallace's team again. Hamill had been plucked from his job as a Co-Op van driver by Wallace and handed his chance towards the end of the previous season that ended in relegation from Division One. He made a goalscoring start to the 1981-82 season – bagging the only goal against Wrexham at Filbert Street – and followed it three days later with the goal that beat Barnsley to make it three games unbeaten at the start of the campaign. Hamill netted from close range after Jim Melrose's overhead kick had been blocked. But he was replaced by new signing Keith Robson for the next game and never played for Leicester again. Hamill ended up joining Northampton Town and scored after 35 seconds on his debut.

SATURDAY 8TH SEPTEMBER 1973

Leicester City's 2-0 win at Arsenal made it five games unbeaten and left them fourth in Division One. Goalkeeper Peter Shilton kept the scoreline blank at the break with several outstanding saves. Leicester turned on the style after the break and were ahead on 52 minutes. Len Glover gathered Keith Weller's pass, cut inside and rifled a shot just inside the far post and the destiny of the points was settled on 76 minutes when Mike Stringfellow headed home Frank Worthington's cross to double the lead.

SATURDAY 8TH SEPTEMBER 1934

Arthur Chandler hit a hat-trick in Leicester City's 5-0 demolition of Midlands rivals Aston Villa at Filbert Street in Division One to write his name in the record books. He was 39 years and 32 days old when he fired home the treble against Villa, making him the club's oldest-ever scorer of a hat-trick. Tommy Mills and Danny Liddle got the other goals in front of a crowd of 28,548.

WEDNESDAY 9TH SEPTEMBER 1964

Leicester City climbed to fifth in Division One, and just one point behind leaders Chelsea, with a 2-0 win over champions Liverpool at Filbert Street. City had been unbeaten in their opening five games and were soon ahead through Frank McLintock's shot that took a couple of deflections on its way past wrong-footed Reds keeper Tommy Lawrence. It took a couple of good saves from City goalkeeper Gordon Banks to deny Roger Hunt an equaliser and the game was put beyond the visitors with ten minutes left when Ken Keyworth lunged to head home Howard Riley's low cross. There was no way back for the champions.

WEDNESDAY 9TH SEPTEMBER 1959

Gordon Banks made his Leicester City debut in a 1-1 draw against Blackpool at Filbert Street. Banks stepped in to replace the injured Dave McLaren and produced a fine save from Ray Charnley's close-range effort in the first half to keep the scoreline blank at the interval. Ken Leek put City ahead after the break and they were in charge, but Jackie Mudie equalised on the break and Blackpool rattled the woodwork with a late free kick. Banks' teammate Albert Cheesebrough also had reason to celebrate after becoming a father for the second time on the morning of the game.

SATURDAY 10TH SEPTEMBER 1994

A 2-1 defeat at Wimbledon made it five games without a win for Brian Little's Leicester City at the start of their Premier League campaign following promotion via the play-offs. David Lowe got the goal for the Foxes at Selhurst Park. Leicester had claimed their first point of the season in their previous game against Queens Park Rangers.

SUNDAY 10TH SEPTEMBER 1995

Julian Joachim got the winning goal for Leicester City at East Midlands rivals Derby County. The three points took City to the top of Division One. Not a bad day!.

SATURDAY 11TH SEPTEMBER 1982

Steve Lynex and Gary Lineker both hit hat-tricks in a 6-0 demolition of Division Two rivals Carlisle United at Filbert Street. Lynex's treble included two penalties, but he handed the ball to Lineker when the Foxes were awarded a third spot kick later in the game and he fired home.

SATURDAY 11TH SEPTEMBER 1971

Malcolm Munro suffered a broken cheekbone on his Leicester City debut at Ipswich Town. City went on to win the game 2-1 with goals from Jon Sammels and Bobby Kellard securing the points.

SATURDAY 12TH SEPTEMBER 1998

Emile Heskey got Leicester City's goal in a 1-1 draw against Arsenal in the Premiership at Filbert Street.

SATURDAY 13TH SEPTEMBER 1986

Steve Moran made a goalscoring debut in a 2-2 draw at Sheffield Wednesday. A few days earlier he had become the club's record signing when he joined from Southampton in a £300,000 deal.

THURSDAY 13TH SEPTEMBER 2007

Former Nottingham Forest manager Gary Megson was revealed as Leicester City's new boss after the departure of Martin Allen.

WEDNESDAY 13TH SEPTEMBER 1961

Tottenham Hotspur winning the league and FA Cup double meant FA Cup finalists Leicester City were entered in the European Cup Winners' Cup. Their first European campaign started with a 4-1 win at Irish Cup winners Glenavon. City fell behind and hit back through goals from Jimmy Walsh (2), Colin Appleton and Ken Keyworth.

SUNDAY 13TH SEPTEMBER 1992

Russell Hoult was dramatically plucked from the stands, while munching a pre-match hot dog, and handed the keeper's jersey for the home game with Wolverhampton Wanderers, after Carl Muggleton suffered a slipped disc in the pre-match warm-up. It was City's first-ever league fixture to be televised live. 'The Hot Dog Kid' kept a clean sheet and was named Man of the Match after the goalless draw.

THURSDAY 14TH SEPTEMBER 2000

Leicester City embarked on their second Uefa Cup campaign in four seasons with a first round first leg tie against former European champions Red Star Belgrade at Filbert Street. Martin O'Neill's team fell behind in controversial circumstances. The Yugoslav supporters in the East Stand set off flares just before kick-off and the red smoke had not cleared by the time Acimovic belted a 30-yard shot past City goalkeeper Tim Flowers. Leicester were level just before the break when Gerry Taggart headed home and Stan Collymore went close to earning them a lead to take into the second leg.

WEDNESDAY 14TH SEPTEMBER 1999

Leicester City used three goalkeepers in a thrilling 3-3 draw at Crystal Palace in a League Cup second round first leg clash. City were in charge at 3-1 ahead in the second half at Selhurst Park through a first-half own goal and strikes from Neil Lennon and Gerry Taggart. The game turned when goalkeeper Tim Flowers was injured. He had come on to replace Pegguy Arphexad and with all the substitutes used, Theo Zagorakis went between the posts for ten-man City. Palace netted twice in three minutes to draw level, but couldn't force a winner in a frantic last 15 minutes.

MONDAY 15TH SEPTEMBER 1969

Andy Lochhead was the hat-trick hero in a 3-1 win over Bristol City in a League Cup second round second replay at Filbert Street. The Robins were ahead after five minutes, but City got the equaliser eight minutes later when Lochhead fired home and he put Leicester ahead seven minutes after the break. He completed his treble on 59 minutes.

FRIDAY 15TH SEPTEMBER 2000

Steve Walsh ended his spell at Leicester City when he joined Norwich City. Walsh had spent more than 14 years at Filbert Street after arriving from Wigan Athletic and clocked up 449 appearances for the Foxes.

TUESDAY 16TH SEPTEMBER 1997

Leicester City returned to European football after a 36-year absence with a trip to Atletico Madrid in the first round of the Uefa Cup. Ironically, Atletico had ended City's European adventure in their previous campaign, but a repeat didn't look likely when Ian Marshall put Leicester ahead from close range after just 11 minutes at the Vicente Calderon Stadium. They held on to the advantage until late in the game. The introduction of substitute Jose Mari by the home side proved to be decisive. He had a hand in goals from Juninho and Vieri that gave the Spaniards a 2-1 lead to take into the second leg at Filbert Street.

WEDNESDAY 16TH SEPTEMBER 1987

Mike Newell had become Leicester City's record signing when he joined from Luton Town for £350,000 just a few days earlier and he could not have asked for a better start to his career with the Foxes. His diving header on his debut sent Brian Hamilton's team on the way to a 4-1 win over Oldham Athletic at Filbert Street. Finnish striker Jari Rantanen also got his first goal for the club and Gary Ford and Ian Wilson were the other marksmen in the Division Two clash.

WEDNESDAY 16TH SEPTEMBER 2016

"There's never been a better time to be a Leicester City fan," was how the BBC journalist concluded their report of Leicester City's first ever game in the Champions League. Leicester, Premier League champions, headed to Bruges in Belgium for their opening Group G game, against FC Brugge. At half-time, City were 2-0 up. Marc Albrighton, considered not good enough for Aston Villa a year or so earlier, bagged the opener after Brugge made a mess of clearing a throw-in and Riyad Mahrez doubled the lead with an inch-perfect, left-footed free kick. Mahrez completed the scoring from the penalty spot in the second half.

SATURDAY 17TH SEPTEMBER 1994

Julian Joachim was the hero as Leicester City claimed their first win of the Premier League season at the sixth attempt. Joachim netted a pair of typically spectacular solo goals in a 3-1 thumping of Tottenham Hotspur at Filbert Street that was captured by BBC television's

Match of the Day cameras. Ossie Ardiles' Spurs had a star-studded line-up including German international striker Jurgen Klinsmann, who found the target for the visitors. Spurs simply couldn't cope with Joachim's pace, however, and David Lowe bagged City's third goal in front of a 21,300 crowd. City had lost four of their previous five games in the Premier League.

SATURDAY 18TH SEPTEMBER 1926

Leicester City's 4-3 win at Everton took them to the top of Division One for the first time in their history. Arthur Chandler got two goals and the others in a historic game came from Ernie Hine and John Duncan.

TUESDAY 18TH SEPTEMBER 2007

Leicester City travelled to Nottingham Forest for their rearranged Carling Cup second round tie and Gary Megson's team earned plaudits by allowing their local rivals to score straight from the kick-off to ensure the game started as the original fixture ended. They had met three weeks earlier and the game was abandoned at half-time due to Clive Clarke's health problems with Leicester trailing 1-0. To reflect this, Leicester allowed Forest keeper Paul Smith to score unopposed in the first minute. The Foxes equalised and then overturned a 2-1 deficit in dramatic style with two goals in the last two minutes. Richard Stearman grabbed the equaliser and Stephen Clemence curled home a last-gasp free kick to make it 3-2.

SATURDAY 18TH SEPTEMBER 1976

Dennis Rofe launched a free-kick from inside his own half that sailed over the head of Queens Park Rangers goalkeeper Phil Parkes at Filbert Street. Everyone there said it was a fluke, with the exception of Rofe. Chris Garland netted Leicester's other – less spectacular – goal in a 2-2 draw.

SATURDAY 19TH SEPTEMBER 1987

Three days after trouncing Oldham Athletic 4-1, Leicester City beat Plymouth Argyle 4-0 at a rain-lashed Filbert Street. The same four players found the target: Mike Newell, Jari Rantanen, Gary Ford and Ian Wilson.

SUNDAY 20TH SEPTEMBER 1987

Ian Wilson left Leicester City to join Everton for £300,000 after starring in the previous day's drubbing of Plymouth Argyle.

SATURDAY 20TH SEPTEMBER 1930

Ernie Hine's 100th goal for Leicester City was a consolation effort in a 4-1 defeat at Arsenal in Division One. Hine reached the landmark in his 185th game for the club.

TUESDAY 21ST SEPTEMBER 1993

Rochdale were hit for six in a League Cup second round first leg tie at Spotland. The travelling Leicester City fans must have feared the worst when Brian Carey's own goal put 'Dale ahead after just five minutes. Mike Whitlow levelled and the Foxes hammered in five more goals in the second half. Steve Walsh, Steve Thompson, David Oldfield, David Speedie and Ian Ormondroyd were the marksmen for Brian Little's side in the romp.

SATURDAY 21ST SEPTEMBER 1985

Tony Sealy scored on his Leicester debut in the 2-1 defeat at Birmingham City after joining the Foxes from Fulham. He didn't get many more.

SUNDAY 22ND SEPTEMBER 1996

Martin O'Neill's team announced their arrival as a Premiership force with a 2-1 win at Tottenham Hotspur. Leicester City started better and it was no surprise when Steve Claridge slid in at the far post to put them ahead after 22 minutes. He was injured while scoring and was replaced by Ian Marshall, who proved to be Leicester's match-winner at White Hart Lane after Clive Wilson had netted a 64th minute leveller for the home side. Marshall headed home the winner for the visitors with four minutes left.

FRIDAY 23RD SEPTEMBER 1938

David Gibson was born in Winchburgh, West Lothian and went on to become a Leicester City legend.

SATURDAY 24TH SEPTEMBER 1977

Frank Worthington made his last appearance for Leicester City in the 3-0 defeat at home to Nottingham Forest. Worthington headed to Bolton Wanderers and the following season was Division One's top goalscorer with 24 goals.

SATURDAY 24TH SEPTEMBER 1938

Mal Griffiths made his Leicester City debut in a goalless draw against Bolton Wanderers at Filbert Street. He joined City from Arsenal for a bargain £750 seven months after marking his Gunners debut with a goal against Leicester. Griffiths went on to help Arsenal win Division One before joining City.

SATURDAY 25TH SEPTEMBER 1926

Leicester City stayed top of Division One after a 4-0 thrashing of Blackburn Rovers at Filbert Street. The goals came from Arthur Lochhead, Ernie Hine, John Duncan and Arthur Chandler.

FRIDAY 26TH SEPTEMBER 1947

David Nish was born in Burton-upon-Trent.

SATURDAY 27TH SEPTEMBER 1997

Ian Marshall and Graham Fenton got the goals in a 2-0 win at Barnsley that lifted Leicester City up to third in the Premiership and secured the Manager of the Month award for Foxes boss Martin O'Neill.

WEDNESDAY 27TH SEPTEMBER 1961

Goals from Gordon Wills, Ken Keyworth and Hugh McIlmoyle secured a 3-1 win for Leicester City over Glenavon in the second leg of their European Cup Winners' Cup first round tie. That completed a 7-2 aggregate win and set up a clash against Atletico Madrid.

THURSDAY 28TH SEPTEMBER 2000

Leicester City's Uefa Cup first round, second leg tie at Red Star Belgrade was switched to Vienna because of unrest in the Serbian capital. They went into the game level at 1-1 after the first leg, but fell behind early on. Muzzy Izzet forced the ball home from close range to level the scores just before half-time, but Red Star stepped up a gear after the break and netted twice more to make it 3-1 on the night and 4-2 on aggregate.

SATURDAY 28TH SEPTEMBER 1985

Gary McAllister made his debut in a 1-0 win over Ipswich Town at Filbert Street that was secured by Alan Smith's strike.

SATURDAY 29TH SEPTEMBER 1990

David Pleat's side suffered a seventh straight defeat at Middlesbrough. They were thumped 6-0 at Ayresome Park and Steve Walsh was sent off. Leicester trailed 1-0 six minutes before the break when Walsh was sent off for a professional foul and Middlesbrough twisted the knife. They found the target three more times before the interval and completed the rout after the break. The loss equalled Leicester's record losing run in the league.

SUNDAY 30TH SEPTEMBER 2001

Peter Taylor was sacked as Leicester City manager. The previous day, City had lost 2-0 at Charlton and that meant they had taken only one point from their opening eight games in the Premiership. Junior Lewis was sent off at Charlton Athletic.

TUESDAY 30TH SEPTEMBER 1997

Leicester City bowed out of the Uefa Cup after a 2-0 defeat against Atletico Madrid in the second leg of their first round clash. That meant the Spaniards went through 4-1 on aggregate, but Leicester made them battle and the outcome could have been different. The referee waved away four penalty appeals with Muzzy Izzet being aggrieved after being sent crashing three times. City were handed a lift when Lopez was sent off, but the Foxes were also left with only ten men after Garry Parker was dismissed. Parker and the crowd were stunned when he was punished for taking a free-kick too quickly. Juninho and Kiko bagged breakaway goals to send Madrid through.

SATURDAY 30TH SEPTEMBER 1995

Emile Heskey's first goal for Leicester City secured a 1-0 win at Norwich City and kept them on top of Division One. Heskey came off the bench for only his third appearance for the Foxes and turned home David Lowe's cross with only three minutes remaining. City boss McGhee handed a debut to defender Franck Rolling and the Canaries line-up included future Leicester players Darren Eadie and Ade Akinbiyi.

LEICESTER CITY
On This Day & Miscellany

OCTOBER

SATURDAY 1ST OCTOBER 1938

Leicester City were on the receiving end of an 8-2 hammering at Leeds United. They suffered an early setback with the loss of goalkeeper Sandy McLaren through injury and the presence of Fred Sharman and then Billy Frame between the posts couldn't prevent the home side's rout.

SUNDAY 1ST OCTOBER 2000

Leicester City ended the day at the summit of the top flight of English football for the first time since August 1963. The 0-0 draw at Sunderland and Thierry Henry's spectacular winner against Manchester United meant Peter Taylor's team were on top of the Premier League. The result stretched their unbeaten start to the season to eight games and goalkeeper Tim Flowers was in fine form. He conceded only two goals in open play during that spell and was named the Carling Premiership Player of the Month.

SATURDAY 2ND OCTOBER 1926

Leicester City's two-week stay at the top of Division One came to an end after a 5-3 defeat at Huddersfield Town. Jack Bamber got two goals for City and Arthur Chandler the other in the defeat.

SATURDAY 2ND OCTOBER 2004

Preston North End goalkeeper Andy Lonergan scored against Leicester City in a 1-1 draw at the Walkers Stadium.

SATURDAY 2ND OCTOBER 1954

A crowd of 42,486 – the highest attendance for a league game at Filbert Street – watched Leicester City and Arsenal battle out a 3-3 draw in Division One. Arthur Rowley netted twice – once from the penalty spot – and Derek Hines got the other in a six-goal thriller.

SATURDAY 3RD OCTOBER 1992

Julian Joachim made his Leicester City debut in a 2-1 win over Barnsley at Filbert Street. Simon Grayson and Bobby Davison got the goals for Brian Little's team.

SATURDAY 4TH OCTOBER 1975

A goalless draw at Manchester United's Old Trafford ended a run of three straight defeats for Leicester City. The result left City looking for their first win of the season after 11 games of the Division One campaign.

WEDNESDAY 5TH OCTOBER 1977

Frank McLintock's Leicester City ended a run of five straight defeats in Division One by battling to a goalless draw at Chelsea. Tommy Williams made his debut for the Foxes at Stamford Bridge.

WEDNESDAY 5TH OCTOBER 1994

Leicester City were in trouble at the bottom of the Premiership and Brighton & Hove Albion piled on the misery for Brian Little's team. The visitors from the Second Division won 2-0 to complete a 3-0 win in the second round of the League Cup. It was City's first defeat against a team from a lower division since Lincoln City triumphed over two legs in 1982. Brighton led going into the second leg through a controversial late goal in the first meeting between the sides and Stuart Munday stunned the home crowd by making it 2-0 on aggregate after just 16 minutes. David Oldfield stepped off the bench to make his first appearance of the season, but couldn't inspire City and Kurt Nogan completed the humiliation with a second goal for the Seagulls with just six minutes remaining.

SATURDAY 6TH OCTOBER 1962

Matt Gillies took his Leicester City team to Division One champions Ipswich Town, while placed fifth in the table. But they had been the victims of a League Cup giant-killing at Charlton Athletic in the previous game and were without playmaker David Gibson through injury. Gillies reshuffled his team with Frank McLintock taking over the inside-left position and Graham Cross stepping in at wing-half. It worked. Cross had a starring role in the match at Portman Road that was won by McLintock's second-half goal.

SATURDAY 7TH OCTOBER 1967

Mike Stringfellow was the goal hero as struggling Leicester City turned the formbook on its head to topple Division One leaders Liverpool at Filbert Street. Three successive defeats had left Matt Gillies' team bottom of the table and it was no surprise when Ian St John struck in the 27th minute to give the Reds the advantage at half-time. City, with full-back Willie Bell making his home debut, hit back after the break. Stringfellow netted twice and goalkeeper Peter Shilton marked his return to the side following an injury with several crucial saves to deny the visitors an equaliser in an exciting climax.

SATURDAY 8TH OCTOBER 1988

Jimmy Quinn rifled home an unstoppable free-kick from 20 yards to clinch a 1-0 win for David Pleat's Leicester City against Brighton & Hove Albion in Division Two. It was only the Foxes' third win in their opening ten games of the season.

SATURDAY 9TH OCTOBER 1926

Arthur Chandler reached the landmark of 100 goals for Leicester City with a double strike in the 2-1 win over Sunderland at Filbert Street. It was his 140th game for the Foxes.

SATURDAY 10TH OCTOBER 1992

Bobby Davison and Julian Joachim were on target in a 2-0 win at Birmingham City that secured a third straight win for Brian Little's Leicester City and lifted them up to fourth in the Division One table.

SATURDAY 10TH OCTOBER 1982

Leicester City's 3-0 win at Bolton Wanderers took them back into the top ten in Division Two. Jim Melrose was the two-goal hero and Alan Young was also on target for the Foxes.

MONDAY 11TH OCTOBER 2004

Leicester City announced they had accepted Micky Adams' resignation as manager. The Foxes were 12th in the Championship at the time and Adams was under pressure from supporters. He had failed to keep City in the Premier League the previous season.

WEDNESDAY 12TH OCTOBER 1960

Leicester City played their first game in the League Cup and there were just 7,070 fans at Filbert Street to see Jimmy Walsh write his name in the record books. Walsh became the first player to score a hat-trick in the competition's history with a treble in a 4-0 demolition of Fourth Division Mansfield Town. Albert Cheesebrough got the other goal and the game marked the only senior appearance in a City shirt for youth team goalkeeper Rodney Slack. The League Cup was introduced to take advantage of the widespread installation of floodlights around the country and to introduce a sudden-death element to the first half of the season when the divisions are still taking shape. Only 87 clubs entered the first League Cup.

SATURDAY 13TH OCTOBER 1973

In a game well remembered by Leicester City fans and Alan Birchenall, the Foxes came close to becoming the first team to halt Leeds United. The sides shared four goals in a breathless first half. City were 2-0 ahead inside the opening 20 minutes. Frank Worthington bagged the opener and Birchenall slammed home a 30-yard volley. Leeds hit back and were level before the break through Mick Jones and Billy Bremner. Don Revie went on to lead Leeds to the First Division title with a record points haul.

TUESDAY 13TH OCTOBER 1964

Mike Stringfellow's goal secured a third successive victory for Leicester City at Anfield. Nine minutes after the break, Billy Hodgson sent over a low cross and Stringfellow rammed the ball into the roof of the net to continue Leicester's jinx over the Reds.

SATURDAY 13TH OCTOBER 1894

Leicester Fosse crushed Notts Olympic in an FA Cup qualifying-round clash. David Skea grabbed a hat-trick for Fosse and there were four apiece for both 'Tout' Miller and Willie McArthur. Johnny Hill rounded up the haul with a double – 13-0!

SATURDAY 14TH OCTOBER 2000

Leicester City's longest ever spell at the top of the top flight of English football came to an end after 13 days. They were beaten 3-0 by Manchester United at Filbert Street and knocked off their Premier League perch. Teddy Sheringham scored twice for the visitors and Ole Gunnar Solskjaer bagged the other.

TUESDAY 14TH OCTOBER 1997

Leicester City skipper Steve Walsh and teammate Julian Watts both spent the night in hospital after the League Cup holders crashed out after defeat at Grimsby Town. Martin O'Neill's team were without six first-team regulars for the third round clash, but were on course for victory when Ian Marshall headed home a Robbie Savage cross after 16 minutes. Former Leicester player Kevin Jobling drew the home side level in the 68th minute and then came the game's turning point. Goalkeeper Kasey Keller raced from his goal, punched Watts rather than the ball and Mariners striker Steve Livingstone accepted the gift. Walsh collided with a post when he tried to clear the ball and joined Watts in the local hospital. Livingstone added another five minutes later to make it 3-1.

SATURDAY 14TH OCTOBER 1967

Mike Stringfellow grabbed a goal double in a 5-1 win at Southampton – but it was Leicester City goalkeeper Peter Shilton who grabbed the headlines. Shilton punted the ball forward from the edge of his area and with the help of a strong wind and the hard surface, watched it bounce over Saints goalkeeper Campbell Forsyth and into the net. That put the seal on City's first-ever win at The Dell and meant Shilton emulated Pat Jennings after the Arsenal goalkeeper netted in the Charity Shield two months earlier. The match was also memorable for Leicester-born striker Alan Tewley, who marked his first start in the senior side with a goal. Jackie Sinclair was City's other marksman.

SATURDAY 15TH OCTOBER 1983

Leicester City's match against Southampton was abandoned after 22 minutes because of a waterlogged pitch. BBC Television's *Match of the Day* cameras were there to capture City winger Steve Lynex doing his breaststroke in one of the many puddles on the pitch before the referee decided the conditions were too bad.

SATURDAY 16TH OCTOBER 1999

Steve Guppy and Tony Cottee got the goals for Leicester City in a 2-1 win over Southampton at Filbert Street. The result lifted the Foxes up to fifth place in the Premiership table.

SATURDAY 16TH OCTOBER 1993

There was late drama in Leicester City's clash at Charlton Athletic. Steve Agnew appeared to have secured a point for City with a late goal, but the Addicks were awarded a controversial penalty in the dying moments and Darren Pitcher smashed the spot kick past Gavin Ward to break Leicester's hearts.

SATURDAY 17TH OCTOBER 1964

Leicester City made their first appearance on BBC Television's *Match of the Day* – and the viewers were thrilled by a 3-2 win over Nottingham Forest at Filbert Street. Billy Hodgson headed Leicester in front after the goalkeeper could not reach a corner, but Forest came back. Colin Addison smacked a shot against the crossbar and Gordon Banks pulled off several fine saves before Forest drew level. City were back in front just 60 seconds later. Bobby Svarc was bundled over in the box and Colin Appleton stepped up to convert the penalty. Forest were level again through a deflected shot, but Leicester snatched maximum points with five minutes left. Appleton swung over a free-kick from the left and Mike Stringfellow got above the defence to steer his header into the bottom corner to leave City eighth in the Division One table.

SUNDAY 18TH OCTOBER 1970

Gerry Taggart was born in Belfast.

MONDAY 19TH OCTOBER 1998

An emotional night at Filbert Street as Leicester City fans implored boss Martin O'Neill to stay during the 2-1 win over Tottenham Hotspur. Fans held posters pleading: "Don't Go Martin!" after Leeds United made public their interest in City's manager. Ironically, the manager's post at Elland Road had been left vacant by George Graham's decision to resign and take over at Tottenham. Graham brought his new team to Leicester and the game went according to the script with Muzzy Izzet belting home a spectacular late winner to secure a 2-1 win for the Foxes. Les Ferdinand, who went on to play for Leicester, had earlier put the visitors ahead. Emile Heskey levelled and Izzet won the game by crashing home an unstoppable volley after a clearance dropped to him.

SATURDAY 20TH OCTOBER 1928

Leicester City's 10-0 win over Portsmouth at Filbert Street remains the biggest league win in the club's history – and is also remembered for Arthur Chandler and the six swans! The meeting between the sides in Leicester eight months earlier had ended in a 6-2 win for the Foxes and they were on course to better that after romping into a 5-0 half-time lead. Chandler's fifth goal made it 7-0 in the 71st minute and legend has it that a flock of five swans flew over the ground – one for each of his goals. A few minutes later, after Ernie Hine had bagged number eight, a sixth swan is said to have appeared as if imploring Chandler to add another goal. He did just that and Hine completed the scoring with his hat-trick strike.

SUNDAY 20TH OCTOBER 1951

Claudio Ranieri was born in Rome. A defender, he played only a handful of games for Roma and spent most of his playing career with Catanzaro. As a manager, he made his name by taking Cagliari up to Serie A with back-to-back promotions.

SATURDAY 20TH OCTOBER 1984

Mark Wallington made his 460th and last appearance for Leicester City in a 5-0 defeat at Sheffield Wednesday. Imre Varadi put three goals past Wallington and he went on to join Derby County at the end of the season.

SATURDAY 21ST OCTOBER 1989

David Pleat's team went into the home date with Swindon Town in deep trouble at the bottom of Division Two. The opening 12 games had brought only one win and a crippling injury list meant 23 players had already been used. Paul Reid proved to be City's match-winner with a pair of stunning strikes. A left-footed player, Reid was often used on the right side of midfield and his ability to cut inside and shoot from range proved to be the difference between the sides. He put City ahead eight minutes after the restart from 30 yards and after Ossie Ardiles' team levelled, Reid blasted home another long-range effort on 66 minutes to secure three precious points.

SATURDAY 22ND OCTOBER 1961

Jack Lorrie and Albert Cheesebrough got the Leicester City goals in a 2-2 draw against West Bromwich Albion in Division One at Filbert Street.

SATURDAY 23RD OCTOBER 1976

Keith Weller was on target twice as Leicester City dished out a 4-1 thrashing to Arsenal at Filbert Street. The other goals came from Steve Earle and a Frank Worthington penalty.

SATURDAY 23RD OCTOBER 1982

Gary Lineker bagged a hat-trick in a 4-0 win at Derby County that kept Gordon Milne's Leicester City in touch with the Division Two pacesetters. He completed his hat-trick with a last-minute header and strike partner Alan Smith got the other.

WEDNESDAY 23RD OCTOBER 1957

Leicester City marked the installation of floodlights at Filbert Street with a friendly against Borussia Dortmund. Willie Gardiner grabbed City's goal in a 1-0 win.

WEDNESDAY 24TH OCTOBER 2007

Gary Megson resigned as Leicester City manager to take over at Premier League strugglers Bolton Wanderers. He was at the Walkers Stadium for just 41 days and was in charge for nine league games. The night before he resigned, Leicester lost 1-0 at home to Sheffield United.

WEDNESDAY 25TH OCTOBER 1961

Leicester City's Uefa Cup second round first leg against Atletico Madrid ended in a 1-1 draw at Filbert Street. Mendoza got a last-gasp leveller for the Spaniards after Ken Keyworth had put City ahead. Keyworth had another goal ruled out.

WEDNESDAY 26TH OCTOBER 1988

Another stunning fightback against Swindon Town at Filbert Street. The previous season, Leicester City overturned a 2-0 deficit with eight minutes left to win a five-goal thriller and there was more drama when the sides clashed again. The visitors swept into a 3-0 lead inside the opening 28 minutes. Gary McAllister gave the home fans hope with a 64th minute penalty and within 11 minutes, the scores were level. Phil King's own goal made it 3-2 and McAllister bagged the equaliser. City went close to finding a winner in a frantic climax.

WEDNESDAY 26TH OCTOBER 1983

Leicester City's 3-0 win over Arsenal at Filbert Street proved to be the season's turning point. Following the previous campaign's promotion, Gordon Milne's team had struggled to adapt to the top flight and went into the clash against Arsenal one place above the bottom having claimed just one win in their opening 14 games. Bob Hazell made his return for Leicester at the back and it was his presence at the other end of the pitch that helped create the opening for Gary Lineker to fire City in front. Steve Lynex doubled the lead before the break and Alan Smith completed the scoring in the last minute. The Foxes went on to climb the table to safety.

SATURDAY 26TH OCTOBER 1991

Steve Thompson made the perfect start to his Leicester City career after making the move from Luton Town. He stepped off the bench at Oxford United to net a stylish winner from the edge of the penalty area. Tommy Wright had bagged City's opener with a dipping volley.

SATURDAY 27TH OCTOBER 1984

Gary Lineker bagged a hat-trick against Aston Villa in just 29 minutes in the first half to send Leicester City on their way to a crushing 5-0 win. Steve Lynex (penalty) and Peter Eastoe were the other marksmen for the Foxes.

WEDNESDAY 28TH OCTOBER 1981

It was six years since Leicester City had won a tie in the League Cup and that miserable run came to an end at Filbert Street. City trailed 1-0 from the second round, first leg at Third Division Preston North End, but avoided an embarrassing exit with a four-goal blitz. Keith Robson levelled the scores on aggregate after 28 minutes with what proved to be his only goal for Leicester; Steve Lynex put them ahead ten minutes later. Early in the second half, an own goal put City further clear and Jim Melrose slammed home a late fourth from close range.

FRIDAY 28TH OCTOBER 1960

John Sjoberg made his Leicester City debut in a 2-1 defeat at Cardiff City. Jimmy Walsh got Leicester's goal and Sjoberg went on to make a total of 413 appearances for the Foxes.

SATURDAY 28TH OCTOBER 2000

Arnar Gunnlaugsson stepped off the bench to get Leicester City's winner against Derby County in the Premiership. Muzzy Izzet got the other goal in a 2-1 win.

SATURDAY 29TH OCTOBER 1983

Leicester City secured their first win of the Division One season at the 11th attempt. Alan Smith and Paul Ramsey got the goals for Gordon Milne's team in a 2-0 win over Everton at Filbert Street.

SATURDAY 30TH OCTOBER 1999

Leicester City climbed to fifth in the Premiership with a 3-0 victory over Sheffield Wednesday at Filbert Street. Gerry Taggart was the hero with two goals and Tony Cottee grabbed the other for Martin O'Neill's side.

THURSDAY 31ST OCTOBER 1974

Muzzy Izzet was born in Mile End, London.

LEICESTER CITY
On This Day & Miscellany

NOVEMBER

SATURDAY 1ST NOVEMBER 1884

History was made on this day. Leicester Fosse played their first-ever competitive match. It wasn't very competitive, though. They thumped Syston Fosse 5-0 at a venue just off Fosse Road with West and Milton Johnson getting two goals each, with Dingley grabbing the other, to get the club off to a winning start.

MONDAY 1ST NOVEMBER 2004

It was announced that Craig Levein was Leicester City's new manager. He quit Scottish Premier League side Heart of Midlothian to take the job. He replaced Micky Adams after his resignation.

WEDNESDAY 2ND NOVEMBER 1988

Leicester City, mid table in Division Two under David Pleat, dumped Division One leaders Norwich City out of the League Cup in a third round tie at Filbert Street. Mike Newell put Leicester ahead in the first half and Paul Reid rifled home a late clincher in front of the Kop after Ali Mauchlen's fearless challenge on the edge of the box had sent the ball into his path.

SATURDAY 2ND NOVEMBER 1963

Leicester City had been Liverpool's bogey team the previous season with victory in the FA Cup semi-final, and a win double in Division One, and pulled off another win at Anfield. Ken Keyworth, the scorer of the opening goal in the win on Merseyside the previous campaign, gave Matt Gillies' team a first-half lead. Liverpool swept forward in pursuit of an equaliser and found City goalkeeper Gordon Banks in his best form. His saves brought applause from the Kop.

SATURDAY 2ND NOVEMBER 1968

Andy Lochhead made his Leicester City debut in a goalless draw at Newcastle United.

SATURDAY 3RD NOVEMBER 1980

Leicester City climbed three places up to third in the Division Two table with a 3-1 win at Watford that was secured by two goals from Bobby Smith – including a penalty – and another from Andy Peake.

SATURDAY 4TH NOVEMBER 1972

George Best was on target at Filbert Street as Leicester City and Manchester United shared four goals in Division One. Jimmy Bloomfield's Foxes went into the game struggling for form. They were 20th in the table, two places above their visitors. Best fired United ahead from an acute angle after 15 minutes and Leicester were level five minutes before the break when Jon Sammels netted. Wyn Davies restored United's advantage on the hour, but John Farrington hauled Leicester level eight minutes later.

THURSDAY 4TH NOVEMBER 1920

Jack Lee was born in Sileby.

SUNDAY 5TH NOVEMBER 1995

Leicester City boss Mark McGhee handed debuts to goalkeeper Zeljko 'Spider' Kalac and Pontus Kaamark at West Bromwich Albion. Kalac was finally granted his work permit having joined from Sydney United in the summer and Sweden international Kaamark arrived from IFK Goteborg for £840,000. McGhee's team were never better than they were at the Hawthorns in the first half. Scott Taylor (two) and Iwan Roberts put them in charge at 3-0 ahead before Kalac blundered to let the Baggies get it back to 3-2.

SATURDAY 6TH NOVEMBER 1993

A 3-0 win over Southend United at Filbert Street sent Leicester City to the top of Division One. The goals came from Julian Joachim, David Oldfield and a Steve Thompson spot kick.

SATURDAY 7TH NOVEMBER 1987

Mark Venus, a target for Leicester City's boo-boys for the past few months, was the hero of a dramatic 3-2 win over Swindon Town at Filbert Street in Division Two. Future Foxes striker Jimmy Quinn bagged Swindon's second as the visitors took a 2-0 lead and City clawed their way back. Paul Ramsey and Steve Walsh were on target to draw the sides level and Venus thumped home an unstoppable 25-yarder in the dying seconds to snatch victory and earn the acclaim of the City supporters.

WEDNESDAY 8TH NOVEMBER 1995

Leicester City goalkeeper Zeljko 'Spider' Kalac ended the League Cup third round replay against Bolton Wanderers with his head in his hands after his blunders gifted the Premier League visitors a 3-2 win they didn't really deserve. City were the better side and Mark Robins and Iwan Roberts found the target, but Kalac's mistakes undid all the good work from Mark McGhee's team.

SATURDAY 9TH NOVEMBER 1957

Matt Gillies' team were finding it tough in the top flight after storming to the Second Division title the previous season and were on the receiving end of a 7-3 hammering at Burnley. Johnny Newman made his Foxes debut after joining from Birmingham City for £12,000 and could do little to stop the rampant Clarets. Leicester did lead twice in the first half thanks to John Doherty's goals and were eyeing a possible point when Derek Hogg netted after 79 minutes to make it 4-3. A late flurry of goals sank Leicester and left Burnley hat-trick heroes Jimmy McIlroy and Albert Cheesebrough to squabble over who should take home the match ball.

SATURDAY 9TH NOVEMBER 1929

Leicester City and Portsmouth clashed at Filbert Street – and there was a stunning reversal of fortunes. The previous season, City had romped to their record 10-0 win and the home fans must have harboured hopes of a repeat with Pompey having shipped 20 goals in their previous three games. Instead, the visitors upset the formbook and claimed a 5-0 win. City were without influential skipper Johnny Duncan and centre-half George Carr was back in the starting line-up despite not being fully fit. Pompey took advantage with Fred Forward netting twice.

SATURDAY 10TH NOVEMBER 1985

Goals from Ian Banks and Gary Lineker weren't enough to save Leicester City from defeat against Manchester United at Filbert Street. Gordon Milne's team were beaten 3-2 in the Division One clash.

WEDNESDAY 11TH NOVEMBER 1998

Weeks after Martin O'Neill's decision to stay at Leicester City rather than join Leeds United, the two sides met at Filbert Street in a cracking League Cup fourth round tie. Leeds took the lead through Harry Kewell's header that slipped through Leicester goalkeeper Kasey Keller's fingers, but there was late drama. Muzzy Izzet pulled City level with three minutes left in spectacular style. Leeds goalkeeper Nigel Martyn raced from his goal to head the ball clear and it fell to the City midfielder, who sent a sweetly-struck volley into the empty net. Izzet was then involved in City's winner in the dying moments. He was felled by Robert Molenaar for a penalty that Garry Parker stepped up to convert to send Leicester through.

SATURDAY 11TH NOVEMBER 1967

Frank Large made his Leicester City debut after joining from Northampton Town and he could not have had a tougher start. The Foxes were thrashed 6-0 at Manchester City in Division One.

SATURDAY 11TH NOVEMBER 1989

Paul Ramsey came off the bench and netted twice in a dramatic 4-3 win for David Pleat's Leicester City against Division Two pacesetters Leeds United at Filbert Street. Paul Moran and Gary McAllister got the other goals for the Foxes as they upset the formbook to win a seven-goal thriller with McAllister rolling home the winner to cap a sensational fightback. Kevin Campbell made his Leicester debut after arriving on loan from Arsenal. He became Pleat's second loan signing after Moran joined from Division One side Tottenham Hotspur.

SATURDAY 12TH NOVEMBER 1955

BBC Television's *Sportsview* programme put Leicester City under the spotlight for the first time and the presence of the cameras inspired the Foxes to a 6-1 demolition of Swansea Town in Division Two. Willie Gardiner was the hat-trick hero for the Foxes and the other goals came from Mal Griffiths, Johnny Morris and Arthur Rowley.

SATURDAY 13TH NOVEMBER 1965

George Best and Bobby Charlton were on the scoresheet for Manchester United in a 5-0 Division One thrashing of Leicester City at Filbert Street.

SATURDAY 13TH NOVEMBER 1982

Leicester City and Newcastle United fought out a thrilling 2-2 draw in Division Two at Filbert Street. Tommy English and Gary Lineker were on target for City and Kevin Keegan bagged both replies for the Magpies.

SATURDAY 14TH NOVEMBER 1970

Leicester City were given a helping hand by their opponents at Filbert Street. They were 3-1 winners over Swindon Town and two of the strikes were own goals. Ally Brown grabbed the other goal for the Foxes to make it four straight wins to keep his side on top of Division Two and on course for promotion.

SATURDAY 15TH NOVEMBER 1958

Leicester City striker Derek Hines netted four times in a 6-3 romp over Aston Villa at Filbert Street. Jimmy Walsh and Bernard Kelly got the other goals in the demolition.

WEDNESDAY 15TH NOVEMBER 1961

Leicester City's Uefa Cup second round second leg tie at Atletico Madrid attracted a crowd of 52,000. The sides were level at 1-1 from the first leg at Filbert Street and City boss Matt Gillies handed Graham Cross a place at the heart of the Foxes' defence on his 18th birthday. Cross acquitted himself well, along with goalkeeper Gordon Banks, who kept out a penalty. The City stopper was beaten by another penalty and Leicester bowed out to the eventual winners. Gillies expressed his displeasure at the officials and their decision to award two penalties following City's exit by 3-1 on aggregate.

SUNDAY 15TH NOVEMBER 1992

Julian Joachim was the two-goal hero for Brian Little's Leicester City in a 2-1 win at Sunderland in Division One that lifted them into the top six in the table.

SATURDAY 16TH NOVEMBER 1996

Leicester City's 3-1 win at Aston Villa gave further proof that Martin O'Neill's team were blossoming into a Premiership force. Steve Walsh was back in the side after a knee operation and Steve Claridge gave Leicester the perfect start with an eighth-minute goal. Villa drew level, but City led at the break after referee David Elleray awarded them a penalty just before the interval and Garry Parker rifled home. Leicester defended well in the second half and made sure of the points with seven minutes left when Muzzy Izzet latched on to Claridge's pass and rounded the goalkeeper to score.

SATURDAY 16TH NOVEMBER 1895

Leicester Fosse's biggest local rivals in their early years came from a few miles up the A6. Their games with Loughborough Town were hard fought and created plenty of interest. The games led to the first "football specials" on the railways and there were clashes between rival fans. Fosse proved they were Leicestershire's premier team with a 4-1 thumping at the Athletic Grounds in Loughborough that came a month after a 5-0 win. Town went ahead in the second meeting through an own goal from Harry Davy, but Fosse stormed back. Richard Davies found the target twice and the other goals came from Matt Bishop and James Lynes.

SATURDAY 16TH NOVEMBER 1957

Leicester City played their first game under the Filbert Street floodlights. The visitors were Preston North End for a Division One fixture and poor visibility meant the lights were switched on from the start of the game that kicked off at three o'clock. City were beaten 3-1 in the historic fixture with Tommy McDonald grabbing the goal for the Foxes.

SATURDAY 17TH NOVEMBER 1984

Ian Banks and Gary Lineker got the goals for Leicester City in a 2-0 win over Norwich City at Filbert Street in Division One to hand Gordon Milne's strugglers a boost.

SATURDAY 18TH NOVEMBER 1967

Len Glover made his Leicester City debut in a 2-2 draw against Arsenal at Filbert Street. Foxes boss Matt Gillies paid Charlton Athletic £80,000 – then a British record for a winger – to bring him to Filbert Street five years after his goal dumped Leicester out of the League Cup. Glover made a sparkling debut. He tormented Gunners full-back Peter Storey throughout and was a whisker away from scoring with a blistering shot that came back off the crossbar in front of the Kop. Frank Large, making his first home appearance for City, opened the scoring for the home side and Jackie Sinclair added a second from the penalty spot. But they had to settle for a point against an Arsenal side that included future Leicester players Frank McLintock, Jon Sammels and George Armstrong. The Gunners fought back to earn a share of the spoils.

SATURDAY 19TH NOVEMBER 1966

A crowd of 25,003 at Filbert Street saw goals from Leicester City strikers Mike Stringfellow and Derek Dougan clinch a 2-1 win over West Bromwich Albion and take the Foxes up to sixth in Division One.

SATURDAY 20TH NOVEMBER 1909

Fred Shinton bagged a hat-trick in just five minutes for Leicester Fosse in a 3-0 win over Oldham Athletic.

WEDNESDAY 21ST NOVEMBER 1962

Alan Smith was born in Birmingham.

SATURDAY 21ST NOVEMBER 1953

Derek Hines took just ten seconds to find the target for Leicester City in the Division Two clash against Lincoln City at Filbert Street. He finished the game with a five-goal haul in a 9-2 romp for the Foxes. The other goalscorers were Arthur Rowley (2), Johnny Morris and Mal Griffiths.

TUESDAY 22ND NOVEMBER 1994

Brian Little cited personal reasons for his decision to resign as Leicester City boss the day after Everton won the Merseyside derby to leave his Foxes side bottom of the Premier League.

WEDNESDAY 23RD NOVEMBER 1994

Leicester City went into the Premier League clash with Arsenal at Filbert Street in disarray. Boss Brian Little had walked out the previous day and City had lost their four previous games. Allan Evans was in charge and will be remembered for leaving with a 100 per cent record as Foxes boss after the team responded with a gutsy performance that secured a third Premiership win of the season. City were ahead after 16 minutes. Ian Ormondroyd took the plaudits from the majority of a 20,774 crowd, but the dubious goals panel later deemed it was an own goal by goalkeeper David Seaman. Ian Wright levelled the scores from the penalty spot, but David Lowe restored City's lead before the break and they held on in the second half to lift the gloom and raise hopes they could survive in the top flight.

SATURDAY 23RD NOVEMBER 1985

Leicester City were struggling at the bottom of Division One and Manchester United setting the pace at the top when the sides clashed at Filbert Street. Gordon Milne's team stunned the visitors with three goals in the opening 30 minutes that secured a famous victory. Gary McAllister put Leicester on their way with a sweetly-struck shot after just seven minutes and Alan Smith doubled the lead before thumping home the third from a tight angle to send the home fans wild.

SATURDAY 23RD NOVEMBER 1935

Leicester City went top of Division Two with victory at Filbert Street. Tony Carroll and Gene O'Callaghan got the goals in a 2-0 win over Plymouth Argyle.

TUESDAY 23RD NOVEMBER 1948

Frank Worthington was born in Halifax.

SATURDAY 24TH NOVEMBER 1979

Derek Strickland and Martin Henderson were on target for Leicester City in a 2-0 win over Wrexham at Filbert Street. The result stretched City's unbeaten run to six games and kept Jock Wallace's team fifth in Division Two.

FRIDAY 25TH NOVEMBER 1994

Brian Little was unveiled as Aston Villa's new boss. Leicester City fans were far from happy. Alan Evans, who had been in caretaker charge of City following Little's departure from Filbert Street, resigned. City fans were incensed because Little had said personal reasons had been behind his decision to quit Leicester just six months after taking them into the Premier League.

SATURDAY 25TH NOVEMBER 1989

A 1-0 win at Stoke City marked the start of a revival by David Pleat's Leicester City. He brought in loan strikers Paul Moran and Kevin Campbell from Tottenham Hotspur and Arsenal, respectively, and they played their part in a crucial victory that sparked a run of six wins in seven games. Both sides needed the points at the Victoria Ground. Stoke were bottom of the table and City just one point and one place above them. Gary Mills struck after 62 minutes to ease the relegation fears of Leicester's fans and move them away from their relegation rivals.

SATURDAY 25TH NOVEMBER 1961

Goalkeeper George Heyes was Leicester City's hero in a 2-1 win at Tottenham Hotspur in Division One. Heyes was beaten after just three minutes by John White's effort and City were level five minutes later through Ken Keyworth's strike from a Howard Riley cross. Hugh McIlmoyle went close to giving Leicester the lead with a header that crashed against the woodwork and then nodded down for Colin Appleton to lash home an unstoppable shot from 25 yards with 20 minutes left. The home side threw everything at Heyes in the last 20 minutes, but he kept them all out to secure maximum points for the Foxes.

SATURDAY 26TH NOVEMBER 1927

The first radio commentary from Filbert Street captured the drama as Leicester City beat Newcastle United 3-0 in Division One. Arthur Chandler grabbed two goals for City and Arthur Lochhead completed the scoring.

WEDNESDAY 27TH NOVEMBER 1895

Arthur Chandler was born in Paddington and he went on to become the record goalscorer in Leicester City's history.

WEDNESDAY 27TH NOVEMBER 1991

Brian Little's Leicester City beat Premier League Everton in the third round of the Zenith Data Systems Cup at Filbert Street. David Oldfield put City ahead with a thunderbolt and Steve Thompson doubled the lead before Peter Beardsley danced through to halve the arrears for the Toffeemen. City held on to the lead.

SATURDAY 27TH NOVEMBER 1976

Leicester City stayed sixth in Division One following a 2-2 draw at Leeds United. Frank Worthington and Steve Earle got the goals for City at Elland Road.

SATURDAY 27TH NOVEMBER 1993

Iwan Roberts made a stunning debut for Leicester City after joining from Huddersfield Town for a fee of £300,000. He netted twice in a dramatic 2-2 draw against Wolverhampton Wanderers at Filbert Street and was a whisker away from completing a hat-trick in a dramatic clash when he just failed to convert a cross.

SATURDAY 27TH NOVEMBER 1926

Foxes legend Arthur Chandler got all five goals for Leicester City in their 5-1 thrashing of Aston Villa at Filbert Street.

WEDNESDAY 27TH NOVEMBER 1996

Goals from Steve Claridge and Emile Heskey powered Leicester City to a 2-0 win over Manchester United in a League Cup fourth round tie at Filbert Street.

SATURDAY 28TH NOVEMBER 2015

Jamie Vardy scored for City against Manchester United at the King Power Stadium to rewrite the record books. The goal meant Vardy had scored in 11 consecutive Premier League games, breaking the record set by Manchester United striker Ruud van Nistelrooy 12 years earlier.

SATURDAY 29TH NOVEMBER 1997

The wait for a win at Coventry City came to an end for Leicester City and their supporters. Their first win at the Sky Blues' home for 22 years came thanks to an opening goal from Graham Fenton and Matt Elliott's penalty.

WEDNESDAY 30TH NOVEMBER 1988

There's never a Russian linesman when you need one! Leicester City and Nottingham Forest battled out a goalless draw in the fourth round of the League Cup in front of a bumper crowd of 26,764 at Filbert Street. But, the scoreline should have been different according to Mike Newell. City's striker crashed a right-foot shot off the underside of the bar in the second half of a game played in a highly-charged atmosphere and is still convinced the ball crossed the line, two decades later. The linesman disagreed and the game ended scoreless. First Division Forest had to play the second half with only ten men after Stuart Pearce was dismissed for a reckless lunge on Paul Reid.

WEDNESDAY 30TH NOVEMBER 1983

A Leicester City legend marked his return to Filbert Street with a goal in a game that brought Foxes striker Gary Lineker face-to-face with his hero. Former City striker Frank Worthington was on target for Southampton, but it wasn't enough to prevent the Foxes running out 2-1 winners in the Division One clash. Alan Smith and Gary Lineker got the goals for Gordon Milne's team in front of 14,181 and that made it back-to-back wins for City as they put their disastrous start to the season behind them.

WEDNESDAY 30TH NOVEMBER 1966

Leicester City stayed fifth in Division One despite a 2-1 defeat at home to Manchester United. David Gibson grabbed City's goal and the replies for United came from George Best and Denis Law.

SATURDAY 30TH NOVEMBER 1968

Everton piled on the misery for Division One strugglers Leicester City at Goodison Park. Rodney Fern was on target for City in a crushing 7-1 defeat that made it eight games without a win for the Foxes. Joe Royle got a hat-trick for the Toffeemen.

LEICESTER CITY
On This Day & Miscellany

DECEMBER

SATURDAY 1ST DECEMBER 1990

Leicester City edged out Newcastle United in a nine-goal Division Two thriller at Filbert Street. David Kelly bagged a hat-trick for the Foxes and Mick Quinn hit a treble for the visitors. David Pleat's City included loan signings Mike Hooper and Terry Fenwick and they led 2-1 at the break through Fenwick and Kelly. David Oldfield and Kelly (penalty) made it 4-1 to the home side, but Newcastle hit back and reduced the deficit to a single goal with two strikes. Kelly appeared to have put the game beyond the visitors with the goal that completed his hat-trick after 86 minutes, but there was still time left for Quinn to bag his third and set up a nervy climax to the match.

TUESDAY 1ST DECEMBER 1964

Leicester City's record away win came at Coventry City on the day Foxes legend Ken Keyworth completed a switch to Highfield Road. He saw his former team storm to an 8-1 win in a League Cup fifth round tie over the Sky Blues, who were playing in the third tier of English football. Graham Cross had a spell in goal for Matt Gillies' team after Gordon Banks was injured and Coventry skipper George Curtis contributed an own goal as City went on the rampage. Full-back Richie Norman was on target twice for City, and they were collector's items. He scored just five times in 365 appearances.

WEDNESDAY 2ND DECEMBER 1998

Leicester City went through to the semi-finals of the League Cup with victory over Premier League rivals Blackburn Rovers at Filbert Street. Neil Lennon grabbed the only goal to set up a semi-final against Sunderland.

SATURDAY 2ND DECEMBER 2000

Leicester City went back up to third in the Premier League with a 3-1 win over Leeds United at Filbert Street that was secured by goals from Robbie Savage, Ade Akinbiyi and Gerry Taggart.

SATURDAY 3RD DECEMBER 1966

Teenager David Nish made a goalscoring debut in the 4-2 win over Stoke City at Filbert Street. Peter Rodrigues, Derek Dougan and John Sinclair got the other goals. Nish went on to play 272 games for the Foxes and score 31 goals.

SATURDAY 3RD DECEMBER 1994

Brian Little was barracked throughout the game as he returned to Filbert Street as manager of Aston Villa. Fans held banners declaring him 'Judas' and 'Liar'. Phil Gee's goal, that put Leicester City ahead, lightened the mood somewhat. Guy Whittingham grabbed a second-half equaliser. There can seldom have been such a hostile atmosphere at Filbert Street.

SATURDAY 4TH DECEMBER 1976

Leicester City were thumped 6-2 by Birmingham City at a frozen Filbert Street. The visitors coped better with the Arctic conditions and none more so than Kenny Burns, who grabbed a hat-trick for the Blues. Steve Kember and Frank Worthington got City's goals.

SATURDAY 5TH DECEMBER 1987

Leicester City and Middlesbrough battled out a goalless draw at Filbert Street in Division Two. The result made it four games without a win and left the Foxes 16th in the table. It proved to be Bryan Hamilton's last game in charge of the club.

SATURDAY 6TH DECEMBER 1980

Leicester City ended a run of four straight defeats in Division One with a 2-1 win at Birmingham City. Jim Melrose got both goals for City and Geoff Scott put through his own goal for the Blues' reply. Scott went on to join Birmingham City.

THURSDAY 7TH DECEMBER 1995

Mark McGhee was unveiled as Wolverhampton Wanderers' new manager after walking out of Leicester City just over 12 months after Brian Little quit the job. Leicester fans were furious and accused McGhee of betrayal. His response was to say: "I think everyone at Leicester knows what type of person I am." The response was emphatic, but unprintable.

SATURDAY 8TH DECEMBER 1984

Gordon Milne's team started their climb towards Division One safety with a 4-0 win at Sunderland. Leicester City stunned the home side with three goals in the first half. Alan Smith led the way with a double strike after 16 and 42 minutes and strike partner Gary Lineker added another. The scoring was completed by Steve Lynex after 71 minutes and City's strikeforce went on to hit top gear. Smith then proceeded to score in five successive games – and Lynex in four – to take the Foxes away from the drop zone, while Sunderland's slump continued and they ended up being relegated.

SATURDAY 9TH DECEMBER 1989

Kevin Campbell got his first goal for Leicester City after arriving on loan from Arsenal. He was on target in a 4-2 win at Blackburn Rovers. Gary McAllister got City's opening goal from the penalty spot and the others came from Simon Morgan and Tommy Wright.

SATURDAY 10TH DECEMBER 1977

Roger Davies, a hero in Derby County's First Division championship-winning season of 1974-75, made his Leicester City debut against the Rams in a 1-1 draw at Filbert Street. Foxes boss Frank McLintock splashed out a club record £250,000 to bring Davies to the club from Belgian football in a bid to boost his side's survival hopes in Division One.

FRIDAY 10TH DECEMBER 1999

Darren Eadie became Leicester City's record signing when he joined from Norwich City for a fee of £3m.

FRIDAY 11TH DECEMBER 1987

Bryan Hamilton was sacked as Leicester City manager with the Foxes 16th in Division Two.

SATURDAY 12TH DECEMBER 1987

Peter Morris took charge of the Leicester City team that was beaten 2-0 at Oldham Athletic in the first game following Bryan Hamilton's departure. Tommy Wright, who went on to become a fans' favourite at Filbert Street, got one of the goals for the Latics in the Division Two clash.

SATURDAY 13TH DECEMBER 1947

Goalkeeper Joe Calvert became Leicester City's oldest-ever player when he went between the posts at Southampton at the age of 40 years and 313 days. City were beaten 3-1.

WEDNESDAY 14TH DECEMBER 1994

Mark McGhee became Leicester City's new manager after quitting Reading.

WEDNESDAY 14TH DECEMBER 1988

Leicester City crashed out of the League Cup after defeat at East Midlands rivals Nottingham Forest in their fourth round replay. The sides had drawn 0-0 at Filbert Street and Forest went ahead in the replay through Gary Crosby. City levelled when Paul Groves headed home a Mike Newell cross. Forest roared back and Lee Chapman stabbed home the winner after a goalmouth scramble.

WEDNESDAY 15TH DECEMBER 1999

Leicester City had never won a penalty shoot-out until the visit of Leeds United for a League Cup fourth round tie at Filbert Street. Their three previous shoot-outs had all ended in defeat, but that all changed after 120 minutes of stalemate. City went first and Icelandic international Arnar Gunnlaugsson kept his cool to slot home the opener. Matt Elliott and Andrew Impey were also successful to keep Leicester ahead at 3-2 and Leeds defender Gary Kelly then blazed over the bar to put the home side in charge. Theo Zagorakis then shot over, but Leeds midfielder Ian Bowyer also cracked under the pressure. He smacked his shot against the crossbar and Muzzy Izzet netted Leicester's next spot kick to send his team through 4-2.

SATURDAY 15TH DECEMBER 1951

A third successive win in December against promotion rivals Cardiff City lifted Norman Bullock's Leicester City up to sixth place in Division Two. Arthur Rowley gave the Foxes the perfect start with a 10th-minute opener and Derek Hines gave the home side some breathing space by doubling the lead just before the hour mark. Fred Worthington completed the scoring with a third goal.

TUESDAY 16TH DECEMBER 1969

Simon Grayson was born in Ripon, Yorkshire. He went on to become the first Leicester City captain to lift a trophy at Wembley.

SATURDAY 16TH DECEMBER 1961

Goals from Albert Cheesebrough and Jimmy Walsh secured a 2-0 win over Manchester City at Filbert Street in Division One.

SUNDAY 17TH DECEMBER 1995

A huge day in Leicester City's history: Martin O'Neill quit as Norwich City manager on the morning of the game with the Canaries at Filbert Street. Mike Walker was at the match working as a television pundit and was expected to become City's next manager after Mark McGhee's departure. Leicester hit back from 2-0 down to win 3-2 and Walker didn't get the job. O'Neill did.

SATURDAY 17TH DECEMBER 1994

Mark McGhee's first game in charge of Leicester City ended in a goalless draw against Premier League table-toppers Blackburn Rovers at Filbert Street. It was the Foxes' first clean sheet of the season and Rovers went on to win the title.

SATURDAY 18TH DECEMBER 1999

Darren Eadie made his Leicester City debut eight days after becoming the club's record £3m signing and couldn't prevent a 1-0 defeat at Derby County in the Premier League.

SATURDAY 18TH DECEMBER 1954

Andy Graver marked his Leicester City debut with a goal in a 3-1 defeat at Chelsea in Division One. Graver became City's record signing when he joined from Lincoln City for a fee of £27,600. The game is also remembered for a bizarre 'shared' own goal. Stan Milburn and Jack Froggatt simultaneously kicked the ball past Foxes keeper Johnny Anderson.

SUNDAY 19TH DECEMBER 1993

Leicester City avoided defeat at Peterborough United thanks to a last-gasp own goal, after Tony Adcock's opener had put the Posh on course for a league double, after victory at Filbert Street earlier in the season.

SATURDAY 20TH DECEMBER 1974

Keith Weller refused to come out for the second half of the game against Ipswich Town at Filbert Street. Weller had a transfer request turned down a few days before the game and got his wish after the game along with a fine of two weeks' wages.

SATURDAY 21ST DECEMBER 1963

Frank McLintock got the only goal for Leicester City in a 1-0 win at Arsenal in Division One.

SATURDAY 22ND DECEMBER 1973

Frank Worthington's late goal settled the local derby against Coventry City at Filbert Street, just three days before Christmas. The win also took Jimmy Bloomfield's team up to fifth place in Division One, but it was the Sky Blues who started the better as they led through a ninth-minute goal. City were level at the break thanks to Len Glover, who blasted home an unstoppable shot from the edge of the penalty area just moments before half-time. Leicester, with new signing Steve Earle in the thick of the action, stepped up a gear after the break. But, they had to wait until two minutes before the end of the match for the decisive goal. Worthington rose to head home Glover's cross to break Coventry's hearts.

SATURDAY 22ND DECEMBER 1934

Leicester City's home game against Portsmouth kicked off with only one official on duty. Referee FW Wort didn't arrive until half-time and one of the linesmen didn't arrive until the third minute. That left AW Smith to take charge and the sides shared four goals in a hectic opening seven minutes. City went on to win 6-3 with Arthur Chandler netting twice. The haul was rounded up by Tommy Mills, Arthur Maw, Danny Liddle and an own goal.

SATURDAY 23RD DECEMBER 1995

Martin O'Neill's first game as Leicester City manager ended in a 2-2 draw at Grimsby Town. The goals came from Iwan Roberts and Steve Walsh.

SATURDAY 24TH DECEMBER 1932

Leicester City were edged out 4-3 at West Bromwich Albion. City's marksmen in the seven-goal thriller in Division One were Arthur Lochhead, John Campbell and Sep Smith.

THURSDAY 25TH DECEMBER 1924

John Duncan bagged six goals in the 7-0 thrashing of Port Vale at Filbert Street. Arthur Chandler had opened the scoring for the Foxes in the Division Two clash in front of a crowd of 22,000. The result kept City fourth in the table.

FRIDAY 25TH DECEMBER 1953

Leicester City stayed top of the Division Two table with a 4-1 thumping of Rotherham United at Filbert Street. Arthur Rowley was the goal hero with a hat-trick and Derek Hines bagged the other for the Foxes in front of a bumper crowd of 30,902.

SATURDAY 25TH DECEMBER 1926

Arthur Chandler made it a happy Christmas for Leicester City fans with a five-goal haul in his team's 5-0 thrashing of West Bromwich Albion at Filbert Street. The result lifted the Foxes up to fifth in Division One.

MONDAY 26TH DECEMBER 1932

Andy Lochhead got his 100th goal for Leicester City in a 2-1 defeat at Portsmouth. It was his 267th game for City.

MONDAY 27TH DECEMBER 1993

For thousands of Leicester City fans, Ian Ormondroyd saved Christmas. He sent a last-gasp header looping into Watford's net to snatch a dramatic 4-4 draw at Filbert Street. The other scorers for Brian Little's team were David Oldfield (2) and a Steve Thompson penalty.

MONDAY 28TH DECEMBER 1959

Albert Cheesebrough gave Leicester City the lead after just 13 seconds of the game at Preston North End. City had to settle for a point after a 1-1 draw. The result made it five games unbeaten for City in Division One.

SATURDAY 29TH DECEMBER 1979

Two goals in the last seven minutes ensured Leicester City ended the decade with a win. Jock Wallace's promotion hopefuls took on Queens Park Rangers at Filbert Street and the visitors went on the defensive after the dismissal of future City defender Bob Hazell. Leicester dominated, hitting the woodwork twice, but couldn't find a way through until Dennis Rofe broke the deadlock. He carried the ball out of defence, the visitors backed off and Rofe belted home a stunning shot from 30 yards. With two minutes left, Martin Henderson doubled the lead with a header from close range.

SATURDAY 29TH DECEMBER 1973

Leicester City's 2-0 win at Arsenal completed a rare double over the Gunners and lifted Jimmy Bloomfield's team up to fifth in Division One. City's two-goal hero at Highbury was Frank Worthington. Worthington ensured he found the target for the fifth successive game with a 12th-minute opener to boost his hopes of an England call-up and he set up the second after 17 minutes. He lashed a fierce effort goalwards that Steve Earle diverted into the net with his head. Both players claimed the goal and it was Earle who eventually got the credit for what was his 100th goal in the Football League.

SATURDAY 29TH DECEMBER 1934

Arthur Chandler scored in a 3-1 defeat at Wolverhampton Wanderers and that made him Leicester City's oldest-ever goalscorer at the age of 39 years and 32 days. It was the last goal of a record-breaking City career that brought 273 goals in 419 appearances.

FRIDAY 30TH DECEMBER 1938

Gordon Banks was born in Sheffield and went on to become a goalkeeping legend for both Leicester City and England.

SATURDAY 31ST DECEMBER 1960

Leicester City hammered Everton 4-1 at Filbert Street in Division One. Ken Leek netted twice for the Foxes while the other strikes came from Howard Riley and Jimmy Walsh.

LEICESTER CITY
On This Day & Miscellany

MISCELLANY

DOING A LEICESTER

The phrase "Doing a Leicester" could mean going to "Skegg-eh" for your holidays or calling everyone "me' duck." It doesn't. "Doing a Leicester" is in the lexicon of politicians, boxers, football managers and anyone else who sets out to conquer the sort of unconquerable odds Leicester City faced at the start of the 2015-16 season. The bookmakers reckoned there was as much chance of City winning the Premier League for the first time in their history as there was of Elvis Presley reappearing. That's the Elvis Presley who died in 1977. It was a 5,000-1 shot. This was a team capable of miracles, however. The previous season, City had stayed up with a late surge that brought 19 points from their last eight games. But in the weeks that followed, City lost both their manager, Nigel Pearson, and their best player. Esteban Cambiasso, he's magic, you know, decided one season with Leicester was quite enough. Without Pearson and Cambiasso, City were sure to struggle. Especially after Claudio Ranieri – "an uninspired choice", according to Gary Lineker on Twitter – was appointed manager. 'The Tinkerman' was known for a successfulish spell at Chelsea, but more recently, his CV showed he had been sacked by Greece after a defeat against the footballing minnows of the Faroe Islands. To the surprise of just about everyone, the eccentric Italian went on to become only the fourth manager to take City to the summit of the top division in English football with a win at Newcastle United on Saturday, November 21 and unlike Willie Orr, Matt Gillies and Peter Taylor before him, he kept them there. City were top at Christmas – they had been bottom 12 months earlier – following a 3-2 win at Everton and though that was followed by a run of only two points from a possible nine, victory at Tottenham Hotspur confirmed the bubble hadn't burst. The 3-1 win at Manchester City – Leicester were 3-0 up after an hour – put them five points clear of Tottenham and Arsenal, but eight days later, on Valentine's Day, the gap was slashed to two after a last-gasp defeat at Arsenal. The experts nodded knowingly. The history books showed Arsenal, Chelsea, Manchester United or Manchester City usually win the Premier League and surely, this was the moment plucky Leicester bowed out of the title race. But this City team simply didn't know its place. They put together another unbeaten run and when Tottenham could only draw at Chelsea on Monday, May 2, the 5,000-1 shots were champions of England.

THE FUTURE'S BRIGHT WITHOUT GARY

The Football League's fixture computer was at its most mischievous in the summer of 1985. A few weeks after leaving Leicester City for Everton in an £800,000 transfer, Gary Lineker discovered he would be heading back to Filbert Street to make his debut for the Toffeemen. Although expected, Lineker's decision to leave Leicester still hurt supporters he had stood alongside as a boy. He remembers crying all the way home from Wembley in 1969 after the FA Cup Final defeat against Manchester City and when asked in a football magazine to name his 'favourite other team', Lineker's reply was Leicester reserves! But after 103 goals in 216 games for City, the prospect of playing for the Division One champions proved to be greater than that of another season spent battling in mid table and afternoons off playing a few frames of snooker with Willie Thorne. So, Lineker went to Merseyside and then came back to face the club and supporters he had left behind. His place in Leicester's starting line-up went to Mark Bright and he had hardly set Filbert Street alight in his first season after joining from Port Vale. Although he failed to find the target, Bright did score 28 goals in 27 games for the reserves and was the obvious choice to replace Lineker in City's forward line when the 1985-86 season kicked off. At the other end of the pitch, City boss Gordon Milne handed a debut to Russell Osman at the heart of the defence following his £240,000 move from Ipswich Town and while he was one of the heroes of Leicester's stunning 3-1 win, the following day's newspaper headlines were all about Bright. Bobby Smith cancelled out Everton's early opener and then Bright smacked a couple of belters past Welsh international Neville Southall to wrap up a sensational 3-1 win. Julie Welch wrote in *The Observer*: "As the champions stumbled to their first pratfall of the season, the locals showed their sympathy for Lineker's poor showing with a rousing chorus of: 'What a waste of money.'" Bright failed to build on that stunning performance, however. He netted only four more times for City, the fans barracked him and he went on to have success at Crystal Palace where he finished top scorer in Division Two, played in the top flight and the 1990 FA Cup Final and formed a partnership with Ian Wright. After hanging up their boots, Lineker and Bright ended up on the same side as football pundits for the BBC.

A TALE OF TWO BROTHERS

For the benefit of the press, Allan Clarke arrived at Leicester City in a wheelbarrow – he was going to score a barrow load of goals – and two decades later, brother Wayne was similarly wheeled out to face the photographers at Filbert Street. The difference is, Wayne probably left in a wheelbarrow as well. He couldn't match his big brother's achievements. In June, 1968, City smashed the British transfer record when boss Matt Gillies got the backing of the club's board to spend £150,000 on Fulham striker Allan Clarke. Leicester paid the Cottagers £110,000 and the fee was made up by Frank Large making the move in the opposite direction to London. A slender and stylish striker, Clarke got his City career off to the perfect start with a debut goal in the 1-1 draw at Queens Park Rangers on the opening day of the season. Eleven days later, he looked worth every penny of Leicester's investment when a stunning hat-trick beat Manchester City at Filbert Street. City ended up in a relegation battle, however, and Clarke's languid displays attracted criticism. He saved his best displays for the big occasion – and they don't get much bigger than the FA Cup semi-final. City faced holders West Bromwich Albion in the last four at Hillsborough and Clarke bagged the only goal with less than three minutes left to send City through to their third FA Cup Final in the 1960s. Again, Clarke was City's top performer on the big day. Leicester were beaten 1-0 by Neil Young's strike, but it was 'Sniffer' who took the man-of-the-match award. After the final defeat, City had five games left to preserve their top-flight status and although Clarke got the only goal against Tottenham Hotspur three days after the defeat at Wembley, Leicester were relegated. Clarke wasn't keen on playing in Division Two and his 16 goals in 46 appearances for City was enough to attract an offer from Leeds United that re-wrote the British transfer fee record for the second time in the space of 12 months. Clarke left for a fee of £165,000 and City made a £15,000 profit. In the summer of 1989, Clarke's brother Wayne headed to Filbert Street from Everton as part of the deal that took Mike Newell to Merseyside. Like his brother 21 years earlier, Clarke marked his Leicester debut with a goal in a 1-1 draw at Hull City, but netted only once more and left for Manchester City just seven months after arriving at City.

WHAT A GOAL!

Joey Gudjonsson looked up and saw that Hull City goalkeeper Boaz Myhill had wandered off his goal line. He then put down his binoculars, took aim and launched a shot from the halfway line that sailed over Myhill's head, into the net and into this book on the page that chronicles the most spectacular goals scored by Leicester City players. The Icelandic international went on to add the winner in City's 3-2 victory in the Championship fixture at the Walkers Stadium in March, 2006. As you will read elsewhere – if you get that far – Peter Shilton got on the score-sheet when playing in goal at Southampton in October, 1967 and another who found the target from long range was Dennis Rofe. He belted home a free kick from just inside his own half in a 2-2 draw against Queens Park Rangers at Filbert Street in September, 1976. Rofe remembers this goal rather differently to everyone else who saw it. He reckons it was a tremendous bit of opportunism on his part. Everyone else says it was a fluke! That word featured prominently in City's dressing room at the start of the 2003-2004 Premier League campaign and it was directed at French midfielder Lilian Nalis. He arrived at the Walkers Stadium in the summer of 2003 and his unstoppable volley sent City on their way to a 4-0 win over Leeds United in front of the Sky Sports cameras in September. "Lilian doesn't speak much English," said City boss Micky Adams, "but he knows what the word fluke means now!" The previous season, Muzzy Izzet left fans breathless with a stunning overhead kick that secured a 2-1 win for ten-man City at Grimsby Town and mention must be made of Alan Birchenall's howitzer against Leeds United at Filbert Street in October, 1973. Later that season, Keith Weller danced through the Kenilworth Road mud and then smacked a left-foot shot into the top corner that put the seal on a 4-0 win at Luton Town in the fifth round of the FA Cup that is remembered as one of City's finest performances of their flamboyant 1970s pomp. Julian Joachim's haul of 31 goals for Leicester include some spectacular strikes. As a teenage whizzkid, he bagged the BBC's Goal of the Month award for his solo goal in an FA Cup third round replay at Barnsley in January, 1993. Better still was his blistering run and cheeky poke through the goalkeeper's legs in the play-off semi-final against Portsmouth later that season.

THE GAFFER

Claudio Ranieri had performed miracles before. Only ever an average player, he spent most of his career at Catanzaro, before he made his managerial breakthrough with Cagliari. The 37-year-old Ranieri inherited a Serie C1 team and following back-to-back promotions, they were a Serie A team – and flourishing. "When we got as high as seventh, I said: 'This is a dream, a fairytale. Football is not like this,'" remembered Ranieri. "Everyone in Cagliari loved me. That is not normal, that is not football." How did he do it ? "It's important to have a very good group of players," he said. "I changed very few and this group kept going until Serie A." Ranieri says he didn't want big signings. "I don't want to break the changing room," he said. "My lads are special. The team is our boss." He took his philosophies with him to Napoli, Fiorentina, Valencia, Atletico Madrid and Chelsea, where he upset supporters by selling Dennis Wise to Leicester, a move that would upset City supporters – and players – as well. 'The Tinkerman', he was forever tinkering with line-ups and formations, did have his successes at Chelsea and kept the press amused with his offbeat musings about parachutes, animals and his mother, among other things, before leaving Stamford Bridge in 2004. He returned to the Premier League with Leicester 11 years later – and the welcome might have been warmer. "Really?" Tweeted Gary Lineker. "Claudio Ranieri is clearly experienced, but this is an uninspired choice by Leicester. It's amazing how the same old names keep getting a go on the managerial merry-go-round." Ranieri may have been an old name, but he was young at heart. He bought his players pizza after they kept their first clean sheet of the season – a 1-0 win over Crystal Palace in the tenth match – and got the best out of a group nobody else wanted. Wes Morgan was too old, Stoke didn't need Robert Huth anymore and as for Jamie Vardy and Riyad Mahrez, who were they? Ranieri told his players he wanted them to be "warriors" and they played their hearts out for him – and each other. Ranieri worked as hard as his players. He would stay up all night examining film of City's opponents, looking for weaknesses, and when it appeared Leicester themselves may falter in the closing weeks, Ranieri knew what to say. "I told my players: 'It's this year or never. In an era where money counts for everything, we give hope to everybody.'"

SEVEN MINUTES OF MAYHEM

The drama didn't end when the referee finally blew his whistle to end Leicester City's astonishing 3-3 draw with Arsenal at Filbert Street in August, 1997. Just ask Steve Walsh. Or rather, don't ask him. The decision to allow seven minutes of added time gave Walsh enough time to power home a late leveller and the Gunners were so incensed that several players surrounded the officials to protest. Ian Wright even raced off the substitutes' bench to get his point across and Walsh, never one to back down, met him head on. "The question I get asked the most," recalled the Leicester legend "is what I said to Wright when he came running onto the pitch. The thing is, I'd rather not say. I always tell people I can't remember." Nobody who was there and didn't leave early will ever forget the late drama that led to the confrontation. City were 2-0 behind after 83 minutes and went on to snatch a point after Dennis Bergkamp's hat-trick had looked like winning it for the Gunners. Along with his wholehearted commitment and crucial goals, Walsh is also remembered for his feuds and battles with Wolverhampton Wanderers striker Steve Bull which provided a compelling subplot to matches between the sides. In fact, you suspect there were those who went to the games just to watch their duel. Walsh admitted his instructions were to "give him a kick early on to slow him down a bit" and he got a black eye for doing just that in November, 1989 during a Division Two clash at Filbert Street. Bull was given a red card for giving Walsh a shiner and the roles were reversed in August, 1992. This time it was Walsh running the taps ahead of schedule after an off-the-ball bust up. In total, Walsh was sent off nine times while playing for City – a club record. He is also among the leading appearance makers for Leicester having played 449 games during 14 years at Filbert Street after joining from Wigan Athletic. He proved to be effective at both ends of the pitch and perhaps his finest moment came in the play-off final at Wembley in May, 1994. It looked like Walsh's season was over eight months earlier after a cruciate ligament injury he suffered at Middlesbrough. He battled back to fitness, though, and his goal double against Derby County sent Brian Little's team into the Premier League and secured the Foxes' first win at Wembley at the seventh attempt.

I WILL GET MY COAT

Peter Eccles wasn't the type to outstay his welcome. He is remembered for having one of the shortest international careers having played just 10 minutes for the Republic of Ireland – and he didn't hang around for long at Leicester City either. David Pleat handed Eccles his debut at the heart of City's defence at Blackburn Rovers in March, 1989 – in the absence of Steve Walsh – and he was substituted at half time. City went on to draw at Ewood Park 0-0 and Eccles never played for City again. The distinction of the shortest-ever Leicester City career is shared by Malcolm Clarke and Tommy Williamson.

Both came on in the 89th minute of fixtures; Clarke came on in the dying moments of a home match against Leeds United in September, 1965 and Williamson earned a footnote in Filbert Street's history by replacing Muzzy Izzet in the final game at the ground against Tottenham Hotspur in May, 2002. Compared to them, Kevin Ellison was a Leicester stalwart. His Foxes career lasted six minutes! At least the striker plucked from non-league Altrincham by boss Peter Taylor got to play at Old Trafford – and he can say that his introduction was the turning point. The scores were level when he came on in the 84th minute – and Manchester United ended up winning the game 2-0. Luigi Glombard wore Leicester's colours for just ten minutes. He joined on loan from Cardiff City and came off the bench in the 2-0 win at Ipswich Town in February, 2007 before returning to Wales. Sascha Lenhart's contribution to Leicester City winning their first piece of silverware for 33 years was just 49 minutes. The winger came on in the League Cup clash against Scarborough at Filbert Street in September, 1996. Lenhart never got another chance for Leicester and probably didn't even notice when Martin O'Neill's team went on to lift the trophy seven months later. Kevin Reed came on as a second-half substitute in the clash with Wrexham in November, 1978 and he didn't do enough to get another chance from Leicester boss Jock Wallace. Graham Brown was another not to complete 90 minutes. He came on for John Sjoberg in the second half of the 1-0 win over Aston Villa at Filbert Street in April, 1970. James Campbell was a regular for City in fixtures during the Second World War, but his first-class career lasted less than 90 minutes as he suffered a head injury in an FA Cup clash at Chelsea in January, 1946.

MANAGERS ON THE MOVE

Above all else, football fans demand a bit of loyalty and that's why you probably won't see Brian Little or Mark McGhee doing their shopping at the Highcross. In the space of 12 months, both walked out of Filbert Street and it is doubtful either will ever be forgiven by Leicester City supporters. City were in disarray when Little arrived in the summer of 1991 having previously steered Darlington to back-to-back promotions. Leicester had escaped relegation to the third tier of English football for the first time in their history and Little set about rebuilding the club's fortunes. At the third attempt, he took City into the Premier League via the play-offs with victory over Derby County following defeats in the previous two finals at Wembley against Blackburn Rovers and Swindon Town. Following promotion, City were immediately installed as favourites to be relegated and set about ensuring the gamblers weren't disappointed. They had to wait until their sixth game for a first victory – Julian Joachim on target twice in a memorable 3-1 win over Ossie Ardiles' Tottenham Hotspur at Filbert Street – and the rumours started that Little would be on his way back to Villa Park after Ron Atkinson was sacked by Villa. Little actually cited personal reasons for his decision to resign as Leicester manager in November 1994 and whatever those personal reasons were, they didn't prevent him becoming Villa boss four days after leaving Filbert Street.Cue outrage in Leicester and thankfully for Foxes fans, they got the chance to let Little know exactly what they thought of him later that month when Villa came to Filbert Street. He was booed, heckled and hissed at throughout the 1-1 draw. McGhee left Reading to take on the job and although a 4-4 draw at Little's Villa when City clawed back a 4-1 deficit with only 13 minutes left raised hopes of an escape, Leicester were relegated. The Scot's team played some dazzling football at the start of the 1995-96 season as they set about earning promotion. Then history repeated itself. Wolverhampton Wanderers sacked their manager; McGhee got itchy feet and was off. Cue more outrage in Leicester. City did get their revenge with a 3-2 win at Molineux in February that was Martin O'Neill's first win as Leicester manager. Thankfully, O'Neill hung around for a while. More than a decade earlier, Jock Wallace's decision to leave Filbert Street for Motherwell in the summer of 1982 caused similar fury. A few months earlier, he had taken City to the FA Cup semi final.

WHAT MIGHT HAVE BEEN

Both grew up supporting Leicester City and idolising Frank Worthington. Gary Lineker made his boyhood dreams come true, Richard Hill was the one that got away. As a teenager, Hill, raised in Hinckley, was on City's books, but he failed to make a first-team appearance and joined non-league Nuneaton Borough in 1983. A move to Northampton Town followed and Hill's haul of 33 goals from midfield in the 1986-87 season helped the Cobblers romp to the Division Four championship and earned a £240,000 move to Watford – in the days when £240,000 was a lot of money. Hill was hit by injuries, however, and after a transfer to Oxford United, he went on to play for Leicestershire non-league side Shepshed Dynamo. He made an appearance at Filbert Street with Dynamo in the County Cup final in 1997-98 and was denied an early goal against Leicester by the woodwork before the Foxes ran out 6-1 winners. Tony Thorpe is another who went on to be a prolific goal scorer in the lower leagues after being released by his home-town club. He had the satisfaction of netting for Luton Town in a 1-1 draw at Filbert Street in February, 1996, but another return to Leicester with Bristol City for an FA Cup fifth round tie in February, 2001 ended in a 3-0 defeat. Carl Heggs also suffered FA Cup heartbreak at Filbert Street. Although never on City's books, Heggs made no secret of his affection for his home-town club and came off the bench in Northampton Town's 4-0 defeat in a third round tie in January, 1998. Leicester made a mistake when they let Dixie McNeil leave the club. After his release in 1966, he went on to score 239 goals in the Football League in spells with Exeter City, Northampton, Lincoln City, Hereford United (twice) and Wrexham. Pat Bonner is another player City really should have hung on to. He was between the posts for the Foxes during the 1975-76 FA Youth

Cup campaign and had a career at the highest level with Celtic and Ireland. Northern Ireland international Ian Stewart, formerly with Queens Park Rangers and Newcastle United, also didn't do enough in a couple of Central League games in 1988 to earn a contract with City. Fans of a certain age may remember central defender Grant Brown making 16 appearances during the late 1980s. Up the A46 in Lincoln, he is regarded as one of the Imps' finest-ever players having made a club record 407 appearances.

DOUBLE TROUBLE

At the time of scribbling – December, 2008 – only ten teams have won the Football League championship and FA Cup double. In 1962-63, Leicester City were on course to join a list that features Manchester United (1994, 1996, 1999), Arsenal (1971, 1998, 2002), Liverpool (1986), Tottenham Hotspur (1961), Aston Villa (1897) and Preston North End (1889). City's 4-3 win over Manchester United at Filbert Street on April 16th, 1963, secured by Ken Keyworth's hat-trick, took them back to the top of the Division One table with just five games left in the season and Matt Gillies' team also had an FA Cup semi-final against Liverpool to look forward to 11 days later. Incredibly, the Foxes took just one point from their remaining top-flight fixtures and ended the season fourth after four straight defeats. That was City's highest finish since 1928-29 when they finished runners-up behind Sheffield Wednesday and while their failed title challenge was a crushing disappointment, Mike Stringfellow's goal in the FA Cup semi-final at Hillsborough gave them the chance to lift the trophy for the first time. City were making their third appearance in the showpiece final and were fancied to beat a Manchester United side who had spent most of the season battling against the drop from Division One. Instead, a Leicester team that included new internationals Gordon Banks, Frank McLintock and Davie Gibson flopped. They were beaten 3-1 with Keyworth on target and that meant Leicester finished the season empty-handed having six weeks earlier been on course to lift two trophies.

ANOTHER ELITE GROUP

On the subject of elite groups… until May 4th, 2008, City were one of only ten clubs to have never played outside the top two divisions of English football. All that changed when a goalless draw at Stoke City's Britannia Stadium wasn't enough to keep Ian Holloway's team in the Championship. Gareth McAuley was a whisker away from rescuing City with a second-half header that smacked against the woodwork, but a 3-2 victory for Southampton against Sheffield United on a dramatic afternoon meant the Foxes ended up being relegated alongside Colchester United and Scunthorpe United. Ironically, the manager who masterminded Southampton's survival at the expense of City went on to become Leicester's next boss after Holloway left. Nigel Pearson was handed the task of leading City back into the Championship.

GOD IS A LEICESTER FAN

As with most clubs, Leicester City have the odd celebrity fan... and no supporter of any of them can be more odd than Foxes fan David Icke! Icke, you may remember, went from presenting snooker on the telly to declaring himself to be God's spokesman on Earth. David Neilson, the actor who played Roy Cropper in Coronation Street, was born in Loughborough and supports City, while television chef Rustie Lee was a regular at Filbert Street. Elsewhere in the world of showbiz, Leicester's leading bands have followed the Foxes. Leicester rockers Family were regulars at Filbert Street and on the cover of the band's live album, Roger Chapman is belting out an anthem bedecked in a classic 1970s City shirt.

Other bands have followed in the shirt-wearing tradition including rockers Kasabian with singer Tom Meighan packing his City shirt when he heads off on tour to promote the band's number one albums. The band's guitarist, Serge Pizzorno, had trials at Nottingham Forest as a teenager and remembers wearing his Leicester socks under Forest's. They are regularly spotted at the Walkers Stadium and when they can't make it, Tom is on the phone to his father every few minutes for updates on City.In the early 1990s, indie hopes Blab Happy wore their team's colours on stage and of the latest bunch of Leicester bands, The Screening are City supporters. While, the man inside Filbert Fox is one of their biggest fans! Showaddywaddy produced ten top-ten singles, including a number one, and guitarist Trevor Oakes produced two sons who played for his favourite team. Scott and Stef both played for their home-town club and the latter picked up a League Cup winners' medal in 2000. Boxing champion Rendall Munroe is another City fan. Munroe won the European super-bantamweight boxing title in March, 2008 with a points win over previously unbeaten Spanish puncher Kiko Martinez that propelled him into the top ten of the world rankings. His favourite football team were less successful and two months later, City were relegated to the third tier of English football for the first time. Mark Selby, a finalist in the 2007 world snooker championships, is a City fan and fellow potter Willie Thorne would go to Filbert Street to perform the half-time draw when he wasn't pocketing 147s or down the bookies. Rather disappointingly, David Gower, the former Leicestershire batsman regarded as possibly the most talented English cricketer of his generation, supports Nottingham Forest.

HE BANGS THE DRUMS

Leicester City's biggest supporter is very big indeed. Lee Jobber tips the scales at around 30 stones – hopefully less by the time you read this – and the matchday experience at the Walkers Stadium simply would not be the same without the sight and sound of him stripped to the waist belting a drum. His topless tub thumping has made him a legend among City fans and has led to him being followed by television cameras and splashed all over national newspapers and magazines. Lee, an affable, cheery man from Braunstone, could have been playing for City rather than supporting them. As a schoolboy, he was a promising goalkeeper on the club's books until a shattering injury ended his footballing ambitions when he was just 15 years old. He dived to save a penalty during training and the force of the shot smashed his wrist. Devastated, Lee headed to the pub for a few years and when he wasn't drowning his sorrows, he was cheering on City. Then he started taking his clothes off. It all started on the opening day of the 2002-2003 season and City's Premier League clash with Southampton at the Walkers Stadium. Lee sat in the stands sweltering uncomfortably and after some encouragement from his friends, peeled off his shirt and spent the second half getting a sun tan while watching City chuck away a 2-0 lead. "After the game," he remembered, "my mate said he would buy me a season ticket the following season if I didn't wear my shirt again for the rest of that campaign, so I agreed. "He never did buy me that season ticket, but at the first game of the next season, I sat down and about ten people said: 'Come on, get your shirt off.' So I took it off and it's been off ever since." Then came the drum. During the 2006-2007 season, the club approached Lee and asked him to add to the atmosphere at home games by standing at the back of the Alliance & Leicester stand with his shirt off beating a large drum. Lee agreed and after sinking a few drinks for some courage, made his drumming debut – next to a bunch of Millwall fans! "Three bangs and you're out of breath," they chanted. Lee had a giggle, got through it and has been drumming ever since. Jobber has gone on to appear on Football's Hardest Away Days on Sky One and applied for the manager's job at City during the wretched 2007-2008 season.

FORGOTTEN HERO

And the winner is… well, everyone already knew. Gary Lineker's 24 goals had helped Leicester City secure 15th place in the top flight in 1984-85, earned an England call-up and made him a transfer target for the country's biggest clubs. So he would surely end the season by being named the Leicester City Supporters' Club's Player of the Year? But that trophy is missing from a collection that includes 80 England caps, the Golden Boot from the 1986 World Cup and a winner's medal from the European Cup Winners' Cup earned when he was with Barcelona. Instead, City's fans handed the Player of the Year award to a player forgotten by many supporters. Andy Feeley, a robust, uncompromising defender and midfielder, walked off with the trophy. Fans were possibly too scared to vote against him because if they had handed out an award for Player Whose Pint You Really Don't Want to Spill, Feeley would have won that as well. Put simply, Feeley was hard. Built like the proverbial outhouse and wearing a plaster cast on his right arm to hide tattoos he was less than fond of, he wasn't exactly afraid of confrontation and his jobs after leaving football included a spell as a prison officer in a unit for the criminally insane. Feeley first came to prominence on August 18th, 1979 when he entered the record books as the youngest captain in Football League history by leading out home-town club Hereford United against York City – aged just 17. But a fiery temperament and injuries meant there were fears his early promise would be unfulfilled. Feeley ended up drifting into non-league football with Trowbridge – where his manager was Alan Birchenall! 'The Birch', a popular member of City's 1970s side, recommended Feeley to Gordon Milne and he was impressed enough to hand Andy his debut at Old Trafford in front of 39,473 fans in March, 1984. The following season, Feeley made 41 appearances in all competitions to pip the soon-to-be-departing Lineker for the Player of the Year award and added 26 more in 1985-86 as City escaped the drop with victory over Newcastle United on the final day of the season. City would have stood a better chance of securing a fifth successive season in the top flight had Feeley not been ruled out for the last two months of the 1986-87 campaign with a knee injury. He left in the summer after rejecting a new deal and ended his career with Brentford and Bury.

THE ENTERTAINER

He loved Elvis Presley and for five glorious years, Frank Worthington was the king of Filbert Street. Worthington left fans breathless with his skills on the pitch, broke hearts off the pitch and was undeniably the biggest personality of a Leicester City team packed with them. He scored 78 goals in his 239 appearances for City and earned eight England caps – scoring twice – while starring for a flamboyant team put together by Jimmy Bloomfield. Worthington only ended up at Filbert Street because of a failed medical! He was set to sign for Liverpool until that misfortune ended their interest and Bloomfield stepped in to sign him from Huddersfield Town in August, 1972 for a £100,000 fee that would prove to be a bargain. 'Wortho' made a goalscoring debut for the Foxes at Old Trafford as George Best grabbed Manchester United's goal in a 1-1 draw. With the talents of Keith Weller and Len Glover helping carve out openings for him, Worthington ended his first season at City with ten goals and added 20 more in 1973-74 as Leicester finished ninth in the top flight and reached the semi-finals of the FA Cup. At the end of the season, he was called up for England and grabbed his first goal for his country in his third appearance, a 2-2 draw with Argentina at Wembley. Worthington only made eight appearances for his country, but the goals kept coming for the Foxes and it was a surprise to most supporters when boss Frank McLintock decided to sell their hero to Bolton Wanderers in September, 1977. His final appearance for Leicester came in a 3-0 defeat at home to Nottingham Forest and he went on to become the top flight's leading scorer in the 1978-79 season with a 24-goal haul for the Trotters. Worthington was soon on the move again and after making his debut for Birmingham City against Leicester, he made a goal-scoring farewell to Filbert Street in November, 1983. Frank, still good enough to play in the top flight around a decade after his pomp with Leicester, lined up against City for Southampton and found the target in a 2-1 defeat in front of a crowd of 14,181. He was warmly received by City fans and his admirers at the ground that night included Gary Lineker, who grabbed Leicester's winner after Alan Smith had opened the scoring. Worthington returned to Leicestershire as player manager of Hinckley Town in 1990 which attracted a few misty-eyed City fans through the turnstiles.

QUE SERA, SERA

Back then, nobody with any brains wanted to go to Cambridge. It was an intimidating place and you were likely to leave there bruised, battered and empty-handed. At the Abbey Stadium in the university city, all the punting was directed by Cambridge United boss John Beck, who set about masterminding a revolution with a bit of help from a player born and raised in Leicester. Dion Dublin's talents escaped the attention of City's scouts – despite growing up just around the corner from Filbert Street – and after a spell at Norwich City, he launched his career at Cambridge. They were in the basement division when he went there and Beck's bruising, unconventional tactics took them to back-to-back promotions and the quarter-finals of the FA Cup in successive seasons. Leicester were also enjoying something of an upturn in fortunes at the start of the 1991-92 season and in September, a 3-0 win over Blackburn Rovers at Filbert Street took them up to third in the Division One table and meant they travelled to Cambridge for a Sunday afternoon fixture flushed with a confidence that was then comprehensively battered out of them. City were on the receiving end of a 5-1 thumping at the Abbey Stadium with Colin Gordon grabbing the consolation. Dublin and future City legend Steve Claridge got two goals apiece for the home side. Leicester went on to avenge the loss with a 2-1 victory at Filbert Street the following April that was secured by goals from Tommy Wright and Phil Gee and kept the Foxes second in the table with two games remaining in the season. Defeats against Charlton Athletic and Newcastle United meant City had to settle for the play-offs rather than automatic promotion and a two-legged semi-final against Cambridge. They returned from the Abbey Stadium with a 1-1 draw after the first leg which set up an unforgettable night at Filbert Street with City aiming to reach Wembley for the first time since the 1969 FA Cup Final defeat against Manchester City. Tommy Wright opened the scoring late in the first half when he got to a near-post corner and stabbed the ball into the roof of the net. Cambridge fell apart after the break. Wright added another and further strikes from Steve Thompson, Kevin Russell and Ian Ormondroyd secured a stunning 5-0 win that sent the majority of the 21,054 crowd wild with delight, and the Foxes back to Wembley – to face Blackburn Rovers – after an absence of 23 years.

REDS SING THE BLUES

Liverpool have lifted more trophies than any other English club. They also have a bogey team – and it's Leicester City. For more than four decades, City have made a habit of chucking a spanner in the works for the Merseyside giants and perhaps the most remarkable of all Leicester's performances against Liverpool came in the 1980-81 season. Jock Wallace's team, promoted to the top flight as Second Division champions, had started the season with back-to-back defeats and then stunned the Reds at Filbert Street through Andy Peake's long-range shot and a strike from Martin Henderson. City went on to complete an astonishing double in January, 1981 by ending Liverpool's 85-match unbeaten run at Anfield. Leicester had lost their previous five games, but ripped up the formbook with Jim Melrose bagging both goals in a 2-1 win. Liverpool's goal came through an Alan Young own goal. City were still relegated at the end of the season. Leicester also completed a league double over the Reds in the 1962-63 season when City were chasing both the Division One championship and FA Cup and they handed Liverpool a double dose of league misery again in the 1964-65 campaign.

REDS DRAWING

City produced a pair of determined performances against Liverpool in 1983-84. Mark Wallington saved a penalty from Graeme Souness to secure a 2-2 draw at Anfield and the sides fought out a thrilling 3-3 draw at Filbert Street later in the season. The following season, Alan Smith and Gary Lineker got the goals for Gordon Milne's team in a 2-1 win at Liverpool.

THREE ON THE BOUNCE

Under Martin O'Neill, City won at Anfield for three successive seasons. They were 2-1 winners in the second game of the 1997-98 season through goals from Matt Elliott and Graham Fenton and the following season, former Everton striker Ian Marshall was City's last-gasp match winner on Merseyside. City followed that in May, 2000 with a 2-0 win at Anfield thanks to strikes from Tony Cottee and Phil Gilchrist. Leicester's winning run at Anfield came to an end the following season with a 1-0 defeat – the goal scorer was former City striker Emile Heskey.

IN THE BIG TIME

All around the streets of Leicester, people were united in joy. Men, women and children sang, danced and embraced. No, I'm not describing the scenes on the day this publication hit the city's bookshops. It was the sight that greeted Leicester Fosse's players, though, when they stepped out of the city's train station on London Road on Monday April 27th, 1908 having earlier that day secured a 1-0 win at Stoke City that took them into the top flight of English football for the first time in the club's 24-year history. The players spent hours trying to weave their way home through the rejoicing throng of fans that had gathered on London Road and Granby Street, so if you thought the traffic around there these days is bad, think again. Fosse had gone into the season confident they could secure a top-two finish and a place among the elite. The club announced record season-ticket sales that brought in £1,167 and ground improvements increased the capacity at Filbert Street to 22,000. The club also signed new players including forwards Jimmy Donnelly and Percy Humphreys and set about climbing out of Division Two. They were beaten only once in the opening 11 games and after Humphreys was allowed to move to Chelsea for a fee of £350, the arrival of Fred Shinton in a deal from West Bromwich Albion helped kick-start the promotion challenge. Fosse were eighth in the table going into the home date with Blackpool on February 15th, 1908 and Humphreys got both goals in a 2-1 win that started a club-record run of seven straight victories. The winning run included a 5-1 thrashing of Bradford City – who would go on to be crowned champions – and came to an abrupt end with a 5-1 defeat at Fulham on April 4th. The battle for the second promotion place went down to the final day of the season. Bradford had already secured the championship and Fosse were level on points with promotion rivals Oldham Athletic, but had a better goal average than the Latics. That victory at Stoke would guarantee promotion for Fosse and they claimed maximum points through a Tommy Shanks strike. He netted from close range after Shinton's shot had been blocked by the Stoke custodian. Fosse keeper Horace Bailey, who had recently been capped by England, was in sparkling form at the other end of the pitch to ensure Leicester held on to their advantage and ended the club's wait for top-flight football.

MATT FINISH

It's what the old place would have wanted. In May, 2002, Matt Piper, born in Leicester and a life-long Foxes fan, netted the last goal at the Filbert Street ground where he was once a ball boy. His diving header secured a 2-1 win over Tottenham Hotspur and ensured there wasn't a dry eye in the house at the final whistle. Sadly, whoever was writing Piper's scripts ran out of ink after that. He was sold to Sunderland for £3.5 million to help ease City's financial problems and then had to retire in the summer of 2007 after undergoing an incredible 16 operations on his knees and ankles. Peter Shilton and Gary Lineker also made their boyhood dreams come true by playing for City. In May, 1963, Shilton stood behind the goal at Wembley watching Leicester lose the FA Cup Final to Manchester United and six years later, he was between the posts for the showpiece game as Manchester City lifted the trophy and sent Gary Lineker sobbing all the way home. Graham Cross was another who grew up supporting City and went on to play for them many times. As a seven-year-old, he would sit on the wall in front of the Popular Side terrace and cheer on the likes of Arthur

Rowley and a decade later he made his debut for his home-town club. Cross went on to play in two FA Cup Finals, two League Cup Finals and set a club record of 599 appearances that probably would have been more if he hadn't been so good at cricket! His decision to help Leicestershire win their first County Championship in 1975 rather than report back for pre-season training wasn't well received at Filbert Street and spelled the beginning of the end for him at City. Andy Peake grew up in Market Harborough supporting City and went on to make more than 150 appearances for his team. He is remembered for a spectacular goal against Division One champions Liverpool at Filbert Street in August, 1980. Richard Smith's claim to fame is that he grabbed the goal that handed City their first win in the FA Cup for seven years. Smith, a regular in the Spion Kop as a teenager, netted the last-minute winner against Crystal Palace in the third round in January, 1991. Another regular in Brian Little's first season at Filbert Street was a life-long City fan. Nicky Platnauer made no secret of his boyhood devotion to City when he joined the club.

SOCCER'S NICEST STRIKERS

Alan Smith was leaving Leicester City – and he was staying at Leicester City. His goals for City during four successive seasons in the top flight meant it was no surprise when it was announced in March, 1987 that Smith would be joining former strike partner Gary Lineker on the way out of Filbert Street after agreeing an £800,000 switch to Arsenal. The deal allowed Smith to stay at City for the rest of the season as Bryan Hamilton's team battled against relegation and that arrangement put him in a strange position when his two teams came face to face at Highbury the following month. Smith lined up for City in the 4-1 defeat and was cheered by both sets of supporters! There were only Leicester tears at the end of the season, however. A goalless draw at Oxford United couldn't keep them up and at the final whistle, Smith peeled his shirt off and threw it into the hordes of Leicester fans behind the goal. Smith had arrived from non-league Alvechurch in the summer of 1982 and for three seasons, Smith and Lineker formed arguably the most feared strikeforce in the country and definitely the nicest! Lineker was never booked or sent off throughout his career, while Smith picked up just one booking in his 217 games for City and when the referee reached for his notebook, he apparently sighed: "There goes my disciplinary record." Smith had much more to be proud of. A tall, elegant striker willing to chase and harry, he bagged 13 goals in his first season as Gordon Milne's team pipped Fulham for the third promotion spot and that haul included a belter in the 5-0 demolition of Wolverhampton Wanderers that City's excitable programme editor described as "one of the best goals seen at Filbert Street for many years". The following season, Smith, Lineker and Lynex bagged 49 top-flight goals between them and after Lineker's departure at the end of 1984-85 it was left to Smith to spearhead City's attack for two seasons. He left City after scoring 84 goals in all competitions and enjoyed much more success at Highbury. Smith scored one goal and set up the other as the Gunners snatched the Division One title in the dying seconds of the 1988-89 season, briefly played alongside Lineker for England and volleyed home the winner in the 1994 European Cup Winners' Cup Final against Parma. He retired through injury at the age of just 32 and went on to work in the media.

LET'S HAVE A COFFEE

There are two books – and now a page in this one – dedicated to the wit and wisdom of a former Leicester City manager – and it's not Gordon Milne. Ian Holloway, appointed City's third manager of the season in November, 2007, would keep reporters waiting until past their deadline before coming into the press room and reeling off priceless soundbytes to leave hardened hacks sniggering. He did just that after only his third game in charge at City – a 2-1 defeat at home to Southampton in December, 2007 that kept Leicester in trouble near the bottom of the Championship. Holloway was unhappy that a section of Leicester fans had targeted striker Carl Cort for stick and said: "To the people who booed – boo to you!" His decision to quit Plymouth Argyle to take the job at Leicester incensed Pilgrims fans and they vented their anger during their side's 1-0 win at the Walkers Stadium in February, 2008. Holloway shrugged: "Apparently, it's my fault that the Titanic sank." Later in the season, he called Sheffield United striker Billy Sharp a "little turkey" after he won the penalty that sent City on their way to a 3-0 defeat at Bramall Lane. Sadly, the quote that stays in the memory from Holloway's six months at the Walkers Stadium was made as the season headed towards its climax. "I don't want to be the only manager to have taken Leicester to the division below the Championship," he said. Unfortunately, that is on his CV. Holloway can hardly take full responsibility for City's relegation, but he was in charge when they dropped out of the top two divisions of English football for the first time following the goalless draw at Stoke City.

OLLY'S FAMOUS WORDS

Holloway's most famous quote came after he had steered Queens Park Rangers to an "ugly" win at Chesterfield. He said: "To put it in gentleman's terms, if you've been out for a night and you're looking for a young lady and you pull one, some weeks they're good looking and some weeks they're not the best. Our performance today would have been not the best looking bird, but at least we got her in the taxi. She weren't the best looking lady we ended up taking home, but she was very pleasant and very nice, so thanks very much, let's have a coffee."

IT'S A FUNNY OLD GAME

In September, 1933, Burnley-based referee H. E. Hull was set to take charge of the top-flight match between Leicester and Chelsea at Filbert Street. He found the dressing room, changed into his kit, walked out onto the pitch and then noticed something unusual. There were too many players and the ball was the wrong shape. Hull had turned up at Welford Road by mistake! Realising he was at a rugby union fixture rather than a football match, Hull headed to Filbert Street where City and Chelsea drew 1-1. The point gained took Leicester up to third in Division One.

OOOPS!

Leicester Fosse reserves travelled to their Sheffield Wednesday counterparts for a Midland League fixture in 1908-09 and ended up doing it all over again after a refereeing blunder led to the game being replayed in its entirety. The referee awarded Fosse a penalty in the dying moments of the game – and then blew the final whistle before they had the chance to take it! That led to complaints from Fosse and the game being played again.

REF NEEDS GLASSES

A piece of refereeing incompetence denied Arthur Chandler a goal against Middlesbrough at Filbert Street in September, 1924. The officials didn't spot that Channy's shot had hit the stanchion in the goal before the ball bounced back into play and no goal was awarded. Not that it mattered much. Although the game finished goalless, City went on to win the Division Two title and Chandler ended up with 32 league goals. He netted 273 times in his City career to be the club's record goalscorer.

KNOCKOUT BLOW

A linesman was in the firing line when Leicester met Wolves at Filbert Street in April, 1934. A stray clearance knocked him unconscious during a match also remembered for a double sending off. Arthur Lochhead and Wolves defender Crook were both given their marching orders in a game that finished 1-1. Perhaps there was some ill feeling between the pair following the sides' meeting at Molineux the previous day! Both games ended in 1-1 draws with Arthur Maw grabbing the Foxes goal in both fixtures.

STICKS

It was November 23rd, 1994 and Leicester City needed a hero. Step forward – and try not to fall over – Ian Ormondroyd. These were desperate times. City were in disarray. They were rooted to the foot of the Premiership after four straight defeats and the previous day, manager Brian Little had announced his resignation while having one eye on the job at Aston Villa. On the morning of the game, John Gregory decided he was off as well and that left Allan Evans in charge for the visit of Arsenal to Filbert Street. Incredibly, City ran out 2-1 winners against the Gunners in front of 20,774 supporters, and Ormondroyd was the hero. At least for a few weeks. The joyless souls at the Premiership Panel decided that the game's decisive strike was a David Seaman own goal and Ormondroyd was denied what would have been the only Premiership goal of his career. The striker only found the target 12 times in 96 City appearances – celebrating each one with the unco-ordinated joy of a schoolboy on the last day of term before the summer holidays – and there were some crucial efforts among them. He was on target in the second leg of the play-off semi-final at Portsmouth in May, 1993 to help send City through to Wembley and the following season he was the last-gasp hero in a dramatic 4-4 draw against Watford at Filbert Street. Ormondroyd also had a hand in the goal that took City into the Premier League in May, 1994. His header in the closing minutes of the Division One play-off final at Wembley was saved by Derby keeper Martin Taylor and Steve Walsh was there to tap home the rebound and send City back into the top tier. The lanky striker had joined City from the Rams along with strike partner Phil Gee in March, 1992 in a deal which sent Paul Kitson in the opposite direction. The gangly hitman with the physique of a dieting pipe cleaner was soon suffering frustration in front of goal. In his second game for Leicester, Ormondroyd had two first-half goals ruled out at promotion rivals Ipswich Town and then fell over his own feet later in the match when he looked to lead a City counter attack! He was later used as a left winger – despite standing a towering 6ft 4ins. tall – and earned cult status among Leicester fans before rejoining home-town club Bradford City in the summer of 1995 following City's relegation from the Premiership.

JAMIE VARDY IS HAVING A PARTY

No wonder Hollywood is interested in the Jamie Vardy story... There's the years of struggle, the booze – and the goals. Eleven of them in 11 successive Premier League games in the 2015-16 season, a record for what's regarded as the best league in Europe. Vardy joined Leicester from Fleetwood Town for £1 million in 2012 and to start with, he didn't know how to cope. So he drank. Aiyawatt Srivaddhanaprabha, son of the club's owner and a vice-chairman of City, gave Vardy a talking to after sniffing alcohol on his breath at training and towards the end of the 2014-15 season, he gave some idea of what he could do. Vardy was quick like a whippet who'd taken a caffeine overdose – he had been a good runner over all distances since his school days – and knew where and when to run. He scored crucial goals at West Brom and Burnley to help keep City in the Premier League and, his energy levels boosted by three cans of Red Bull before the match, he found the target on the opening day of the following season, the one Leicester started as 5,000-1 outsiders for the Premier title. Vardy kept drinking Red Bull before games – and kept scoring. Ten goals in ten consecutive Premier League matches – starting with a penalty at Bournemouth on Saturday, August 29 – equalled the record set by Dutch marksman Ruud van Nistelrooy when he was playing for Manchester United more than a decade earlier. Vardy got his chance to beat that against Manchester United of all teams at the King Power Stadium on Saturday, November 28. Van Nistelrooy sent a Tweet to Vardy wishing him luck and after 24 minutes, he got his chance. Christian Fuchs slid a pass forward behind the centre backs for Vardy to chase. He got there first and steered his shot where goalkeeper David De Gea couldn't reach it, just inside his far post. The ball nudged the woodwork on its way into the net – and Vardy raced away to celebrate with the United fans who had been chanting van Nistelrooy's name at him all afternoon. "Me!" shouted Vardy in response. "Me! All me!" The goal made Vardy, playing for Fleetwood Town in front of 700 fans in the Conference four years earlier, the most talked-about striker in the world. Arsenal wanted him at the end of the season, but unlike Gary Lineker, Alan Smith and Emile Heskey before him, Vardy decided to stay at Leicester.

BLONDES HAVE MORE FUN

Tottenham Hotspur won the Worthington Cup, Leicester City suffered last-gasp heartbreak, but all the headlines were about Robbie Savage. Just the way he likes it then? Martin O'Neill took his City side back to Wembley for the third time in four seasons in March, 1999 to face Spurs and they faced them without Frank Sinclair. He was dropped on the eve of the game for a breach of club discipline and that controversy was nothing compared to what followed when the game got under way. City probably created the better chances in the first half and then came the game's flashpoint. In the 63rd minute, Savage, City's chief mischief maker and pantomime villain, took a tumble after a collision with Spurs defender Justin Edinburgh. Referee Terry Heilbron gave Edinburgh his marching orders and Spurs' players, clearly incensed by what they believed to be play-acting on Savage's part, set about exacting retribution. As tempers reached boiling point, Savage was the victim of several crunching tackles and while he survived, City didn't. The game was in its final minute and heading for extra time when Steffen Iversen pulled the ball back from the right-hand byeline, City keeper Kasey Keller got a hand to it, but Allan Nielsen was perfectly placed to head home the winner. The late drama was hard on City defender Rob Ullathorne. As he had done two years earlier in the final against Middlesbrough, O'Neill had handed one of his players a man-marking job and Ullathorne's shackling of David Ginola would have surely earned him the man-of-the-match award had it not been for Nielsen's late match winner. Not that anybody seemed to notice Ullathorne or even that Spurs had lifted the cup. The national press were more concerned in condemning Savage following Edinburgh's sending off. Savage, more determined than most blondes to prove that they do indeed have more fun, stunned nobody in particular when he later admitted that Edinburgh hadn't made contact in the incident that led to his dismissal. If nothing else, his honesty about his dishonesty was refreshing. City's defeat at Wembley was hard on Tony

Cottee. He had netted five times in previous rounds – including strikes in both legs of the semi-final win over Sunderland – and the loss meant he had to wait to claim his first winner's medal. A couple of weeks after the loss to Spurs, Cottee was on target in a 2-0 win for City at White Hart Lane to register his 200th goal in the Football League.

FOREIGN LEGION

The Leicester City side that took on Arsenal at Highbury in a Premier League fixture in February, 1999 was the most cosmopolitan in the club's history. Martin O'Neill's starting line-up included representatives of nine different nations. They were: Kasey Keller (USA), Pontus Kamark (Sweden), Frank Sinclair (Jamaica), Matt Elliott (Scotland), Robbie Savage (Wales), Theo Zagorakis (Greece), Neil Lennon (Northern Ireland), Arnar Gunnlaugsson (Iceland) and Muzzy Izzet, who went on to play for Turkey. Robert Ullathorne and Steve Guppy were the only Englishmen in the starting line-up and French goalkeeper Pegguy Arphexad was on the bench for City. Their combined efforts weren't enough to stop Arsenal winning 5-0 with French striker Nicolas Anelka firing in a hat-trick for the Gunners. City enjoyed better fortunes when they relied on home-grown talent in the Division Two fixture against Watford at Filbert Street in October, 1969. Ten of the 12 players on duty had come through the club's youth and reserve team systems. They were: Peter Shilton, David Nish, John Sjoberg, Graham Cross, Rodney Fern, Malcolm Manley, Alan Woollett, Ally Brown, Paul Matthews and Murray Brodie. Brodie, making his first-team debut just eight days after his 19th birthday, bagged City's third goal in the 3-1 win after earlier strikes from Len Glover and David Nish. Four days later, Brodie was on target again in a 2-1 win over Middlesbrough, but was then injured in his third appearance for City at Preston North End and never played for the club again. He could not regain his place in the side after recovering from injury, joined Aldershot and went on to make a club-record 514 appearances for them. Leicester Fosse had eight Scottish players in the starting line-up for their first home league game against Rotherham Town on September 8, 1894. David Seka, born in Arbroath, was the hat-trick hero for Fosse in a 4-2 win. Seven days earlier, he had become Fosse's first goalscorer in the league in a 4-3 defeat at Grimsby Town. He ended the campaign with 23 goals from 30 games and that remained a season's best haul by a Fosse player for 15 years. Fred Shinton broke the record in 1909-10 when he bagged 32 goals.

GONE IN SIXTY SECONDS

Leicester City supporters celebrated, danced and then their hearts sank – all in the space of 60 breathless seconds. City thought they had drawn level against Wolverhampton Wanderers in their first appearance in the FA Cup

Final in April, 1949 and a few seconds later, their challenge for the trophy was effectively over. They weren't given much chance going into the game. Leicester were scrapping for survival at the bottom of Division Two and were underdogs against their top-flight opponents. In the first half, they lived down to that billing as Jesse Pye's goal double put Wolves on course to lift the trophy. That was no surprise after City's preparations had been wrecked in the weeks before the game. Don Revie, a key figure in getting Leicester to Wembley, had been ruled out after a nose injury that led to a near fatal loss of blood and the makeshift line-up included full-back Jimmy Harrison playing at centre-forward and Jack Lee taking on the unfamiliar inside-forward role. Unsurprisingly, they were on the receiving end in the first half and then two minutes after the re-start, City were back in the game after boss John Duncan made changes to his forward line during the interval. Wolves goalkeeper Bert Williams couldn't hold on to Ken Chisholm's powerful drive and Mal Griffiths turned the loose ball home to hand City a lifeline. The outcome of the game was then settled in the space of a few seconds. Leicester thought they were level in the 64th minute when Chisholm steered the ball into the net from the tightest of angles after good work from Griffiths. But the effort was ruled out for a marginal offside spotted by the linesman and with City still shell-shocked, Wolves went up the other end of the pitch and Sammy Smyth's stunning solo goal put the game beyond the Foxes. City had good reason for optimism going into their first game at Wembley having caused a sensation in the semi-finals. The draw pitted Leicester, who were 20th in Division Two at the time, with Division One leaders and eventual champions Portsmouth. City, making only their second appearance at the semi-final stage, were 3-1 winners with Revie the architect of a famous victory. He netted twice and Chisholm got the other goal as City ripped up the formbook to silence the Pompey chimes. There was a happy ending to the season for City and their supporters as they preserved their Division Two status on the final day.

CAN YOU SEE US ON THE BOX?

Leicester City's first appearance in a Football League game broadcast live on terrestrial television had a starring role from 'The Hot Dog Kid'. City goalkeeper Carl Muggleton suffered a slipped disc in the warm up before the clash with Wolverhampton Wanderers in September, 1992 and that meant 19-year-old Russell Hoult had to quickly polish off his pre-match meal and take his place between the posts for his Foxes debut. Hoult, raised in Whitwick, showed why he had been named City's Young Player of the Year in 1991 with a man-of-the-match display in a goalless draw. Hoult went on to concede only one goal in his opening five league appearances for City – and then shipped seven in a League Cup hammering at Sheffield Wednesday. City made their television debut in the FA Cup Final in 1949 – but not many fans tuned in to watch the 3-1 defeat against Wolverhampton Wanderers. Apparently, there were only 35 television sets in Leicester and the surrounding district capable of receiving the live broadcast. Six years later came the first broadcast of highlights from a City game at Filbert Street. The BBC programme Sportsview screened the best bits of Leicester's Division Two clash with Swansea City – and there were plenty of them in a 6-1 win for the Foxes. Willie Gardiner was City's hat-trick hero and the other goals came from Mal Griffiths, Johnny Morris and Arthur Rowley. The *Match of the Day* cameras came to Filbert Street for the first time in October, 1964 to capture all the drama as City edged out Nottingham Forest 3-2. Mike Stringfellow was Leicester's match-winner with a header five minutes from the end, but goalkeeper Gordon Banks was the hero. He received a boot in the face from Colin Appleton in the first half and commentator Kenneth Wolstenholme of "some people are on the pitch" fame later described City fans as "rather justifiably booing Addison". Billy Hodgson put City ahead and less than a minute after Forest levelled, Colin Appleton restored the advantage after Bobby Svarc had been upended. Forest equalised again before Stringfellow had the final word.

STAYING UP

Think of *The Great Escape* and you probably think of Steve McQueen, secret tunnels and motor bikes. Unless you're from Leicester, that is. In that case, you probably think of Saturday May 11th, 1991 and a match between Leicester City and Oxford United at Filbert Street that the Foxes had to win to avoid the drop into the third tier of English football for the first time in their history. It had been a wretched season for City. An opening-day win over Bristol Rovers at Filbert Street was followed by seven straight defeats – including a 6-0 humbling at Middlesbrough – and with the team in desperate relegation trouble and crowd figures dwindling below 10,000, manager David Pleat was sacked at the end of January. Gordon Lee was appointed caretaker boss and although there were signs of improvement, City showed all the survival instincts of a suicidal lemming as the relegation battle entered the closing weeks. They threw away a lead at relegation rivals West Bromwich Albion, losing 2-1, and back-to-back defeats against Swindon Town and Ipswich Town meant the Foxes' fate would be determined on the final day of the season. City took on Oxford United knowing they had to better West Bromwich Albion's result at Bristol Rovers to stay in Division Two and the early news from Twerton Park was not encouraging. Rovers had a player sent off in the 24th minute to settle City's nerves. A corner fell to Tony James and he scooped the ball into the roof of the net from close range to give Leicester a priceless lead. City continued to dominate and the Baggies could only draw 1-1 at Bristol Rovers to ensure Leicester stayed up at their expense. Along with Bristol Rovers' ten men, James was the hero, but City were saved as much by the Football League's ruling at the start of the season that only two teams would be relegated from Division Two rather than three. Had three teams gone down, City would have suffered the drop. Forty-two years earlier, Jack

Lee had been City's hero when City had a similar escape. In May, 1949 – just seven days after losing the FA Cup Final against Wolverhampton Wanderers at Wembley – they needed a point at Cardiff City to survive and Lee popped up with the crucial equaliser at Ninian Park.

THE SWEET FA CUP

Leicester City reached the semi-finals of the FA Cup for the first time in their history in 1934. Then it all went wrong. City's clash with Portsmouth at St. Andrew's on March 17th, 1934 attracted a then-record attendance of 66,544 to Birmingham City's ground and the Foxes had happy memories of the venue. In the fifth round of the competition, they had been 2-1 winners at Birmingham with Arthur Chandler grabbing both goals. Chandler had then been City's marksman in the 1-0 win at Preston North End in the quarter-finals that took the Foxes through to the last four for the first time. Their debut at the semi-final stage was ruined by misfortune. City fell behind early on while distracted by fans spilling onto the touchline after fencing collapsed behind the goal and worse followed with defender Sandy Wood being left dazed and with a broken nose following a collision with a photographer. Andy Lochhead did score for City in the first half, but it was Pompey striker John Weddle who grabbed the headlines. He had been in the Portsmouth line-up that was on the receiving end of a 10-0 thrashing at Filbert Street in October, 1928 and gained some revenge for that humiliation with a hat-trick in the 4-1 win that ended City's Wembley hopes.

48 YEARS LATER...

Leicester City didn't exactly have the best of luck in the 1982 FA Cup semi-final either. The good news was they were playing just up the road at Villa Park, so it was a bit like a home fixture; the bad news was they had to face favourites Tottenham Hotspur. Jock Wallace's team had beaten top-flight opposition on the way to the last four – Alan Young's double powered them to a 3-1 win over Southampton in the third round – but Spurs were the cup holders and could call upon the talents of Ossie Ardiles and Glenn Hoddle. They really didn't need any help from Lady Luck. City fell behind to Garth Crooks' first-half strike and then Leicester were hit by a double blow. Tommy Williams was carried off with a broken leg and Ian Wilson scored a spectacular own goal to put the game beyond the Foxes. His attempted back pass to Mark Wallington looped over his head and dropped into the net to complete a miserable afternoon for City.

MOVING HOME

Filbert Street was the home of Leicester's leading senior football team from November 7, 1891 until May 11, 2002. The club's first competitive match against Syston Fosse in November, 1884 was played at a private field off Fosse

Road and the remaining fixtures in that debut season were staged at Victoria Park. Back then, Victoria Park was often known as The Racecourse and many fans opted to watch rugby union matches on the adjoining pitches rather than follow the fortunes of the city's fledgling football team. Fosse switched to a private ground for the start of the 1887-88 season. The Belgrave Road Sports Ground was hired, but didn't have any changing facilities and the teams got ready for matches at the White Hart Hotel that was almost a mile away from the ground. Fosse only stayed there for one season, however. They were outbid for the use of the facilities by the rugby union club and were on their way back to Victoria Park for the 1888-89 campaign. The following season, Fosse rented an enclosed canal-side pitch on Mill Lane that was owned by the Town Council. They were there for two seasons and then the Leicester Corporation decided they needed it for building purposes, so Fosse ended up renting the Aylestone Road cricket ground. Fosse only played eight games there and then moved to the ground that would be their home for almost 111 years. Legend has it that on the suggestion of a niece of senior Fosse committee man Joseph Johnson, open land between Aylestone Road and Walnut Street had been earmarked and 3.75 acres were secured on lease from the Corporation to secure the club's new home. Johnson, who had four sons play for Fosse, guaranteed the rent and work began on laying a pitch and enclosure, bounded at one end by Filbert Street. The venue was known as the Walnut Street ground and the first match there was a 3-2 win for Fosse reserves against Melton Swifts on October 17, 1891 with Billy Davis the first Leicester scorer at the ground.The club's last game there was the 2-1 win over Tottenham Hotspur in the Premier League and City then moved over the road to the Walkers Stadium. A friendly against Athletic Bilbao marked the stadium's opening on August 4, 2002 with Jordan Stewart on target for Leicester and six days later, Brian Deane was the Foxes' two-goal hero in the 2-0 win over Watford in the first competitive fixture at the ground.

BRUNO

A decade after Gary Lineker left The City of Leicester School, another future England international walked through the school gates. As a teenager, Ian Thompson was a match-winner for England Schools at Filbert Street, joined Leicester City and even appeared on a team photograph. Sadly, the powerfully-built striker's promise was unfulfilled. Thompson, a talented cricketer like Lineker, was hit by injuries and after his release by City without making a first-team appearance, he ended up playing in local football – including a spell at Shepshed Dynamo. Emile Heskey was also still a pupil at the Evington School when he made his international breakthrough by winning caps for England under-16s and he was just two months past his 17th birthday when handed his City debut in the 2-0 Premier League defeat at Queens Park Rangers in March, 1995.His first goal came the following season. Heskey stepped off the bench to get the winner against Norwich City and keep Mark

McGhee's side on top of the table. Heskey went on to secure Martin O'Neill's first win as City manager in the 3-2 success at Wolverhampton Wanderers. He was on target twice in the win against the club McGhee joined after quitting City. Heskey made an instant impact in the Premier League on City's return to the top flight. He netted both goals in a 2-1 win over Southampton in the first home game of the campaign – including a rampaging run and shot that was an early contender for Goal of the Season. 'Bruno' ended the season with a Coca-Cola Cup winner's medal. His late equaliser forced a replay in the final with Middlesbrough and Steve Claridge grabbed the only goal at Hillsborough. Heskey added another League Cup winner's medal in 2000 and the final victory over Tranmere Rovers came just a few days after he had marked his first full appearance for England with a man-of-the-match performance in a goalless draw against Argentina at Wembley. A few days after the win over Tranmere – and a starring role alongside hat-trick hero Stan Collymore in a 5-2 demolition of Sunderland at Filbert Street – Heskey was off to Liverpool in an £11 million deal that was the third biggest signing by a British club at the time. Emile ended his first full season at Anfield with a 22-goal haul as the Reds won the FA, League and UEFA Cups and was one of England's heroes in the 5-1 win against Germany in Munich in September, 2001. He scored the last goal in the romp.

RAISING A SMILE

The 1980s was a dark decade for English football. The disasters at Heysel and Hillsborough made it ugly times for the beautiful game, so up popped fanzines to put a smile back on the face of football. These unofficial publications gave fans the chance to voice opinions that the club programme and local paper would have been unlikely to print. The title For Fox Sake gives you some idea of the mood of Leicester supporters when the first issue appeared during the 1990-91 battle against the drop into the third tier of English football. The Fox also came out around the same time. An early issue of The Fox had Leicester boss David Pleat on its cover with his head in his hands in the dug out with the caption: "Calling International Rescue". The mix of well-written nostalgia, humour and cartoons has made The Fox a good seller among supporters and when City enjoyed their early 1990s revival under Brian Little, the publication's replica shirts from the 1960s and 1970s were often spotted on the terraces. The Fox remains the only City fanzine, but there have been a few others.

WHERE'S THE MONEY GONE?

…came out during another troubled time for City – and the title was even chanted at Filbert Street as Leicester crashed out of the Premier League in 1994-95. The supporters who put together WTMG wanted to know why a club that had brought in funds by the sale of star players including Gary Lineker and Alan Smith could not sustain a top-flight football team or keep their manager following the departures of Brian Little and Mark McGhee in the space of 12 turbulent months. The pages of the fanzine bristled with humour and resentment and it picked up several awards from football magazines. WTMG disappeared when City started their revival under Martin O'Neill. There wasn't anything to be angry about any more.

WHEN YOU'RE SMILING

There was another City fanzine that came out around the same time as Where's The Money Gone? Named When You're Smiling after the City supporters' anthem, it was backed by Foxes Against Racism and along with the usual features, it also gave publicity to local bands before disappearing after a few issues.

CITY'S TOP 10 ALL-TIME LEADING GOALSCORERS

273 ....Arthur Chandler
265 ....Arthur Rowley
156 ....Ernie Hine
117.............Derek Hines
114.............Arthur Lochhead
113 ....George Dewis
103 ....Gary Lineker
97 ....Jack Lee
97 ....Mike Stringfellow
95 ....Johnny Duncan

Unbelievable as it may seem now, the arrival at Filbert Street of the player who went on to become the leading goalscorer in Football League history caused outrage among Leicester City supporters. Arthur Rowley tops the Football League's scoring charts with 433 goals – 54 more than second-placed Dixie Dean – and he scored 251 of those for City with another 14 coming in the FA Cup. Rowley came to Leicester in the summer of June, 1950 as a replacement for popular, Sileby-born forward Jack Lee. Lee, himself eighth on City's list of record scorers with 97 goals, was sold to Derby County for £16,000 with Rowley being brought in by boss Norman Bullock on the same day from Fulham. At the time, City fans were fuming, but it turned out to be a good bit of business. After an impressive first season with the Rams, Lee was hit by injuries, while Rowley set about re-writing City's record books. He bagged a late winner at Bury on his debut and went on to end his first season with a 28-goal haul. In the Division Two championship-winning season of 1956-57, Rowley netted 44 times. That haul made him the leading scorer in the country for the second time and remains the most goals scored by a Leicester player during a season. Rowley scored an incredible 16 hat-tricks for City during his eight years with the club and 'The Gunner' predictably marked his final appearance at Filbert Street with a goal for Shrewsbury Town reserves in February, 1963. Similarly, there wasn't much fanfare when Arthur Chandler arrived at City in June, 1923 from Queens Park Rangers. At the age of 27, many believed he was past his best – and they were all spectacularly wrong. 'Channy' is City's record goalscorer with 273 goals in all competitions that includes six in the record 10-0 pasting of Portsmouth at Filbert Street in October, 1928.

LAST-DAY DRAMAS

Leicester City went to the top of Division Two with victory in their penultimate game of the 1922-23 season – and still ended up missing out on a top-two finish and promotion. City had been among the challengers at the top for most of the season. They put together what was then a club record nine-game unbeaten run and were seldom out of the top three. Leicester went top of the table with a 2-0 win over Bury at Filbert Street in their penultimate league fixture on April 28th thanks to Tom Smith's double, but two days later they were knocked off the summit following victory for West Ham United. The Foxes still went into the final game of the season at Bury in the second promotion spot, but City headed to Gigg Lane without the injured John Duncan, Mick O'Brien, Billy Thomson and Albert Pynegar. City were beaten 2-0 with future Foxes boss Norman Bullock on target for the Shakers and missed out on promotion on goal average – despite finishing as the division's top scorers. City scored 65 goals and conceded 44 to leave them with a goal average of 1.477, while West Ham's record was 63–38 for an average of 1.657 and that was enough to take them into the top flight at Leicester's expense. As it turned out, the key result during the season was a shocking 6-0 defeat at home to the Hammers in February.

THE NEXT SEASON

The following season, City inflicted last-day agony on East Midlands rivals Derby County. The Rams needed a 5-0 win in the clash at the Baseball Ground to pip Bury for the second promotion place and they looked on course to do just that when they opened up a 3-0 half-time lead against City. Leicester shipped a fourth goal to leave Derby on the brink of promotion – and then battened down the hatches. Derby couldn't grab a fifth goal and missed out on promotion.

BORO DENIED

Leicester denied Middlesbrough promotion to the top flight on the final day of the 1987-88 season. Boro needed maximum points to go up and were beaten by Peter Weir's opener and a long range Gary McAllister shot as David Pleat's team wrapped up a 2-1 win at Ayresome Park.

MILNE'S SWAP OF HORRORS

Gordon Milne got Leicester City promoted to Division One in his first season at the club, then kept them in the top flight for three seasons. Despite all that, he is probably best remembered by City fans for a transfer deal that has left supporters scratching heads ever since. Jim Melrose had arrived from Partick Thistle in the summer of 1980 for a fee of £250,000 and he top scored with nine goals as Jock Wallace's team battled in vain against the drop. That haul included the winner at Liverpool and a hat-trick on the last day of the season at Norwich City that condemned the Canaries to the drop alongside City. Melrose added 14 more goals the following season – including two in the epic FA Cup quarter-final victory over Shrewsbury Town – despite starting 11 games on the bench. Wallace left at the end of the season for Motherwell. In came Milne and within a month of taking over he had got rid of crowd favourite Melrose in a swap deal that brought Tommy English to Filbert Street from Coventry City. English had hardly endeared himself to City fans when netting a hat-trick for the Sky Blues in a 4-1 win at Highfield Road in March, 1981 which dealt a massive blow to Leicester's hopes of staying up. His goal scoring touch deserted him when he rejoined former Coventry boss Milne. He found the target only three times in 28 appearances as City were promoted and after misfiring again the following season, English was on his way out. After spells at Rochdale and Colchester United among others, Tommy played for non-league Harwich and Parkeston alongside younger brother Tony and his teenage son.

RAM LEGEND

Roger Davies is a Derby County legend for his goalscoring feats in the side that won the Division One championship in 1974-75. A few junctions down the M1 in Leicester, they would rather forget all about him. Frank McLintock bought Davies from Belgian side Bruges for £250,000 in December, 1977 in the hope he would score the goals that would keep the Foxes in the top division. But he scored just four times in 18 appearances – and one of those looked like an own goal – as City were relegated and he netted twice more the following season before heading off to play in America.

BACK TO THE FUTURE

The club's future was going to be put to the vote and everyone with a Leicester City tattoo held their breath. City were coming out of administration in February, 2003 with the help of a consortium led by chairman Jon Holmes and he decided the best way to make a new start would be to change the club's name back to the one they had ditched almost 84 years earlier! He suggested the club should be called Leicester Fosse again believing it would make the club unique. Ironically, Fosse had been wound up, taken over and renamed in the summer of 1919 because it owed the United Counties Bank the sum of £3,150 3s 3d. Anyway, the city's tattooists rubbed their hands in anticipation as Holmes' proposed name change was put to the vote. On their way into the Walkers Stadium for the game with Wimbledon on February 22nd, City fans were each handed a card with the letter 'C' and 'F' on it, so they could cast their vote during the half-time interval. Leicester fans among the crowd of 31,438 voted overwhelmingly against changing the club's name and confirmation at the final whistle of the 4-0 victory came with the announcement: "City will be City forever!" It had all started with a group of former schoolmates in a garden shed. The history books tell us that in the spring of 1884, a group of Old Wyggestonians met in a garden shed just off Fosse Road in Leicester and decided to form a football club. Frank Gardner was among the co-founders. He was elected the club's first secretary and treasurer and years later, claimed to have made the following rather bold declaration at the meeting: "As the Fosse is known throughout the land, so shall the new club be known in the future."

ANOTHER FOSSE

The name wasn't that unique, however. The club's first opponents were Syston Fosse! The sides met at a private playing field just off Fosse Road on November 1st, 1884 after a carpenter had made a set of goalposts reportedly painted amber and black. Leicester wore black jerseys with a diagonal blue sash and long white trousers for the historic fixture and they powered to a 5-0 win. There were two goals apiece for West and Hilton Johnson and Dingley got the other.

ROOSTER!

Kevin Russell owed his cult status at Leicester City to his vital goals – and John Wayne! As a boy, he was given the nickname 'Rooster' because of his love for the classic Western Rooster Cogburn that starred 'The Duke' and it stuck with him throughout his football career. City fans chanted 'Rooster' and it was suggested Russell got his nickname because he ran around like a headless chicken. 'Rooster' thought there was no such thing as a lost cause and that's just as well because his City career looked like being one. In the months following his £150,000 move from Wrexham in the summer of 1989, Russell spent so much time in hospital that he probably got invited to the staff parties and had to wait until the nerve-jangling climax of the 1990-91 season to show City supporters what he could do. Caretaker boss Gordon Lee handed Russell his chance against Middlesbrough in March, 1991 after a run of four straight defeats had left City in danger of a first-ever drop into the third tier of English football. 'Rooster' responded with a goal in a thrilling 4-3 win. He added another from the penalty spot in a 2-0 win at Notts County and ended the season with five goals as City survived on the final day of a dramatic campaign. Russell had a similar impact towards the end of the following season when the Foxes were battling away at the other end of the table and his two winning goals in the space of four days fired Brian Little's team to the brink of the Premier League. His late winner against Tranmere Rovers at Filbert Street on April 15th lifted Leicester into the second promotion place and Russell ensured they stayed there with another dramatic goal at promotion rivals Blackburn Rovers three days later. Russell charged down Rovers goalkeeper Bobby Mimms' clearance and then joyfully ran the ball into the empty net in front of the thousands of travelling Leicester fans. City missed out on a top-two spot and Russell went on to have a crucial role in the play-off semi-finals against Cambridge United. He grabbed the opener in the 1-1 draw at the Abbey Stadium and added another in the 5-0 romp that followed in the second leg and took Leicester back to Wembley after 23 years. Russell drew a blank in the final against Blackburn Rovers at Wembley and to the surprise of most supporters, he left for Stoke City in the summer.

IS THERE ANYBODY THERE?

Around 2,500 fans turned up to watch Leicester Fosse take on local rivals Loughborough Town in December, 1890 – but they didn't see much! The 1-1 draw was played out in heavy fog and legend has it that Fosse goalkeeper Charlie Walker was left on the pitch at the final whistle and it wasn't until 20 minutes later that his team-mates in the changing room noticed he was missing. Walker was found still on the pitch and reportedly said he thought the game was still going on and that Fosse were piling on the pressure at the other end of the pitch! At least the game went ahead. In 1885-86, Fosse set off to take on Leicestershire rivals Old Loughburians and after failing to find the ground, they reportedly spent the afternoon at the races!

ROUGH ON LUFF

Fosse's clashes with Loughborough led to the first reports of football violence in Leicester's history and there were some fiery exchanges on the pitch. In 1893-94, Fosse were accused of "downright ruffianism" by the Leicester press after the FA Cup clash between the sides. There was a 34-minute delay while Luffs defender Jack Kent had a broken leg treated on the pitch. Fosse won the fourth qualifying round match 1-0. The rivalry at Football League level came to an end after the 1899-1900 season as Loughborough finished bottom of Division Two for the second time in three seasons and were not re-elected. Fosse were sorry to see them go having won nine of their ten league matches and drawn the other, but Woolwich Arsenal were glad to see the back of them. The Gunners' record defeat remains the 8-0 mauling they suffered at Loughborough in 1896. Loughborough also had two goals disallowed!

SPOT OF BOTHER

Leicester City went into the record books for all the wrong reasons at Anfield in August, 1974 – they conceded the quickest penalty in Football League history with just 19 seconds on the clock. City kicked off the game at Liverpool, a pass from Malcolm Munro was intercepted by Steve Heighway and he was brought down by Leicester keeper Mark Wallington. Alec Lindsay stepped up to convert the spot-kick and he was only the second Liverpool player to touch the ball in the match. Lindsay went on to add another penalty in a 2-1 win for the Reds. Keith Weller netted City's reply.

WANDERING INTO TROUBLE

Fosse's early rivals included Burton Wanderers and after a match between the sides in January, 1897, Wanderers full-back Cunningham sank a few post-match pints with his team-mates and then headed off to more pubs in the city to challenge all comers to a fist fight! Someone took him up on his offer and put him in hospital.

GREW DON'T KNOW WHAT YOU'RE DOING

Mark Grew had some big boots to fill – and didn't. Grew was signed by Leicester City boss Gordon Milne in the summer of 1983 as a possible replacement for long-serving goalkeeper Mark Wallington. Wallington and the club were in a contract dispute and that prompted Milne to bring in Grew from West Bromwich Albion for a £60,000 fee. Grew had spent eight years at the Hawthorns, making his debut in a Uefa Cup tie against Galatasaray, and made 33 league appearances for the Baggies.He was handed the goalkeeper's jersey for the opening match of the 1983-84 season against Notts County at Filbert Street and had a horror debut. Martin O'Neill's free kick whistled past him and former Foxes striker Trevor Christie added a hat trick in the Magpies' 4-0 romp. Four days later, Luton Town were 3-0 winners at Filbert Street and Grew was powerless to prevent further defeats against West Bromwich Albion (0-1), West Ham United (1-3) and Tottenham Hotspur (0-3), which meant he had shipped 14 goals in his first five appearances for the Foxes and probably helped speed up negotiations between Wallington and City. Wallington was back between the posts for the trip to Coventry City and while he couldn't stop a 2-1 defeat at Highfield Road – which made it six straight defeats for the Foxes and a worst-ever start to a league campaign – he kept his place and Grew was relegated to the reserves. After just five games Grew moved on to Ipswich Town and made an unhappy return to Filbert Street at the start of the following season. Television viewers watched him theatrically rip his gloves off and throw them on the ground in front of a joyful Kop after being beaten by Steve Lynex's last-gasp winner. Grew went on to have a successful career at Port Vale and was between the posts for the Valiants when they knocked Tottenham Hotspur out of the FA Cup in the fourth round in 1988.

THE BEST OF THE BEST

Wallington is fourth in the list of average goals per game conceded by City's goalkeepers. He was beaten 607 times in 460 appearances – an average of 1.319 per game – and Peter Shilton tops the list with an average of 1.118 goals conceded per game in his 339 appearances. George Hebden is second with 1.135 goals conceded per game in his 104 games.

AN INNOVATIVE FOX

Fosse goalkeeper Jimmy Thraves had a key role in the introduction of the penalty kick. In February 1891, he was between the posts for Notts County in an FA Cup tie against Stoke City. Thraves was beaten by a shot which defender Jack Hendry punched off the line and Stoke were awarded a free kick. Thraves spread himself right in front of the player taking the kick and smothered his effort. This proved to be crucial as Notts ran out 1-0 winners and the FA later decided to bring in the penalty kick just a year after rejecting the suggestion. Thraves joined Fosse the following year and got off to a stuttering start. He was late for his debut at Mansfield Town after missing his train connection, but went on to be an ever-present for the next four and a half seasons, making 148 consecutive appearances for Fosse.

MILLER MISSED

The penalty kick was introduced for the fixtures played on September 1st, 1891 and on that day, 'Tout' Miller netted from the spot for Burton Wanderers against Great Bridge Unity. Miller went on to join Fosse and missed Leicester's first penalty kick awarded to them at Football League level against Newcastle United at Filbert Street on October 20th, 1894, in a 4-4 draw.

THE FIRST OF MANY

Harry Bailey scored Fosse's first-ever penalty in a friendly against Notts County on September 14th, 1891 and Billy Dorrell grabbed the first in competitive fare in the FA Cup tie against Rushden on October 15th, 1892.

DR. WHO

Leicester City's Youth Academy has produced among others, Gary Lineker, Emile Heskey and Dr. Who! Matt Smith was a prolific goalscorer for City's under-15 and under-16s and was showing plenty of promise according to long-serving Academy manager Jon Rudkin until a serious back injury ended his footballing ambitions. Smith was forced to hang up his boots and a decade later, it was revealed he had landed one of the biggest roles on British television. BBC bosses confirmed in January, 2009 that Smith would be the 11th actor to play Dr. Who having previously had several minor roles.

KNOCKOUT

Heskey was known as 'Bruno' for his resemblance to former world heavyweight boxing champion Frank Bruno and his team-mates, when he played for Leicester Schools, included another who was to bid to conquer the world with his fists. Neil Linford remembers playing alongside Heskey at the heart of what must have been a no-nonsense defence before deciding to concentrate on boxing. He was a top-class amateur with Belgrave Amateur Boxing Club – boxing for England and winning the bronze medal at the European under-19 championships – before turning professional. The biggest night of his career came in Portsmouth in March, 2003 and he planned to walk into battle for his WBU world title fight with Tony Oakey wearing a Leicester City shirt until he was advised against it. At the time, City and Portsmouth were scrapping it out for promotion to the Premier League and it was feared Linford's show of support for Leicester would inflame tensions. Linford had the home favourite on the floor in the 10th round of a gruelling fight before losing a points decision.

NEVER MADE HIS MARK

As a teenager, Mark Walsh was a promising player on Leicester City's books who played alongside Heskey and later became a professional boxer after being released by the Foxes.

DEVOTED

Kevin Concepcion is another Leicester boxer who made no secret of his devotion to the Foxes. Concepcion, the elder brother of another professional boxer, Martin, walked to the ring for his fights in Leicester to the same post-horn gallop tune that greeted City's arrival on the pitch.

THE CUP THAT DIDN'T CHEER

For six years, the FA Cup had all the romance of a slap round the face for Leicester City supporters. Following a run to the fifth round in 1984-85 that was ended by Millwall after wins over Burton Albion and Carlisle United, City didn't win a game in the competition for the next six years. City's reputation in the FA Cup was built in the 1960s when they reached three finals and was left in tatters by third-round defeats against Bristol Rovers, Queens Park Rangers, Oxford United, Manchester City, Barnsley and Millwall. Admittedly, the draw was not kind. They were handed only one home match in that six-year barren spell and were beaten 2-1 by Barnsley in January, 1990. The third round defeat at Millwall the following season was even more devastating. Tony James' goal put David Pleat's team in front and they were just four minutes away from the fourth round when it all fell apart. Steve Walsh and Paul Ramsey were sent off, Millwall netted twice in the dying minutes and Leicester hearts were broken again. The summer of 1991 brought Brian Little to Filbert Street, and with the new manager came plenty of optimism. He got rid of some players, brought in a few, and gave confidence to those left shell-shocked by the previous season's battle against relegation that was won on the final day thanks to Tony James' goal against Oxford United. Under Little's leadership, City were soon among the contenders for promotion and the FA Cup draw handed the chance to test themselves against top-flight opposition. They were drawn at home to Crystal Palace and although they had the better of the chances, City couldn't make the breakthrough and the scoreline was blank with the game just seconds away from a replay at Selhurst Park. City had a final chance when they were awarded a free kick. Gary Mills lifted the ball over to the far post where Richard Smith was lurking unmarked, and rather unexpectedly, to crash his right-foot volley into the roof of the net and spark wild celebrations. Smith was interviewed by Sky Sports as he left the pitch and then headed into the city for a few drinks that he didn't have to pay for. It didn't last, however. The Foxes were drawn at home to Bristol City in the fourth round and in icy conditions, the Robins skated through to the fifth round with livewire winger Junior Bent the inspiration for the visitors and Paul Kitson on target for the Foxes.

CITY AND SIR MATT'S FINISH

Maybe it wasn't *Mission Impossible*, but it wasn't far off. Leicester City headed to Old Trafford on May 17th, 1969 to face a star-studded Manchester United side, including George Best and Denis Law, needing maximum points to secure their top-flight survival. As if that wasn't enough, United were also determined to give manager Sir Matt Busby a fitting send off as manager in his final game in charge. Three weeks earlier, City had been beaten by Manchester City in the FA Cup Final and after the game, the Foxes were left needing seven points from their remaining five games to stay in Division One for a 13th successive season. Allan Clarke secured victory for City over Tottenham Hotspur and after defeat at Ipswich Town, Ally Brown's debut brace clinched two more priceless points against Sunderland and Graham Cross grabbed City's goal in a 1-1 draw against Everton. All of which meant Frank O'Farrell's team needed to win at Manchester United to stay up. Skipper David Nish gave them the perfect start with a goal in the opening minute. By the fourth minute, City were behind with Best and Law the marksmen for United. The Reds went on to add a third and although Rodney Fern pulled a goal back for Leicester, it wasn't enough to keep them in Division One.

DEVILISH PERFORMANCE

Manchester United were top of Division One when they took on Leicester City at Filbert Street on November 23rd, 1985 and were blown away inside a breathless opening 30 minutes! City handed a debut to loan signing Laurie Cunningham, formerly with United, but it was Gary McAllister and Alan

Smith who got the goals that fired the Foxes to a famous win. McAllister put Gordon Milne's team ahead in the seventh minute – dancing past a couple of challenges before rifling his shot into the corner of the net – and Smith's brace in the space of 15 minutes meant there was no way back for United. Smith doubled the lead and then thumped home number three from what seemed an impossible angle in front of 22,008 disbelieving fans. City continued to struggle, however, and only secured their safety on the final day of the season when a 2-0 win over Newcastle United at Filbert Street was enough to keep them up at Ipswich Town's expense.

TIME FOR A REST

Gary Mills needed to put his feet up at the end of the 1991-92 campaign. He was an ever-present for Leicester City throughout the season – making a club-record 61 appearances in Division One, the FA Cup, the League Cup, the Zenith Data Systems Cup and the play-offs – as Brian Little made an instant impact at Filbert Street. Unsurprisingly, Mills was named the Supporters' Club's Player of the Season for his efforts. Mills, who collected a European Cup winners' medal while still a teenager at Nottingham Forest, went on to lead out City in the 1993 Division One play-off final against Swindon Town. Twelve months later, he made a memorable contribution to the play-off victory over Derby County – despite not getting on the pitch! He was working as a summariser on local radio and reacted with plenty of enthusiasm when Steve Walsh's second goal hit the back of the net to take Leicester into the Premier League!

SEVEN OF THE BEST

Mark Wallington set a Leicester record by making 331 consecutive appearances between January 4th, 1975 and March 6th, 1982. His run was ended in the unforgettable FA Cup quarter-final against Shrewsbury Town. He was dazed by a collision with Shrews striker Chic Bates and two goals flew past him while he was seeing stars rather than the ball. In the days before substitute goalkeepers, he was replaced by Alan Young and then Steve Lynex and City romped to a 5-2 win that booked a semi-final against Tottenham Hotspur. Young and Lynex both reckoned that keeping a clean sheet meant they had done better than Wallington, but it was Nicky Walker who was between the posts for City at Chelsea three days later and the Foxes were beaten 4-1 at Stamford Bridge.

46ER

The club's first ever-present was Jack Lord. He achieved the feat in Leicester Fosse's debut season in the Midland League and Gary McAllister became the Foxes' first 46-game ever-present in 1988-89. A decade later, Steve Guppy was City's first ever-present in the Premier League. Guppy played all 38 top-flight games as Martin O'Neill's team clinched tenth spot. He also played both FA Cup matches and all eight games in the League Cup campaign that ended with the heartbreak of a last-gasp defeat against Tottenham Hotspur in the final. The following season, Guppy's consistent form on City's left wing earned a call up to England's squad for the friendly against Belgium that ended in a 2-1 win at Sunderland. After that, Guppy was hit by injury and never played for England again.

SAVE IT WITH FLOWERS

Tim Flowers was in the best form of his career – but still couldn't get his own manager to pick him! Flowers had a starring role as Leicester City climbed to the top of the Premier League after the opening eight games of the 2000-2001 season. He kept six clean sheets to help City to the summit of English football for only the fifth time in the club's history and was named the Carling Player of the Month for September. So Flowers had to fancy his chances of an England recall, especially when City boss Peter Taylor was placed in temporary charge of the national team. Taylor had previously been a successful coach of England under-21s and controversially lost his position when Glenn Hoddle took charge. He went on to take a job often referred to as the second most important in the country behind that of Prime Minister following Kevin Keegan's resignation as England manager in October, 2000 after defeat against Germany in a World Cup qualifier. Taylor was appointed caretaker manager for the friendly against Italy in Turin the following month while the Football Association searched for a successor to Keegan and he looked certain to hand Flowers a recall. Flowers had earned the last of his 11 caps for his country two and a half years earlier against Morocco and had impressed since joining City in the summer of 1999 from Blackburn Rovers for a fee that would rise to £1.4 million. Instead of handing Flowers a recall, Taylor gave the goalkeeper's jersey to David James in Turin. He also appointed David Beckham captain of his country for the first time and Leicester striker Emile Heskey started the game in the forward line. England were beaten 1-0 and although Taylor was set to take charge of the friendly with Spain the following February, Sven-Goran Eriksson took charge before then. Flowers never got the chance to play for England again and injury problems meant that he announced he would be retiring at the end of the 2002-2003 season. Leicester fans were hoping he would mark his last appearance with a goal! Flowers came off the bench in the final match of the season at Wolverhampton Wanderers and when City were awarded a spot kick, the travelling supporters pleaded with Foxes boss Micky Adams to give him the chance to score what would have been the only goal of his career. But the ball was handed to Trevor Benjamin and he netted City's goal in the 1-1 draw.

LEICESTER AND THE LIP

More than three decades after the game, Leicester City fans still breathe a sigh of relief when they watch their side's winning goal hit the back of the net. City's epic FA Cup fourth round tie with Leatherhead in January, 1975 is featured on a BBC DVD of the competition's greatest matches and for the most part, it is X-rated stuff for Foxes supporters and best watched from behind the sofa. At the time, it looked like a great draw for City. They were paired with a team from the Isthmian League and although Jimmy Bloomfield's team were drawn away, the fixture was switched to Filbert Street. Leatherhead's giant-killing bid would be spearheaded by Chris Kelly and his pre-match boasts that his minnows would dump out City earned him the nickname 'The Leatherhead Lip'. Even his team-mates must have thought he was bonkers. Although City weren't having the best of times in the top division – they were one place off the bottom and without a win in 12 games when the sides met – Leicester could still call upon the talents of Keith Weller and Frank Worthington against the part-timers from Surrey. The previous season, City had reached the semi-finals and bowed out to Liverpool after a replay and had eased to a 3-1 win over Oxford United in the third round to set up the clash with Leatherhead. The BBC cameras and 32,090 fans headed to Filbert Street to see if Kelly could back up his boasts. He almost did. To the astonishment of the crowd, Leatherhead stunned the Foxes by racing into a 2-0 lead with Kelly netting the second goal and then came the game's turning point. Kelly looked set to bag Leatherhead's third and surely put the game beyond City after rounding goalkeeper Mark Wallington following a swift counter attack, but Malcolm Munro came to Leicester's rescue by sliding across to hack the ball off the line. That escape woke City from their slumbers. Jon Sammels pulled a goal back on 54 minutes before Steve Earle bagged the leveller with 16 minutes remaining. Weller grabbed the third with just ten minutes left to complete City's stunning comeback and ensure they avoided humiliation. Leicester's reward for their great escape against Leatherhead was a fifth-round trip to Arsenal, which was another epic tie. After the sides battled out a goalless draw at Highbury, the replay ended 1-1 at Filbert Street after extra time, and City were beaten in the second replay by an extra-time goal.

THE HIDING OF ALL HIDINGS

The football reporter of the Leicester Mercury had had enough. Leicester Fosse were already heading for relegation – and then this…

"Fosse have taken a good many beatings in their time," he wrote in the edition dated April 22nd, 1909, "but they have never participated in such a farcically absurd game as that at Nottingham yesterday.When to the score of 12-0 is added the fact that Bailey made a number of good saves and the Forest goalkeeper was never seriously troubled once during the 90 minutes, it will be seen that the beating was such a one that Fosse have never previously known since they have been a club." As it turned out, the

12-0 thumping that remains the club's heaviest defeat – and will hopefully remain so – owed much to a few thumping heads among the Fosse players. The scoreline raised a few eyebrows. Only four days earlier, Fosse had beaten FA Cup Finalists Manchester United 3-2 and with Forest also threatened by relegation, the other teams in the survival scrap demanded an investigation into the lopsided scoreline in Nottingham. The investigation came at Leicester's Grand Hotel on May 6th, 1909 and it revealed that the day before the game at Forest, Fosse's players had been to the wedding of former team-mate 'Leggy' Turner in the city and that the celebrations had continued into the early hours. The league accepted this and Fosse escaped punishment. They finished bottom of the table and then had to endure the season's post script from the Mercury's football reporter. He wrote of a season "of falsified predictions, hopes rent in tatters, past feats obscured and fond beliefs shattered, a season of disappointment, depression and almost interminable disaster. Can one wonder that many who follow their fortunes are in despair ? Or can one blame them? "But let it be the feeling of which a poet wrote: 'Despair is hope just dropped asleep/For better chance of dreaming.'" Poetry in a *Mercury* football report, eh? Times have changed a bit. Fosse's humbling in Nottingham is still the equal record victory in a top-flight fixture along with West Bromwich Albion's hammering of Darwen in 1892 and is still Forest's biggest-ever league victory. Perhaps Forest had gained extra motivation from the drubbing suffered by neighbours Notts Olympic in an FA Cup qualifying round tie on October 13th, 1894. Fosse handed out a 13-0 hammering with a hat-trick for David Skea and four apiece for 'Tout' Miller and Willie McArthur.

LIGHTS, CAMERAS...

The 1981 film *Escape To Victory* stars among others, Michael Caine, Sylvester Stallone, Pele and a Leicester City player! Caine, Stallone, Pele and Bobby Moore all played the parts of Allied prisoners of war who hatch a plot to escape their German prison camp during the half-time break of an exhibition match against a German team. Russell Osman, who went on to play for City, is against the idea. "But we can win this," he says with all the conviction of a footballer who has never acted before and so the team go out for the second half to battle out a 4-4 draw. At the time the film was made, Osman was with Bobby Robson's Ipswich Town and he went on to make 120 appearances for City. Stallone was in goal for the Allies and made the penalty save that ensured the game finished level – with a bit of help from a pair of Leicester keepers. Gordon Banks helped Stallone prepare for the film and then Paul Cooper stepped in to act as Stallone's stunt double in several scenes and the stumpy keeper must have been pleased with that. There were also roles in the film for Ossie Ardiles and Osman and Cooper's Ipswich team-mates John Wark and Kevin O'Callaghan.

"DO I FEEL LUCKY?"

Leicester City's former Filbert Street home gets a mention in the 1971 classic *Dirty Harry*. Sort of. Clint Eastwood starred as the rule-bending, sharp-shooting cop Harry Callahan and at one point he is speeding through the streets of San Francisco in pursuit of some nasty piece of work or other and orders his partner to: "Throw a left at Filbert." He meant Filbert Street in the American city.

FAVOURITE SON

An Evening With Gary Lineker was a successful play that was turned into a television comedy drama. The story, written by Chris England and Arthur Smith, tells of a couple who head to Majorca to discuss their marriage problems and end up getting wrapped up in England's pursuit of the 1990 World Cup in Italy led by Leicester's favourite footballing son. The television adaptation was shown in 1994 and starred Paul Merton, Clive Owen, Martin Clunes and Caroline Quentin. Lineker himself turned up at the end of the show.

MONEY WELL SPENT

On his arrival at Filbert Street in November, 1936, Jack Bowers became a Leicester City hero sparking an astonishing climb up the Division Two table. Struggling in 17th place when he joined, City ended up being crowned champions! Bowers had been the top flight's leading scorer three times in four seasons with East Midlands rivals Derby County and that convinced City boss Frank Womack to spend a club record £7,500 to bring him to the club. That was more than double the previous highest outlay of £3,450 which was spent on Len Barry nine years earlier. Bowers wasted little time in repaying City's investment. After marking his debut with a goal in a 3-1 win at Swansea Town, he went on to score in each of his first six games for City, all of which ended in victory to start a sensational climb up the table. His first six games for the Foxes brought 12 goals – including a hat-trick in a 5-1 demolition of Barnsley – and his brace in a 4-1 thumping of Tottenham Hotspur on the final day of the season ensured City finished on top of the table. He finished his first season at City with 33 goals – despite missing the first three months of the campaign! Bowers added another ten goals on City's return to the top flight and when World War II broke out in 1939, he had an incredible record of 219 goals in 282 appearances. He went on to be assistant manager at Derby.

CONSECUTIVE FOR CHANNY

Arthur Chandler holds the record for scoring in the most consecutive games for City. His goal in the 3-0 win at Derby County on December 6th, 1924 marked the start of a run of 'Channy' finding the target in eight successive games. He ended the season with 32 goals in Division Two as City were crowned champions.

ACCURATE ARTHUR

Arthur Rowley scored in seven consecutive games for the Foxes during the 1951-52 season. His goal-den sequence started with City's third goal in a 3-1 win over Coventry City and he added strikes against West Ham United, Sheffield United, Barnsley, Hull City, Blackburn Rovers and Queens Park Rangers.

CRAZY KEEPERS

For a generation of Leicester City fans, Mark Wallington was their team's goalkeeper. His record-breaking run of 331 consecutive games in goal for City came to an end in an unforgettable clash at Filbert Street. City hosted Shrewsbury Town in the quarter finals of the FA Cup in March, 1982 and were given the perfect start by Larry May's early header. Chic Bates' boot then separated Wallington from his senses and left him seeing stars rather than the ball as it flew past him twice and into City's net to give the Shrews the lead. Wallington groggily – and reluctantly – left the pitch and his place between the posts was taken by striker Alan Young. He wasn't that badly missed up front thanks to Shrewsbury defender Colin Griffin. He rolled the ball into his own net to level the scores and make Filbert Street erupt. Young's spell in goal came to an end when he was left dazed after being clattered and winger Steve Lynex pulled on the goalkeeper's jersey to become City's third stopper. Young went back in goal after his head had cleared and Lynex went on to set up Jim Melrose's goal that put the Foxes ahead again at 3-2. That goal knocked the stuffing out of Shrewsbury and further goals from Gary Lineker and Melrose completed a 5-2 win that took City through to a semi-final clash against Tottenham Hotspur. Young and Lynex joked afterwards that they should be in goal for City's next fixture because they had kept out Shrewsbury while Wallington had been beaten twice. Instead, Nicky Walker took the number one jersey shirt for the clash at Chelsea three days later that was lost 4-1.

CAPITAL TRIO

City also used three goalkeepers in a League Cup second round, first leg tie at Crystal Palace in September, 1999. Martin O'Neill's side looked set to take a lead back to Filbert Street for the return leg when an own goal and strikes from Neil Lennon and Gerry Taggart opened up a 3-1 lead at Selhurst Park. But the game turned when goalkeeper Tim Flowers was injured. He had come on to replace Pegguy Arphexad and with all the substitutes used, Theo Zagorakis went between the posts for ten-man City. Palace netted twice in three minutes to draw level, but Zagorakis kept them out in the last 15 minutes.

WEMBLEY WOE

Only Leicester City could stop Tottenham Hotspur securing their place in the record books at Wembley on May 6th, 1961. Seven days earlier, Spurs had clinched the Division One championship and were aiming to become the first team in the 20th century to complete a league and cup double. City had finished the season sixth and boss Martin Gillies dropped the bombshell of all bombshells when he announced the line up for City's second FA Cup Final. He had decided to drop striker Ken Leek and replaced him with Hugh McIlmoyle. Leek had scored in every round on the way to the final – including a strike in the semi-final win over Sheffield United – and had also starred in City's stunning 3-2 win at White Hart Lane earlier in the season. When quizzed about the decision that stunned City's fans, Gillies said: "There seems to be some kind of mystery in the minds of many people. It is quite absurd to suggest that I made the change for any reason but the interest of the side. I made the change purely and simply because I consider McIlmoyle to be the player in form, and that is all." That didn't quite add up. Since the semi-final, Leek had scored three goals in four league games and McIlmoyle had been on target four times in seven appearances. To add to the mystery, the pages of the boardroom minute book that covered the pre-cup final meeting have been removed. Despite the controversy, City actually settled quicker on the big day before disaster struck in front of a crowd of 100,000. In the 18th minute, City full-back Len Chalmers came out of a challenge with Les Allen with a leg injury and in the days before substitutes that meant Leicester had to battle on for the rest of the game with only ten fit players. Chalmers was handed the role of outside-left and Gillies' reshuffle led to Frank McLintock moving into defence and striker Ken Keyworth dropped back. Although they battled on, City were undone by a couple of late goals as their legs tired. Bobby Smith put Spurs ahead in the 69th minute and seven minutes later, a mis-hit from the injured Chalmers sent the Londoners away on the counter-attack and Terry Dyson put the game beyond Leicester with the second goal. That meant Spurs wrapped up the first league and cup double since 1897 and City's squad headed off to Rhodesia and South Africa for a five-match tour.

IT'S NO JOKE

Peter Shilton didn't realise what he had done until he got home and turned on the television. Only then did he understand that his Leicester City team-mates weren't winding him up! Shilton had been between the posts for the City team that stormed to a 5-1 win at Southampton in October, 1967, and was surprised to find himself on the score-sheet alongside Mike Stringfellow (two), Alan Tewley and Jackie Sinclair. "It was a windy day and I belted the ball down the pitch," remembered the Leicester-born legend. "I saw it drop into the net and presumed somebody got a touch before it went in. I thought the lads were winding me up when they told me it was my goal. I realised they were telling the truth when I got home and turned the television on! A week earlier Pat Jennings had scored against Alex Stepney and everyone seems to remember that. They don't seem to remember my goal!" Shilton never found the target again in a record-breaking career that started with Sunday morning kickabouts at the club's Belvoir Drive training ground that was next to his family's home and went on to span 1,391 first-class matches and 125 caps for England.

SPOT ON HERBERT

Herbert Bown also found the target for Leicester Fosse, but his goal against Hull City in March, 1917 came from the penalty spot. Bown was also off target in another spot kick attempt.

KEEPER TURNED STRIKER

City's goal scorer in the Midland League clash at Mansfield Town in November, 1940 was the Stags' reserve goalkeeper! City turned up for the World War Two fixture with only 10 players and Wright took the opportunity to strike a blow in his battle for Mansfield's goalkeeping jersey by twice putting the ball past the player chosen instead of him. Wright lined up at outside right for City and netted both their goals in the game, which was won 4-2 by the Stags.

COTT-GLEE

The pages of Tony Cottee's scrapbook had something missing... From the start of his playing days on the school field, Cottee kept a record of every goal he scored. All those goals – including 116 for boyhood heroes West Ham United and another 72 for Everton – and not one of them in front of Manchester United's fans at Old Trafford. At the age of 32, Cottee thought his chance had gone and then came the 'prank' phone call that changed all that while he was playing in Malaysia with Selangor. "My family's business is insurance," he explained, "and we used to insure Steve Walford's house. He was assistant manager at Leicester and my dad rang me up to say there was a chance Martin O'Neill might be interested in signing me. I thought it was a wind up!" The clubs agreed a £500,000 fee in August, 1997 and Cottee was on his way to Filbert Street to relaunch his career. He had a spell on loan at Birmingham City and on his return, was named in the starting line-up for the clash at Old Trafford on January 31, 1998. It looked like a home banker. United were unbeaten in front of their home fans since the start of the season and had dropped only two points. Earlier in the campaign Juventus had left Manchester empty handed after a 3-2 defeat in a Champions League tie. So it was something of a surprise when Cottee handed City a first-half lead with his first goal at the Theatre of Dreams. Muzzy Izzet put the ball into United's penalty area and Cottee nipped in to lift his shot over goalkeeper Peter Schmeichel and into the net in front of a stunned and silent Stretford End. Emile Heskey almost doubled the lead before the break and City hung on to secure their first win at Old Trafford in 17 attempts. The Sports Mercury hit the streets that night with the front-page headline: "Cott-Glee !" and there was more to come from the rejuvenated marksman. He went on to claim the first domestic winner's medal of his career after helping City lift the Worthington Cup with victory over Tranmere Rovers at Wembley in February, 2000. At the end of the season, Cottee and Steve Walsh applied for the manager's positions after the departure of Martin O'Neill in the summer of 2000. Cottee says they both felt the club needed "consistency rather than upheaval" and as it turns out, he was right.

HARD ON HAMILL

When is being a match-winner not enough? When you're Stewart Hamill and Jock Wallace is your manager. Hamill was handed the number 11 shirt for Leicester's home date with Wrexham on September 5th, 1981 and grabbed the only goal. Three days later, he did it again, firing City to a 1-0 win over Barnsley at Filbert Street – and never played for Leicester again! Hamill wasn't even on the bench for the trip to East Midlands rivals Derby County that came four days after his heroics against the Tykes and he went on to join Scunthorpe United on loan after falling out of favour with Wallace. The Foxes boss had plucked Hamill from Scottish part-timers Pollok, and a job as a Co-op van driver, in September, 1980 to hand him his chance with City. He made eight appearances in the top-flight as Leicester struggled to live up to Wallace's early-season prediction that they would win Division One and then resurfaced the following season for those match-winning heroics before heading for the exit. After leaving Leicester, Hamill then drifted into non-league before marking his return to the Football League with Northampton Town with a goal after just 35 seconds of his debut against Tranmere Rovers, as the Cobblers stormed to the Fourth Division championship.Hamill had a spell at Scarborough and was in the line-up for their first-ever match in the Football League in August, 1987 before returning to Leicestershire to play for Lutterworth Town and Houghton Rangers in the Senior League. Jack Lee hung around a bit longer than Hamill at Filbert Street. The Sileby-born striker made 163 appearances and netted 97 goals before leaving for Derby County in a £16,000 transfer that caused outrage among Leicester fans. His career as a county cricketer with Leicestershire was rather brief – despite making a dream start to his debut. In July, 1947, he was selected for the County Championship fixture at Glamorgan's Cardiff Arms Park and became one of a select group to take a wicket with their first ball in first-class cricket. He had Glamorgan opening batsman A. H. Dyson caught and also took a catch in the Welsh team's first innings. His bowling figures were 1-13 from four overs. Lee didn't get the chance to bowl in the second innings – and never played for Leicestershire again.

BACK AT WEMBLEY

Third time lucky? Not a bit of it. Believe it or not, but there was a time when Leicester City went into the FA Cup Final against Manchester United as red-hot favourites. It was May, 1963 and City were fancied to lift the trophy at the third attempt having failed in previous finals in 1949 and 1961, against Wolverhampton Wanderers and Tottenham Hotspur respectively. Seven days earlier, they had finished the Division One season in fourth place after being top of the table with just five games remaining, while United had narrowly escaped relegation from the top flight. City had been unbeaten in their two meetings in the league. They met twice in as many days and after drawing 2-2 at Old Trafford, Leicester were 4-3 winners the following day at Filbert Street with Ken Keyworth the hat-trick hero and Denis Law bagging a treble in reply. It proved to be Leicester's last win of a season that promised so much and ended with Matt Gillies' team missing out on any silverware. They ended the league season with four defeats away from home and perhaps still suffering from the disappointment of missing out on what would have been the club's first ever championship, City's stars then went on to freeze on the big day at Wembley in front of a 100,000 crowd. City's line-up included three new internationals – Gordon Banks, Frank McLintock and David Gibson – while Colin Appleton had represented the Football League and Graham Cross had recently gained his first cap for England under-23s. Yet it was United's Pat Crerand who proved to be the match-winner with a masterly display in midfield, setting up the opening goal for Denis Law in the 29th minute. Law took Crerand's pass, spun and rifled his shot past Banks. City struggled to get into the game and it took until the 37th minute before Cross had their first shot of note. United felt they should have been further ahead at the break and went on to double their lead 12 minutes after the interval after an uncharacteristic mistake by Banks. He mishandled a shot which gifted David Herd the chance to pounce and net the rebound. City were back in it with just nine minutes left. Keyworth's diving header handed them a lifeline, but another mistake by Banks allowed Herd to net his second goal, and United's third, to put the game beyond the Foxes and leave them still waiting to win at Wembley.

FALSE STARTS

You've read about the dream debuts, now here are the false starts. Malcolm Munro's Leicester City debut ended in agony. At the age of 18, the Melton Mowbray-born stopper was handed a place at the heart of City's defence for the trip to Ipswich Town in September, 1971 and he left Portman Road in an ambulance after suffering a broken cheekbone. City still won the game 2-1 and Munro endured an unhappy return to Ipswich on the opening day of the 1973-74 season when he scored an own goal in a 1-1 draw. Neil Lennon is a Leicester legend for his starring role in City's midfield during the Martin

O'Neill era. His debut for City in February, 1996 after joining from Crewe Alexandra for a fee of £750,000 would be best described as mixed. Lennon set up City's opener for Neil Lewis against Reading at Elm Park and then conceded the penalty that allowed the Royals to grab a 1-1 draw. Leicester boss David Pleat spent £100,000 to bring Marc North to Filbert Street from Grimsby Town in March, 1989. Pleat had initially signed North as a teenager when he was a goalkeeper, but he came to Leicester as a striker on transfer deadline day having starred for the Mariners in their run to the last 16 of the FA Cup.

After making his debut against Birmingham City, North was handed his first start for the Foxes in the last home game of the season against Crystal Palace. He put City ahead and ended up being stretchered off after suffering a broken shin bone. The game ended in a 2-2 draw. The goalkeeping mishaps of giant Aussie Zeljko 'Spider' Kalac are chronicled elsewhere in this book, but no chapter on horror debuts by City players would be complete without mention of his debut at West Bromwich Albion in November, 1995. City swept into a 3-0 half-time lead through Scott Taylor's goal double and another from Iwan Roberts and then Kalac dropped a couple of clangers. Mark McGhee's team held on for maximum points in front of the television cameras.

MADRID MISERY

Thirty-six years after their first misadventure, Leicester City headed back into European competition and history repeated itself. City lifting the Coca-Cola Cup after victory over Middlesbrough in the final replay at Hillsborough in April, 1997 ensured their qualification for the following season's Uefa Cup. Their League Cup success in 1964 hadn't been rewarded with the chance to take on the continent's cream and City's only previous involvement in European competition had been in the 1961-62 season when Tottenham Hotspur winning the Football League and FA Cup double meant Leicester represented England in the European Cup Winners' Cup. Their interest back then was ended by Atletico Madrid after some controversial refereeing decisions in the second leg – and more than three decades on, Martin O'Neill's team suffered a similar fate. City's supporters headed over to Spain in their thousands for the first leg – and many were soon wishing they hadn't. The conditions on many of the coaches were described as insufferable, but the mood of the travelling fans was lifted just 11 minutes after the action got underway at the Vicente Calderon Stadium. To the astonishment of most of the 35,000 crowd, Ian Marshall put City ahead when he hooked home from close range and Leicester set about hanging onto their lead. The introduction of winger Jose Mari turned the game Madrid's way as he helped unlock City's defence, but it was a familiar face who levelled the scores. City's effective shackling of Brazilian Juninho had been one of the keys to their Coca-Cola Cup success five months earlier and he got his revenge for new club Atletico. He grabbed the equaliser with the help of a deflection off Steve Walsh and

Christian Vieri's late penalty ensured Atletico held a 2-1 advantage going into the second leg at Filbert Street two weeks later. Roared on by a crowd of 20,776, City launched wave after wave of attacks from the opening whistle and felt they should have been awarded four penalties with Muzzy Izzet having three appeals rejected after he was sent crashing. The sending off of Antonio Lopez gave City a boost, but the advantage was controversially wiped out when Leicester playmaker Garry Parker was also dismissed. Parker was handed his marching orders for taking a free kick too quickly and with him went City's hopes of overturning the deficit. Leicester were deflated by the sending off and Madrid went on to snatch victory with late goals from Juninho and Kiko that took them to a 3-1 win on aggregate.

CITY'S TOP 10 ALL-TIME APPEARANCE MAKERS

Graham Cross....................599
Sep Smith...........................586
Adam Black 556
Hugh Adcock.....................460
Mark Wallington...............460
Willie Frame......................459
Steve Walsh........................449
Mal Griffiths......................420
Arthur Chandler...............419
John Sjoberg......................413

Graham Cross holds the record for making the most appearances for Leicester City. In a first-team career with his home-town club spanning more than 14 years, Cross played for City 599 times and would surely have made 600 appearances if he hadn't been so good at cricket. He was a sporting all rounder and his decision to help Leicestershire win cricket's County Championship for the first time in their history in 1975 rather than report back for pre-season training with City spelled the beginning of the end of his time at Filbert Street. His first visits to City's home had come as a seven-year-old when his heroes were Arthur Rowley and Johnny Morris. Cross went on to make his debut as a 17-year-old and marked his first appearance with a goal against Birmingham City. He went on to spend his 18th birthday playing at the heart of Leicester's defence in front of 50,000 fans as City took on Atletico Madrid in the second leg of their second-round tie in the European Cup Winners' Cup. City were beaten 2-0, but Cross emerged with plenty of credit. He also played in two FA Cup Finals and two League Cup Finals during Leicester's golden era in the 1960s and says the best memory of his career with the Foxes came at Blackpool's Bloomfield Road ground on April 8th, 1963. Ken Keyworth's goal secured a point for City from a 1-1 draw and that was enough to take Leicester to the top of Division One. Adam Black actually betters Cross's tally of 495 + 3 appearances for City in the Football League with 528 appearances. Sep Smith had the lengthiest first-team career with Leicester. Smith made his debut on August 31st, 1929 and then 19 years, 249 days later he made his final appearance on May 7th, 1949.

HE'S NO SAINT

There are only two Matt Elliotts. There was the towering, commanding presence at the back for Leicester City and then, er, there was the towering, commanding presence up front. Martin O'Neill needed all his persuasive powers to bring Elliott to Filbert Street in January, 1997. Having previously convinced Neil Lennon not to go to Coventry City – can't have been that difficult – O'Neill then secured Elliott's signature in a £1.6 million deal when he looked to be heading for Southampton. Elliott missed out on City's Coca-Cola Cup triumph because he was cup tied and instead took on the role of television summariser in the matches with Middlesbrough. He had a crucial role to play in the Premier League and it was Elliott's goal in the penultimate game against Sheffield Wednesday that finally made City safe and helped them to a ninth-place finish. City's impressive start to the following campaign – they were third after nine games – led to Elliott's call-up for Scotland. Elliott, born in Wandsworth and with an accent to match, qualified through a Scottish grandmother and was on the bench throughout his adopted country's World Cup campaign in France in the summer of 1998 after helping the Foxes finish tenth. That was followed by another tenth-place finish and an appearance in the Worthington Cup Final in the 1998-99 season. Elliott's comfort on the ball, aerial prowess and powerful shooting meant O'Neill would often push him into City's forward line and it was from this position that he powered the Foxes through to their third League Cup Final in four years. He headed home the only goal of the two-legged semi-final against Aston Villa and then bagged both in the final victory over Tranmere Rovers at Wembley in February, 2000, which earned him the man-of-the-match award and led to more chances up front – particularly after Stan Collymore suffered a broken leg in a 3-0 defeat at Derby County at the start of April. City went on to finish eighth and Elliott had his first taste of European football at club level the following season in the Uefa Cup. After O'Neill's departure, Elliott went on to lead out City in their first game at the Walkers Stadium on the opening day of the 2002-2003 season and went on to skipper Micky Adams' team to promotion back to the top flight. City were relegated the following campaign, however, and Elliott retired in January, 2005 having been troubled by a knee injury for two seasons. He made 271 appearances for City.

JOCK'S SOS

Who better to help rescue Leicester City from relegation than a player once rated the best in the world? Manager Jock Wallace took City to the Division Two championship in 1979-80 and predicted they would add the

Division One crown the following season after seeing Andy Peake's wonder goal and a Martin Henderson strike sink Liverpool at Filbert Street. The title challenge didn't materialise, however, and as well as suffering FA Cup humiliation at Exeter City in a fourth round replay, Leicester also found themselves battling against the drop from the top flight. They were one place off the foot of the table in February, 1981 with 11 games of the season left when Wallace announced his intention to bring Dutch star Johan Cruyff to the club. Although 33 years old and beyond his peak, Cruyff had once been rated as the best player in the world. He was named Player of the Tournament after the 1974 World Cup where he was part of the Netherlands side that thrilled the world with their 'Total Football' on their way to the final where they were beaten 2-1 by West Germany. He was named European Footballer of the Year in 1971, 1973 and 1974. Cruyff retired from international football in 1978 having scored an impressive 33 goals in 48 appearances for the Dutch and was without a club in February, 1981 after a spell in the North American Soccer League. The news that Leicester were bidding to sign him dominated back pages. Wallace reportedly put together a deal offering Cruyff between £4,000 and £5,000 per game and was convinced the payment would be recouped by an increase in attendances at Filbert Street. The Leicester Mercury dated February 24th, 1981 revealed that Wallace had agreed terms with Cruyff and Foxes fans held their breath. But Wallace missed out on what would have been one of the biggest signings in the club's history. Two days after he predicted Cruyff was on his way to Leicester in the Mercury, the Dutchman's agent informed Wallace that he was on his way to Spanish club Levante after a lucrative deal had been agreed. Levante reportedly offered Cruyff 50 per cent of gate receipts for their matches and that offer was too good to turn down. City battled on without him and although they claimed Arsenal's scalp at Filbert Street and then finished the season with back-to-back wins over Birmingham City and Norwich City, it wasn't enough to prevent an instant return to Division Two for Wallace's team.

RECORD BREAKERS

Leicester City's 2008-2009 season went into the record books for the wrong reasons and the right reasons. They kicked off their first campaign outside the top two divisions in English football and went on to set a new club record unbeaten run. City's last-gasp 2-1 win over Bristol Rovers at the Walkers Stadium on November 1st, 2008 kick-started a 23-match unbeaten run in League One that powered the Foxes into a 12-point lead at the top and set them on their way to promotion back to the Championship at the first attempt. The previous longest unbeaten league run had been 19 games and Nigel Pearson's team set a new record with a 1-0 win at Bristol Rovers in February, 2009 that made it 20 matches unbeaten. It took a Max Gradel goal seven minutes into injury time to extend the run seven days later and that was followed by a draw against Stockport County and a 4-0 trouncing of Cheltenham Town before the run was ended by a 2-0 defeat at Tranmere Rovers on March 11th, 2009.

THE OTHER SIDE OF THE TRACKS

Nigel Pearson, the manager at the helm when City put together their longest unbeaten run in the league, was an unlikely Leicester hero. For a start, he was born in Nottingham and then he tried to stop the Foxes claiming their first piece of silverware for 36 years. Pearson was at the heart of Middlesbrough's defence in the Coca-Cola Cup Final in 1997 which was won by Steve Claridge's extra-time strike in the replay at Hillsborough. On top of all that, Pearson then condemned City to their first season outside the top two divisions. He was in charge of the Southampton team that survived on the last day of the 2007-2008 season at City's expense. Fortunately, he made amends for all that.

THE ONLY WAY IS UP

Leicester's previous longest unbeaten run in the league had started on February 6th, 1971 with a goalless draw at Hull City. They had stretched the without-a-loss sequence to 17 games by the end of a season that finished with City lifting the Division Two championship. The Foxes then started the 1971-72 top-flight campaign with a draw at Huddersfield Town and a win over Nottingham Forest before a 2-0 defeat at Derby County.

A GAME OF CARDS

A bit of advice. If you have a late-night game of cards with Dennis Wise, make sure you sleep with one eye open afterwards. Sadly, Wise's spell with Leicester City is remembered more for the impact he had on team-mate Callum Davidson's cheekbone than the impact he had on the pitch. Wise was a legend with Chelsea where he won the FA Cup twice, along with the League Cup and the European Cup Winners' Cup and it cost City £1.6 million to prise him away from Stamford Bridge in the summer of 2001. He made his debut for Peter Taylor's team in a 5-0 opening-day defeat at home to Bolton Wanderers that wasn't exactly the perfect way to start City's final season at Filbert Street. City struggled, Taylor was sacked and Wise's continued poor form attracted plenty of criticism from the stands. At the end of the campaign, Leicester were relegated from the Premier League after six seasons in the top flight and part of the preparations for the promotion bid under Micky Adams' leadership was a pre-season tour of Finland. There the squad trained, played friendlies and had a game of cards that got a bit out of hand. Wise was sent home for inflicting a double fracture of Davidson's cheekbone after dishing out some retribution while the Scottish international lay asleep. City then announced the decision to sack Wise with two years of his contract still left to run. The club were ordered by the Football League to reinstate him and after that decision was overturned, Wise announced his intention to sue the cash-strapped club for lost earnings totalling £2.3 million. It came to nothing and Wise ended up joining Millwall with his return to City for a fixture in December, 2002 much anticipated by Foxes fans. It was another former City player who put the Lions in front with just 14 seconds on the clock. Steve Claridge shrugged apologetically when his name was read out over the Tannoy. To be fair, he simply couldn't miss the target. There was a happy ending, however, and not just for the groundsman who got a Christmas bonus when picking up the coins that had been hurled at Wise throughout. City ran out 4-1 winners with James Scowcroft finding the target twice for Adams' team. The other goals came from Matt Elliott and Paul Dickov. Wise then went on to add to his villain status at Leicester by becoming something of a hero at Midlands rivals Coventry City.

HEADING FOR THE TOP

On January 1st, 1979, Leicester City supporters headed for the Filbert Street exits talking about the teenage striker who looked destined for the top. A few probably talked about Gary Lineker as well. City boss Jock Wallace handed debuts to David Buchanan, Bobby Smith and Lineker in the 2-0 win over Oldham Athletic in Division Two and it was Buchanan who made the headlines. He was on target at the age of just 16 years and 192 days to become the club's youngest goalscorer and Smith added the other, while 18-year-old Lineker drew a blank, was dropped and had to wait three months for a wet night at Notts County to open his account for City. That scrambled effort marked the start of one of the most prolific goalscoring careers of the modern era. Never booked or sent off in 15 years as a professional, Lineker, the son of a Leicester marker stall trader, is the second highest goalscorer for England and a national hero. He first came to prominence with a 17-goal haul in Division Two in 1981-82 and the following season he became the first City player since Arthur Rowley in 1956-57 to score 25 league goals in a season as Gordon Milne's team put together a 15-match unbeaten run that helped Leicester pip Fulham for the third promotion spot. Lineker continued to flourish in the top flight and his 22-goal haul in 1983-84 earned a first England cap as a second-half substitute against Scotland at Hampden Park. The goals kept coming and after 24 the following season, Lineker was sold to Division One champions Everton in June, 1985 for £800,000. In total, he netted 103 times in 216 appearances for City and after 40 more goals in his only season with the Toffeemen, the former City of Leicester School pupil came to global prominence at the 1986 World Cup in Mexico where his six strikes earned him the Golden Boot as the tournament's highest scorer and a £2.75 million move to Barcelona. Lineker went on to score 48 times for England in 80 appearances and would have levelled Sir Bobby Charlton's record had he netted with a penalty against Brazil at Wembley in May, 1992. His final appearance for England came in that summer's European championships in Sweden after manager Graham Taylor replaced him with former City strike partner Alan Smith in a clash with the hosts. Lineker ended his playing career with former Leicester boss Gordon Milne at Nagoya Grampus Eight in Japan.

INTO EUROPE

As it turned out, Leicester City still had reason to celebrate following defeat in the 1961 FA Cup Final. Tottenham Hotspur's 2-0 win completed a league and cup double and that meant City were England's representatives in the following season's European Cup Winners' Cup. The first-round draw sent them to Irish Cup holders Glenavon and in front of a crowd of 10,000 at Windsor Park, City fell behind to Sid Weathercup's opener before easing to a 4-1 win through goals from Jimmy Walsh (2), Colin Appleton and Ken Keyworth. City went on to wrap up a 7-2 aggregate win with a 3-1 victory in the second leg at Filbert Street. Gordon Wills, Ken Keyworth and Hugh McIlmoyle were the marksmen and 10,445 were there to see it. The second round pitted City against Spanish giants Atletico Madrid and Matt Gillies' team had home advantage in the first leg. Their preparations were far from ideal with goalkeeper Gordon Banks arriving at the ground only 40 minutes before kick-off having been on the bench for England against Portugal at Wembley earlier that day. Ken Keyworth gave the majority of the 25,527 crowd reason to cheer by putting City ahead having earlier had an effort controversially ruled out, which proved to be crucial. City looked set to take the lead with them to Spain, but Mendoza popped up with a late leveller for Madrid. Gillies sprang a surprise before the second leg when his team sheet revealed that Graham Cross would spend his 18th birthday at the heart of City's defence in front of more than 50,000 fans. Cross, a goalscorer on his debut on the final day of the previous season, was making only his fourth start for City and while he impressed with a mature display, it was the performance of the officials that dominated Gillies' post-match thoughts. He was enraged by the decision to award Madrid two penalties. Banks kept out the first, but was beaten by the second and the home side went on to complete a 2-0 win and a 3-1 aggregate victory.

VIVA

City were set to go back to Spain at the end of the season to take on the Spanish national team as they prepared for the World Cup in Chile, but the FA blocked Gillies' team from playing matches in Santander and Bilbao.

WHICH GOAL?

Aston Villa defender Chris Nicholl grabbed the headlines after grabbing all the goals in the game with Leicester City at Filbert Street on March 20th, 1976. Nothing too unusual in that. Except that the game finished 2-2!

Nicholl scored two goals at both ends just seven days after Stuart Boam's own goal had gifted City a 1-0 win at Middlesbrough in Division One. A decade earlier, Graham Cross grabbed all the goals in City's 2-1 win over Nottingham Forest at Filbert Street. He made amends for putting the visitors ahead by bagging both goals for the Foxes. Leicester legend Steve Walsh holds the club record for scoring the most own goals. He scored against City seven times with his spectacular long-range effort in the 2-1 defeat at Arsenal in the Premier League on December 26th, 1997 taking him past Dai Jones and Graham Cross's tally of six own goals each.

TO BE FRANK

Walsh's team-mate Frank Sinclair also forgot which way he was kicking a few times. At the start of the 1999-2000 season, he scored an own goal in the opening-day 2-1 defeat at Arsenal, followed seven days later with another in the 2-2 draw against former club Chelsea at Filbert Street. Perhaps his most spectacular own goal came in the Premier League game at Middlesbrough in March, 2002. His back pass from 40 yards left Ian Walker stranded and was the only goal of the game as the Foxes headed for relegation. On the occasion Sinclair was supposed to put the ball past the Leicester goalkeeper, he blew it. Sinclair returned to his former club with Lincoln City for a Johnstone's Paint Trophy tie in September 2008 and after two hours of goalless and tedious football, the game went into a penalty shoot-out. As the drama reached its climax, Sinclair was handed the job of keeping the visitors in the tie and walloped his spot-kick high, wide and pretty ugly, much to the delight of City's fans behind the goal.

DOUBLE TROUBLE

City defenders Stan Milburn and Jack Froggatt shared an own goal in the 3-1 defeat at Chelsea in December, 1954. They managed to somehow simultaneously kick the ball and send it into the Foxes' net.

FLYING STARTS

Best not miss the kick-off when Matty Fryatt is in the starting line-up. He holds the record for scoring the quickest-ever goal for both Leicester City and previous club Walsall. Fryatt went into City's record books on April 15th, 2006 with a goal after just nine seconds of the home game with Preston North End in the Championship. He was also on target for Walsall after nine seconds of their clash with AFC Bournemouth on March 12th, 2005. His early goals didn't set either City or Walsall on their way to victory. Both teams were eventually beaten 2-1. Fryatt joined City from the Saddlers in January, 2006 to boost the battle against the drop from the Championship and his six goals helped fire the Foxes to safety. Twelve months later, he was almost on his way out of Filbert Street. But, in the whirlwind of signings that followed Martin Allen's appointment as City boss in the summer of 2007, perhaps the best bit of business was the transfer that didn't happen. Allen decided striker Fryatt was worth more than the £1 million Wolverhampton Wanderers bid for him and while a few months later he wasn't even worth a place in the first team, there was to be a happy ending to Fryatt's story. He scored only three goals throughout a wretched 2007-2008 season that ended with Leicester being relegated to the third tier of English football for the first time in their history. The following campaign Fryatt became City's first striker since Derek Dougan 42 years earlier to net 20 goals before Christmas. He reached the milestone with back-to-back hat-tricks at the Walkers Stadium against Dagenham & Redbridge in the FA Cup second round, and Southend United in League One.

TEN TEN TEN

Before Fryatt's whirlwind goal, the record for City's fastest strike was shared by three players with a time of ten seconds. On March 28th, 1953 Tom Dryburgh got City off to the perfect start against Swansea City at Filbert Street and Leicester went on to win 2-1. Eight months later, Derek Hines' goal after ten seconds set City on their way to a 9-2 demolition of visitors Lincoln City. Hines added four more goals in the Division Two clash. City went on to win the title and a crucial win as their next Division Two championship-winning season was clinched with the help of a quick strike. Ian McNeill rifled home after ten seconds of the clash at title rivals Nottingham Forest on March 30th, 1957 to set up a crucial 2-1 victory.

MATT THE GENT

Who says nice guys always finish last? A criticism aimed at Matt Gillies during his decade in charge of Leicester City was that he was "too gentlemanly" for the cut and thrust of professional football. But that didn't prevent him becoming one of the most successful managers in the club's history. Gillies kept the team in the top flight for ten years, took them to Wembley for the FA Cup Finals in 1961 and 1963 and twice led them to League Cup Finals. He first came to Leicester as a player. After spending a decade with Bolton Wanderers and captaining them in the First Division, Gillies joined City for £9,500 in January, 1952 and boss Norman Bullock's investment proved to be wise. Gillies had a key role at the heart of City's defence in the side that won the Second Division championship in 1953-54 – missing only three of the 42 games – but lost his place during the following season's struggle. Gillies made a total of 111 appearances for City and was also known for his tactical insights. He had already turned down the offer of a coaching job in Italy when he became coach at Filbert Street in April, 1956. Following manager David Halliday's departure in November 1958, with City struggling in the top flight, Gillies took on the caretaker manager's job and City's instant revival under his leadership led to him landing the job permanently two months later. His transfer dealings were shrewd – the £7,000 he paid Chesterfield for goalkeeper Gordon Banks was considered a gamble at the time – and Gillies became the first Leicester manager to guide the team to silverware when he led them to the League Cup in 1963-64 with victory over Stoke City. The following season, Leicester were beaten in the final by Chelsea. Gillies suffered with a stress-related illness while he was at Filbert Street, but his departure in November, 1968 was prompted by the sacking of his long-serving coach Bert Johnson. Gillies was quick to praise Johnson's input during his decade in charge and followed him out of Filbert Street after he was dismissed. Although the spell in charge at Nottingham Forest that followed was unsuccessful, Gillies did bring Martin O'Neill to the City Ground and the switch to Leicester's East Midlands rivals did nothing to harm his place in the affections of Foxes supporters. His death in December, 1998 led to a perfectly-observed minute's silence before the Premier League game against Blackburn Rovers.

POST-HORN GALLOP

Leicester City started a new era at the Walkers Stadium on August 10th, 2002 and many fans were fuming before the game had even kicked off! City marked the switch from Filbert Street to their plush new home with a game against Watford in the second tier of English football in front of a crowd of 31,022. Many among them were stunned when City ran onto the pitch for the historic fixture and there was no post-horn gallop played over the public address. That probably sparked more post-match conversations than the stadium or the 2-0 win over the Hornets secured by Micky Adams' team by a brace from striker Brian Deane. The tune had accompanied Leicester teams onto the pitch since 1941 and was dispensed with following the move from Filbert Street. Not for long it wasn't. City fans rang the club and *Leicester Mercury* offices demanding the tune was brought back and Foxes officials obliged and the post-horn gallop was soon being blasted out again. It didn't do the team any harm. They went on to win 16 home games in their first season at the Walkers Stadium – setting a new club record on their way to promotion to the Premier League. The post-horn gallop was chosen as a reference to Leicestershire's hunting tradition and dates back to the 19th century when it was used as a coachman's tune to signal mail was arriving. According to the internet, the tune is also a traditional finale at formal dinner functions.

LIVE VERSION

The club went a step further at the start of the 2003-2004 season. They brought in Henry Shipley to play the post-horn gallop while wearing riding boots and jodhpurs. Henry had previously played in brass bands that performed at Filbert Street in the 1930s and 1940s and enthusiastically blew his bugle to accompany the Leicester team's arrival for home games for two seasons. The club decided after that to change their pre-match entertainment and that meant the end for Henry and his bugle! He was told he would no longer be able to play the post-horn gallop when City ran out and instead was offered a slot 15 minutes before kick-off. Henry declined because he felt the ground would be half full when he played the song and that it wouldn't be worth his effort.

SEEING RED

Leicester Fosse showed plenty of fighting spirit at Bolton Wanderers in March, 1905. Bob Pollock and Ike Evenson showed too much of it and both were dismissed for fisticuffs. Incredibly, Fosse hung onto the lead given to them by Arthur Collins' strike to win the Division Two clash. There have been three other occasions when two Leicester players have been sent off in the same game. Kevin MacDonald and Alan Young ran the bath water early during the 2-1 loss at Brighton & Hove Albion in April, 1981 that confirmed relegation from the First Division for Jock Wallace's team and equally dispiriting was the double dismissal at Millwall in the FA Cup a decade later. City headed to The Den without a win in the competition for five years and Paul Ramsey and Steve Walsh were sent off as the Lions cancelled out Tony James' opener for Leicester with goals in the 86th and 89th minutes. David Lowe and Brian Carey were dismissed in the 2-1 defeat at Wimbledon in the Premier League in September, 1994. Lowe had earlier grabbed the Foxes' goal. City had a club record eight players dismissed during the 1994-95 season, which ended in relegation.

THE FIRST

Willie Freebairn was the first Leicester player to be sent off. The Fosse full back was dismissed in the Division Two clash at Lincoln City in April, 1897 for abusing a linesman. Freebairn had earlier scored in the 2-1 defeat.

FILBERT FIRST

David Walker went into the record books as the first player to be dismissed at Filbert Street. He was sent off against Clapham Orient in April, 1911, but his goal still proved to be the winner in a 2-1 victory for Fosse.

FILBERT FLOP

Ade Akinbiyi was a £5 million flop for Leicester City and his career at Burnley got off to the worst possible start following his £600,000 transfer from Stoke City. Akinbiyi was sent off just two minutes after stepping off the bench to make his Clarets debut against Sunderland in March, 2005. He was given his marching orders for trying to elbow and head-butt George McCartney.

TAKING A DIP

Steve Lynex is remembered for his place in Leicester City's 1980s strikeforce alongside Gary Lineker and Alan Smith – and his breaststroke! Lynex, an exciting winger who bagged 60 goals in 240 games, got the chance to show off his swimming skills at a soaking Filbert Street on October 15th, 1983. City and Southampton splashed around in front of the Match of the Day cameras in atrocious conditions until the officials abandoned the game after 22 minutes. Perhaps the moment that helped decide the officials to end the farce came when Lynex slid face first through a puddle and simulated a breaststroke! Harder to accept for Leicester fans must have been the decision to abandon the home game against Newcastle United in February, 1936 with City leading 2-1 and just 10 minutes left on the clock.

FILBERT STREET ABANDONMENTS

City's path to the FA Cup Final in 1961 was delayed by the weather. Their fourth-round tie against Bristol City at Filbert Street was abandoned at half-time because of a waterlogged pitch with the score goalless and three days later, City were 5-1 winners. Thirty-one years later, the sides met at the fourth-round stage of the FA Cup at Filbert Street after the game was given the go ahead despite severe frost and the Robins coped better to run out 2-1 winners in front of the Match of the Day cameras. In total, six games were abandoned at Filbert Street and the club's first game to fall victim to the weather came at Darwen on December 30th, 1894. The game was abandoned after just two minutes when the goal posts were blown down by a gale. They ended up playing a friendly that Fosse lost 6-0 before the sides met again 16 days later – and the conditions weren't much better! The referee allowed one set of goal posts to be moved onto the adjacent cricket pitch and Darwen's players took measures to combat the severe elements. They strapped their boots in swathes of felt to cope with the mud, puddles and sand that covered much of the pitch and they dealt with the conditions better than Fosse. Darwen led 7-0 at half-time and went on to win the game 8-2. City fared better when their clash at Reading in the 2002-2003 season had to be played again. The original fixture on January 1st, 2003 was washed out at half-time with the scoreline blank and Leicester went on to win the rearranged fixture 3-1 on their way to promotion.

WHAT A START!

Jimmy Bloomfield was appointed Leicester City manager in the summer of 1971 – and saw his new team lift a trophy after his first game in charge. Arsenal winning the league and FA Cup double in 1970-71 meant the following season's Charity Shield curtain raiser was between newly-promoted Leicester and Liverpool, who had lost to the Gunners in the FA Cup Final.

The meeting at Filbert Street was settled by Steve Whitworth's strike – his only goal in 400 appearances for City in all competitions! Bloomfield had got the job after the departure of Frank O'Farrell to Manchester United and set about putting together one of the most exciting teams in City's history. His first signing was Jon Sammels from Arsenal after the player admitted he was "95 per cent" certain to join Ipswich Town. Sammels remembers Bloomfield's footballing philosophy. "Jimmy didn't fill your head with tactics and what he wanted you to do," he said. "He put together a skilful team and didn't complicate things. He used to say: 'I've brought you here because you are good players, so go out there and play.' We played football the right way." Bloomfield made his intentions clear with the further additions of Keith Weller, Alan Birchenall and after a 12th place finish in his first season in charge, he brought in Frank Worthington after a move to Liverpool fell through because of a failed medical. City finished 16th in 1972-73 and the following season, they were in contention for honours. They were fourth in January after a 5-0 thumping of Ipswich Town, with Worthington the hat-trick hero, and the following month, their 4-0 win at Luton Town in the fifth round of the FA Cup led to comparisons with world champions Brazil! Leicester went on to finish ninth and lose to Liverpool in an FA Cup semi-final replay. They finished seventh in 1975-76 and the following season, City ended up 11th despite a disappointing spell of only one win from their final ten games that included a 5-0 humbling at home to West Bromwich Albion. Less than a week after the end of the season, Bloomfield resigned and one of the club's most exciting eras was over. Bloomfield still had a role to play in Leicester's future. He was in charge of the Leyton Orient side beaten by Larry May's header on the final day of the 1979-80 season which resulted in Jock Wallace's City being promoted to the top flight as Division Two champions. Jimmy died in April, 1983.

OUT OF LUCK

Patrick Kisnorbo's scrapbook is unlikely to have many cuttings from the 2007-08 season. He was wrongfully dismissed twice during a wretched campaign that ended with his Leicester City team being relegated outside the top two divisions of English football for the first time in their history. City were outside the drop zone when they headed to Ipswich Town in December, 2007 and with six minutes to go before the break at Portman Road, the scores were level at 1-1. Iain Hume cancelled out Pablo Counago's opener for the home side and the Town striker was then involved in the game's turning point. He went down under a challenge from Kisnorbo that won the ball outside the penalty area. Despite that, referee Phil Joslin took the advice of his linesman and decided to dismiss Kisnorbo and award Ipswich a penalty. Alan Lee converted the spot kick, Ipswich added a third in the second half through Jonathan Waters and then the Football Association decided to rescind Kisnorbo's red card. Unfortunately, it happened all over again later in the same season. There were just ten minutes gone in struggling City's clash at Sheffield United in April, 2008 when Billy Sharp took a tumble and Kisnorbo was red carded by referee Mike Pike after he had pointed to the penalty spot. James Beattie stepped up to convert the penalty and went on to complete a hat-trick in just seven minutes that left the Foxes deep in trouble at the bottom of the Championship. City boss Ian Holloway was fuming afterwards. "Sort your life out, Billy Sharp," he said. "You ain't on my Christmas list, you little turkey. That was the biggest blunder I've seen in a long time." At least Holloway was handed a boost a few days later with the news that Kisnorbo's red card had been wiped off and that meant he would be eligible for the final four games of the season. Kisnorbo didn't finish the campaign, though. City needed to beat Sheffield Wednesday at the Walkers Stadium in their penultimate game of the season to secure their survival and all was going well when Iain Hume gave the Foxes an early lead. But they suffered a massive setback on 20 minutes when Kisnorbo was stretchered off with a broken leg and the Owls went on to win 3-1 and beat the drop. Eight days later, City's proud record of never having played outside the top two divisions in English football was ended following a goalless draw at Stoke City.

GETTING SHIRTY

Leicester City's away strip in the 1983-84 season was so unlucky that they only recorded a single victory wearing it – and still ended up losing the game! City's ghastly green and gold strip did not bring Gordon Milne's team much luck. They were 2-0 winners at Chelsea in the second leg of their League Cup second round tie in October, which left the scores level on aggregate following City's 2-0 defeat at Filbert Street. Leicester then lost the game on penalties and never won another game in the strip before it was ditched at the end of the season.

BATTLE OF THE FOSSES

Leicester Fosse kicked off their first-ever match against Syston Fosse on November 1st, 1884 wearing black jerseys with a diagonal blue sash and white trousers. Although the kit lasted only two seasons, the shirt made a comeback in City's 2002-2003 Premier League campaign as part of the change strip for Micky Adams' top-flight team.

CAMBRIDGE COLOURS?

Fosse wore a new strip for the start of the 1886-87 season. They wore chocolate and blue halved shirts and white shorts. There was another change four seasons later with Fosse kicking off their debut season in the Midland League wearing white shirts and dark shorts. That kit lasted until the 1899-1900 campaign when Leicester took to the pitch in Cambridge blue shirts and dark blue shorts. The club switched kits again for the 1901-02 season. Fosse wore dark blue shirts with light blue collars and sleeves and white shorts which was worn for two seasons. In the summer of 1903, the club decided to change to a strip of blue shirts and white shorts that were established as Leicester's colours.

NOT ALRIGHT

City have ditched their traditional blue-and-white strip on a couple of occasions. They wore an all-white kit in 1972-73 that proved to be unpopular and lasted only that season. Then there was the all-blue strip worn in 1966-67 and again in 1992-93. On the latter occasion, it lasted for four seasons.

A TROPHY AT LAST

Eighty years of hurt for Leicester City supporters ended at Filbert Street on April 22nd, 1964. Previously beaten in three FA Cup Finals, City lifted their first major trophy since being formed in 1884 with skipper Colin Appleton getting his muddy mitts on the League Cup after a 4-3 aggregate win against Stoke City. Football League secretary Alan Hardaker could hardly contain his excitement. He enthused: "This is the cure for most of soccer's ills… more games like this." Admittedly, the League Cup was his idea, but there was no denying the drama served up by City on their way to the trophy. Wins over Aldershot, Tranmere Rovers, Gillingham and Norwich City clinched a two-legged semi-final against West Ham United. City were 4-3 winners at Filbert Street and goals from Frank McLintock and Bobby Roberts wrapped up a 6-3 aggregate win and took Matt Gillies' team through to the final to face Stoke. Leicester travelled to the Potteries for the first leg and it took Gordon Banks' acrobatics and the woodwork to keep out Stoke in the first half. Banks could do nothing to prevent Keith Bebbington lashing Stoke into a 62nd minute lead and it took a superb piece of opportunism from David Gibson to ensure City went into the second leg level. A clearance was deflected into his path and Gibson lifted a perfectly-weighted chip over the goalkeeper's head and into the net from 20 yards to leave Stoke stunned. Leicester were soon ahead in the second leg played seven days later. Mike Stringfellow latched onto John Sjoberg's clearance to thump home the sixth-minute opener and after Stoke levelled two minutes after the restart, City stepped up a gear. Gibson's near-post header put them back in front and Howard Riley's left-foot shot made it 3-1. Stoke's second goal in injury time came too late to deny City. The following season, City got through to the League Cup Final again and this time they met Chelsea in the two-legged final after wins over Peterborough United, Grimsby Town, Crystal Palace, Coventry City and Plymouth Argyle. The quarter-final win at the Sky Blues was by an 8-1 scoreline and must have been unpleasant viewing for Ken Keyworth. He completed a move from Leicester to Coventry on the day of the match! The first leg of the final ended in a 3-2 defeat at Chelsea with Colin Appleton and Jimmy Goodfellow on target before a goalless second leg at Filbert Street meant the trophy headed to London.

GETTING HOT AND SWEATY

For Leicester City fans, the last home game of the season means sunshine, tension and The Birch looking shattered! For every season since 1979-80, Alan Birchenall MBE has set off on a charity run around the Filbert Street and Walkers Stadium pitches, dragging some of football's biggest names along with him including David Beckham and Graeme Souness. All have joined him for a lap or two before kick-off and helped raise more than £700,000 for 70 charities across Leicestershire. The Birch was awarded the MBE for his charity work in 2004 and five years later, he was named an Honorary Freeman of the City of Leicester. He admits to being "quite embarrassed" by the accolades that have followed since he hung up his boots. Birchenall, of course, was part of one of the most exciting teams in Leicester's history. Along with Jon Sammels and Keith Weller, he was among the first signings made by Jimmy Bloomfield after he became City manager in the summer of 1971. He was an energetic striker and midfielder and the left foot that he dubbed 'The Claw' memorably sent the ball crashing into the Leeds United net at Filbert Street in October, 1973. He found the target 14 times in 183 appearances for the Foxes and went on to rejoin the club in a public relations role he was clearly well suited to. There was nothing in the job description about running around the pitch before the last game of the season, though. That came about after a member of the Supporters' Club approached The Birch during the 1979-80 season and asked for help raising funds for charity. "I didn't fancy abseiling or chucking myself out of a plane," said Birchenall, "but I had only just finished playing, so I was still fairly fit and came up with the idea of running round the pitch for 90 minutes before the last home game." He has been doing it ever since, but admitted: "I've lost count of the times I've said this is the last run." The most laps Birchenall has completed is 63 and he has never ran less than 50 – and he usually does it in sweltering conditions. "It's usually the hottest day of the year when I do the run," he laughed. "I can only remember one year when it wasn't baking hot." The Birch remembers with fondness the year when £75,000 was raised to help former team-mate Keith Weller receive cancer treatment that prolonged his life.

POOR STARTS

Leicester City's future and past combined to ensure the Foxes had the worst possible start to the 1983-84 season in Division One. Martin O'Neill belted home the opener for Notts County at Filbert Street and former City striker Trevor Christie fired home a hat-trick to secure a 4-0 win for the Magpies. City went on to survive the drop despite losing their first six games, while O'Neill made amends for that goal by becoming one of the best managers in Leicester's history.

TROTTER THRASHING

Leicester had a similarly disastrous start to the 2001-2002 campaign – their last at Filbert Street. Bolton Wanderers left with the points after a 5-0 thrashing and City went on to be relegated from the Premier League.

TAKE THAT

Legend Steve Walsh won't remember the opening day of the 1987-88 season with any fondness after breaking the jaw of Shrewsbury Town striker David Geddis and being handed an 11-match suspension.

RAMPANT ROWLEY

The opening day of the 1950-51 season marked the start of a glorious Leicester career. Arthur Rowley made his debut, scoring the winning goal in a 3-2 win at Bury. He went on to score 265 goals for the Foxes.

EXPLOSIVE

Leicester City were quick out of the blocks at the start of the 1971-72 season. Already boosted by winning the Charity Shield with victory over Liverpool at Filbert Street, they started the Division One campaign under Jimmy Bloomfield by scoring the fastest goal of the opening day's fixtures. Ally Brown was on target with just 45 seconds on the clock at Huddersfield Town and City went on to claim a point from a 1-1 draw.

TOFFEE TIME

Gary Lineker's debut for Division One champions Everton on the opening day of the 1985-86 season was ruined by Mark Bright's brace that fired Leicester City to a 3-1 win at Filbert Street. Bobby Smith also netted for Leicester.

M69 DERBY

The footballing cities of Leicester and Coventry are separated by the M69 and much more besides. They simply don't get on and as with any rivalry, there's plenty of history to it. The sides were locked in a battle against the drop from the top division in 1968-69 and the manner in which their derby battle at Highfield Road was decided didn't do an awful lot for relations between the rivals. Leicester had booked their place in their fourth FA Cup Final of the decade with a 1-0 win over holders West Bromwich Albion at Hillsborough and then three days later they headed to Coventry for an April Fool's Day relegation clash that wiped the smile off City's faces after the euphoria of the win over the Baggies. The game was goalless with just seven minutes to go. Foxes substitute Brian Greenhalgh was brought down as he charged towards goal and the referee awarded a penalty. The ball was placed on the spot and then the referee consulted his linesman and much to Leicester's astonishment, changed his mind about the penalty award and instead decided to give the Sky Blues a free kick. City were deflated and while they protested and rued their luck, the Sky Blues made the most of their good fortune to race up the other end where Neil Martin was on target within seconds of the Foxes having placed the ball on the penalty spot! Leicester went on to be relegated and lose the FA Cup Final, while the Sky Blues survived by the skin of their teeth. Fast forward almost two decades to the final day of the 2007-2008 season and City and Coventry were fighting it out to avoid the drop into the third tier of English football. On an afternoon of unbelievable tension, the survival scrap went down to the closing minutes and with relegation rivals Southampton winning against Sheffield United and the Sky Blues losing at Charlton Athletic, City knew grabbing a winning goal at Stoke City would save themselves and send Coventry down. But the goal didn't come and it was the Foxes who suffered the drop. City can take satisfaction, however, from recording one of the biggest wins in their history at Highfield Road. Ken Keyworth made the switch from City to the Sky Blues on December 1st, 1964 and then saw his former employers beat his new club 8-1 in a League Cup fifth round tie with two goals apiece for Mike Stringfellow, Billy Hodgson and Richie Norman.

BUST UPS

Rewind to December, 1954 and we find Leicester City struggling at the bottom of Division One. The club's directors asked manager Norman Bullock to resign at the end of the season, but events in a Whitley Bay hotel brought forward his departure from Filbert Street. After a 2-0 defeat at Newcastle United in February, 1955, Bullock was involved in an incident that led to him resigning immediately while inside-forward Johnny Morris was handed a 14-day suspension. The pair had a history of conflict with Morris being briefly transfer-listed during pre-season after requesting to train with former club Derby County. Morris ended up staying with City, but his conflict with Bullock clearly had not been resolved. Unsurprisingly, City suffered the drop at the end of the season, but their points total of 37 was the highest achieved by a relegated team since 1937-38.

VOTED OUT

The biggest match in the opening weeks of the 1999-2000 season was City boss Martin O'Neill against Barrie Pierpoint, the club's Chief Executive Officer. The simmering conflict between the football and commercial sides of the club reached boiling point in September, 2000 when club chairman John Elsom and Sir Rodney Walker, chairman of the plc, both resigned. That led to an EGM being called and Elsom and Walker had the backing of both

O'Neill and Leicester legend Gary Lineker and their challenge came from the so-called 'Gang of Four'. They became a gang of one following the resignation of Roy Parker, Gilbert Kinch and Philip Smith at the EGM and Pierpoint was voted off the board. Elsom put together a new board of directors that included former chairman Martin George and ex-director Bill Shooter.

HYPERBOLE

A bust up between City chairman Milan Mandaric and boss Martin Allen led to the latter leaving the club in August, 2007 after just 96 days and four games in charge. Quite why they fell out will probably never be known, but another book could be filled with all the rumours that went around Leicester after Allen left the club. The incident most widely believed to have signalled the end for Allen was his apparent reluctance to sign former Chelsea striker Jimmy Floyd Hasselbaink after Mandaric had lined up the transfer.

FILBERT FOX

Filbert Fox, Leicester City's fluffy, feisty mascot, made his debut in 1992-93 and has been conducting the crowd's chants and mischief-making ever since. He has brought along girlfriend Vicky Vixen to matches and Cousin Dennis has also made a few appearances. When he isn't watching his favourite football team or doing good deeds in the local community, Filbert is winning awards. In February, 2009, Filbert scooped the Leicester Mercury's Mascot of the Year award for the third successive year – and he earned his trophy the hard way. He took on rivals including Charlie Fox from Leicestershire County Cricket Club and Leicester Tiger from, er, Leicester Tigers at 10-pin bowling, shooting basketball hoops and then a test of football dribbling skills. At the end of it all, Filbert was the winner.

OTHER MASCOTS

Unlike some other mascots, Filbert Fox has managed to steer clear of major controversy. In January, 2006, Wolverhampton Wanderers' mascot Wolfie famously came to blows with one of Bristol City's Three Little Pigs at Ashton Gate and Swansea City's Cyril The Swan has faced a charge of bringing the game into disrepute. Cyril was hauled in front of a three-man commission at the Welsh FA in April, 1999 after the referee at Swansea's FA Cup clash with Millwall took exception to his celebration of a goal by his team. He was banished from the touchline, the club were fined £1,000 and a nine-foot tall swan left the hearing to face the press! Cyril is well loved in Swansea and Hartlepool United's mascot H'Angus The Monkey is so popular in his home town that he was voted mayor in 2002! H'Angus takes his name from a famous incident in the town's history. In the early 19th century, British forces battled to stop Napoleon and his French forces invading and when a monkey was washed ashore from a shipwreck off the Hartlepool coast, he was hanged by locals fearing he was a French spy. The good folk of Hartlepool have since been known as 'monkey hangers'. H'Angus The Monkey made his debut at Hartlepool's Victoria Ground in 1999 and became so popular that the club backed H'Angus – or rather Stuart Drummond who wore the costume – to run for mayor. "Vote H'Angus" implored the campaign posters: "He gives a monkey's." Incredibly, he won and made headlines all over the world.

TEARS UNDER THE TOWERS

At the age of 21, David Nish became the youngest player to captain a team in the FA Cup Final when he led out Leicester City at Wembley in April, 1969. Ninety minutes or so later, he became the fourth Foxes skipper to suffer defeat in the domestic game's biggest final. City's preparations for their fourth final – and third of the decade following defeats against Tottenham Hotspur and Manchester United in 1961 and 1963 respectively – were far from ideal. They were scrapping for survival at the bottom of Division One after only one win in their previous eight games and boss Frank O'Farrell had injury worries. John Sjoberg was ruled out through injury, while Len Glover played despite not appearing to be fully fit and David Gibson had to pass a late fitness test. It took some determined defending to keep out Manchester City in the opening minutes and then Allan Clarke helped get the Foxes into the game. His rasping shot was superbly saved by Harry Dowd and from the resulting corner, Rodney Fern's cross flashed across goal and Manchester City breathed a sigh of relief. They did so again moments later when Peter Rodrigues shot just wide from five yards out. The cross proved to be costly. In the 23rd minute, Mike Summerbee cut the ball back from the right-hand byeline and Neil Young's sweetly-struck shot flew past Peter Shilton's fingertips and into the top corner. The *Sports Mercury* reported that night: "It was rather ironic that Leicester should withstand the early sustained pressure and then go behind just as they seemed to be getting a grip on the game." Inspired by Clarke, City had their chances after the break and Andy Lochhead missed the best of them. His miscued shot sent the ball over the crossbar when he was well placed just a few yards from goal. That was City's best chance of an equaliser and although beaten at the final whistle, at least they had the satisfaction of having the game's outstanding player in their side. Clarke, who cost City a then British transfer record fee of £150,000 when he joined from Fulham the previous summer and had netted the only goal in the semi-final win over holders West Bromwich Albion, was named man of the match. The result sent an eight-year-old Gary Lineker sobbing all the way back home to Leicester and that night's *Sports Mercury* reported: "Manchester City were clearly the more polished, assured side and deserved their victory."

THE START OF AN ERA

On the morning of December 17th, 1995, Martin O'Neill was Norwich City's manager and Mike Walker was the red-hot favourite to take over at Filbert Street after Mark McGhee walked out to join Wolverhampton Wanderers. All that changed on a dramatic day. After a bust-up with Norwich chairman Robert Chase, O'Neill quit as Norwich boss just hours before the Canaries took on City at Filbert Street. Walker was at the game in the role of television analyst and there was plenty to analyse as City overturned a 2-0 deficit to snatch a 3-2 win with Emile Heskey grabbing the winner. Five days later, O'Neill was named Leicester's new manager and one of the most successful eras in the club's history began. Not that there was much indication of the thrills to follow in the opening weeks of O'Neill's reign. City were dumped out of the FA Cup by Manchester City after a 5-0 thumping at Maine Road, crowd favourite Julian Joachim was sold to Aston Villa and after achieving his first win as Leicester boss at the tenth attempt at McGhee's Wolves, O'Neill came under fire from some fans after a defeat at home to Sheffield United on March 30th. Three days later, City kick-started their promotion charge with a win at Charlton Athletic courtesy of Steve Claridge's first goal for the Foxes and four days later, Iwan Roberts was the goal hero at Crystal Palace. City went on to end the season with four straight wins to secure a play-off spot. Garry Parker got the only goal of the two-legged semi-final against Stoke City and the Foxes were back in the Premier League after Claridge's last-gasp goal beat Crystal Palace in the play-off final at Wembley. Tipped for relegation the following season by the bookies, City, boosted by the arrival of Matt Elliott from Oxford United, finished ninth and claimed their first trophy for 33 years. After City and Middlesbrough battled out a 1-1 draw in the Coca-Cola Cup Final at Wembley, Leicester won the replay at Hillsborough thanks to Claridge's extra-time strike. Under O'Neill's management, Leicester went on to secure four successive top-10 finishes in the Premier League and reach two more cup finals. They were beaten by Tottenham Hotspur in the 1999 Worthington Cup Final and the following season, were back at Wembley to lift the trophy after a 2-1 win over Tranmere Rovers. O'Neill left at the end of the 1999-2000 season to join Celtic and soon ended Rangers' domination of Scottish football.

PROMOTED ON THE BEACH

The battle for promotion in 1982-83 went to the final day of the season and beyond. Leicester City's players had their feet up and were enjoying the sunshine on their end-of-season break when they finally discovered what league they would be playing in the following campaign. Back then, there were three automatic promotion places up for grabs and City looked set to miss out. They showed some promise with a 6-0 demolition of Carlisle United secured by hat-tricks from Gary Lineker and Steve Lynex, and Gordon

Milne's team went on to kick-start their charge in front of the lowest home league gate at Filbert Street since the war. There were just 6,155 fans there in February, 1983 to watch Gary Lineker's double fire City to a 3-2 win over Shrewsbury Town that took them up to fourth. Four days later, City followed with a 5-0 thumping of promotion rivals Wolverhampton Wanderers that included a thunderbolt from Alan Smith and two goals from Steve Lynex. City kept the run going. Lineker became the first Leicester player since 1957 to net 25 times in a season with a brace in the 3-2 win over Rotherham United that stretched the unbeaten run to ten games and set up a crucial trip to third-placed Fulham. Ian Wilson was City's hero with a shot that bobbled into the net to secure three priceless points at Craven Cottage. Leicester went on to snatch third spot from the Cottagers with just two games remaining in the season. They tightened their grip on the final promotion place with a 2-1 win at Oldham Athletic. Robbie Jones marked his debut with the goal that put City on their way to victory and left them the favourites to go up on the final day of the season. City took on relegation-threatened Burnley in front of a bumper crowd of 29,453 at Filbert Street knowing that victory would secure promotion. They could only draw 0-0, but defeat for Fulham at Derby County meant that would be enough for the Foxes. City celebrated at the final whistle and then waited for their promotion to be confirmed after a controversial ending at the Baseball Ground. The referee had ended the game 75 seconds early after a pitch invasion by Rams fans and Fulham demanded that the game be replayed. The Football League decided to hold an enquiry and ruled that the result should stand, so City were promoted after ending the season with a 15-match unbeaten run.

THE TELETEXT STRIKER

If Leicester City's players and supporters needed any added confidence before the FA Cup quarter-final against Wycombe Wanderers in March, 2001, they only had to look at Teletext. There they would find Wycombe boss Lawrie Sanchez appealing for unattached strikers to contact him after an injury crisis robbed him of eight forwards. Roy Essandoh's agent read the story – which had been initially posted on the club's website – contacted Sanchez and so started the beginning of the end for Leicester boss Peter Taylor. City were red-hot favourites going into the contest. They had beaten York City, Aston Villa and Bristol City to reach the quarter-finals and seven days before the visit of Wycombe, they beat Liverpool 2-0 at Filbert Street to lift them up to fourth in the Premier League. Wycombe were struggling a couple of divisions below, but frustrated City in the first half and it took a flying save from Leicester goalkeeper Simon Royce to keep out Steve Brown's long-range shot. Five minutes after the interval, Brown helped put Wycombe ahead. His free kick picked out Paul McCarthy to head home and City suffered another blow on the hour when Robbie Savage had to limp off. But they were level on 67 minutes when Muzzy Izzet converted Darren Eadie's cross and most of a 21,969 crowd breathed a sigh of relief. There was more drama to come and when Wycombe had a 78th minute penalty appeal turned down after Brown's cross was blocked by Stefan Oakes, boss Sanchez was so incensed that his protests led to him being sent from the dugout. Sanchez, no stranger to FA Cup romance having scored Wimbledon's winner against Liverpool in the 1988 final, watched the rest of the match on a television and saw the game come to an astonishing climax. Deep into injury time, Wycombe had a corner that was nodded across goal to Essandoh and he jumped unmarked to steer his header past a flat-footed Royce and into the top corner in front of a stunned Kop. Brown was rather churlishly sent off for his celebrations and seconds later, City were out. It was a shocking upset and worse was to follow for City as their season fell apart. They suffered a club record eight successive defeats in the Premier League. The run was ended by a 4-2 hammering of Tottenham Hotspur at Filbert Street before the season ended with a 3-1 defeat at Leeds United which meant City finished the season 13th having been top in October.

DOWN TO THE WIRE

The battle for First Division survival in 1985-86 went all the way to the last game of the season. Not that anybody seemed to care. Unthinkable though it may seem now, there were just 13,171 fans at Filbert Street on May 3rd, 1986 to see the relegation scrap reach its conclusion. Gordon Milne's Leicester City needed to beat Newcastle United and hope relegation rivals Ipswich Town slipped up at Sheffield Wednesday to stay in Division One. City went into the game having taken just one point from their previous four games – their last win had come at Ipswich – but Ali Mauchlen walloped home the opener from long range and Ian Banks netted the second from the penalty spot to secure a 2-0 win. That was enough. Ipswich were beaten at Hillsborough resulting in their relegation alongside West Bromwich Albion and Birmingham City.

SAME OLD SAME OLD

Twelve months later, City had a new manager and a similar problem. Bryan Hamilton was at the helm with Milne moved into a general manager's role and the partnership got off to a good start with City climbing as high as ninth in October with a 3-1 win over Nottingham Forest at Filbert Street. Then it all went wrong. Seven days after that, City were beaten 2-0 at Charlton Athletic and their slide down the table was underway. Although there were back-to-back four-goal maulings of Queens Park Rangers and Manchester City in the space of four days at Filbert Street, Leicester's away form was appalling. They suffered 17 straight defeats on their travels, so it was far from ideal that their Division One fate would be decided on the final day of the season at Oxford United. City ended their wretched away form with a goalless draw at the Manor Ground, but it wasn't enough to keep them up.

SORRY BORO

The following season, City were involved in more final-day drama – and this time it was at the other end of the table. Unfortunately, it was Middlesbrough rather than Leicester going for promotion and goals from Peter Weir and Gary McAllister secured a 2-1 win for David Pleat's team at Ayresome Park and denied the Teessiders a First Division berth.

ENGLAND EXPECTS

Back in 1974, England came calling for Leicester City's stars. City team-mates Peter Shilton, Keith Weller and Frank Worthington all lined up for their country in friendlies against Northern Ireland, Scotland and Argentina. They had starred in a City side that boss Jimmy Bloomfield steered to ninth place in Division One in 1973-74, and through to the semi-finals of the FA Cup before bowing out to Liverpool after a replay. Weller got the only goal in the 1-0 win over Northern Ireland with a rare header and Worthington was on target in the 2-2 draw with Argentina. England were beaten 2-0 at Hampden Park. David Nish, who had spent six years with City before leaving for East Midlands rivals Derby County, was also in the teams that faced Northern Ireland and Scotland.

THE BIGGEST STAGE

Gordon Banks, of course, was between the posts for England when they lifted the World Cup in 1966 and two decades later, Leicester players were in the thick of the action again. Gary Lineker and Peter Shilton, both born in Leicester and former City players, had key roles at opposite ends of the pitch in Mexico in 1986. Lineker's six goals earned him the Golden Boot for being the competition's top scorer, while Shilton was in goal throughout the tournament and beaten by Maradona's infamous 'Hand of God' goal in the quarter-final defeat against Argentina. Lineker and Shilton also represented their country at the next World Cup in Italy four years later when England reached the semi-finals before bowing out to Germany on penalties.

HIGHS & LOWS

Horace Bailey became the first Leicester player to represent England when Fosse's goalkeeper lined up for his country in the 7-1 thrashing of Wales in Wrexham in March, 1908. Bailey was described by the Leicester Mercury's football reporter as having "an eye like a hawk and cat-like agility" and he helped the United Kingdom XI strike gold at the 1908 Olympics. He made five appearances for England – shipping just three goals and watching 35 fly in at the other end – and if they were the highlights of his career, the lowlight came when he was in goal for Fosse in the record 12-0 defeat against Nottingham Forest in April, 1909.

BOYS FROM BRAZIL

According to *The Sunday Times*, it was just like watching Brazil – on a muddy pitch in Luton. At the final whistle of the FA Cup fifth round tie at Kenilworth Road on February 16th, 1974, the reporter breathlessly told his copy taker he hadn't seen anything like it since the last time he watched Brazil. Believe it or not, he was talking about Leicester City. After Frank O'Farrell left for Manchester United, Jimmy Bloomfield took on the Leicester manager's job in the summer of 1971 and won a trophy in his first game in charge! City lifted the FA Charity Shield with a 1-0 win over Liverpool in a game that pitted the champions of the top two divisions together and Bloomfield went on to put together a team that thrilled the nation. Despite that, before the FA Cup tie at Luton, there were those who fancied the Hatters' chances of pulling off an upset. Although seventh in the top tier, City hadn't scored in their previous two games and took on a home team on their way to promotion to Division One. Conditions were not expected to suit flair players such as Frank Worthington and Keith Weller and the key figure for the Hatters was Leicester legend Rodney Fern. He had made the move from Filbert Street in the summer of 1972 after 187 appearances and 40 goals for City and when he sent an early header flashing just over the bar, the home crowd sensed an upset. Steve Whitworth also hacked a shot off City's goal-line before the Foxes took charge. The opening goal came when Alan Birchenall sent Dennis Rofe racing away down the left flank and Steve Earle got to his cross before the defender to steer his shot into the corner of the net. Weller was inches away from doubling the lead after another slick attack and City hit top gear after the break. The lead was doubled when Len Glover twisted and turned his way past the mesmerised full-back and then sent over a cross that Earle headed into the top corner. Weller carved out number three. He won the ball in midfield, accelerated away and crossed for Frank Worthington to head home. Weller then completed the scoring with the best goal of the lot. He danced his way through the mud and several challenges before smacking an unstoppable left-foot shot into the top corner of the net. It was later voted Goal of the Season by ITV viewers.

DE-PLEATED

David Pleat arrived at Filbert Street with a reputation. Actually, he arrived with two reputations, but we won't mention the other one. Leicester City were in desperate trouble in December, 1987. They sacked manager Bryan Hamilton after sliding into the relegation places in Division Two and were in the middle of a run of seven games without scoring a goal. The manager's job probably wasn't the most attractive in football and Pleat was highly rated, but circumstances brought Pleat and City together. After getting Luton Town into the top division and then keeping them there, he masterminded a revival at Tottenham Hotspur – leading them to the FA Cup Final in 1987 and turning them into championship challengers – before a tabloid smear campaign led to his departure from White Hart Lane. As with most relationships, all went swimmingly with Pleat and City before the cracks started to appear. His first signing was classy left-winger Peter Weir from Aberdeen and City set about playing their way out of trouble. They put together a run of five wins in six games which made them the form team in the division and a final day win at Middlesbrough denied the Teessiders promotion and ensured Leicester went into the following campaign tipped as title favourites along with Chelsea. All did not go according to plan in the summer, however, with Russell Osman leaving for Southampton. Weir followed him out of Filbert Street a few months later because his family couldn't settle in Leicester. Still, the signings of Jimmy Quinn, the division's top scorer the previous season, and goalkeeper Martin Hodge, among others, meant there was plenty of optimism going into the 1988-89 campaign. It proved to be misplaced. They got as high as ninth in December, but the play-off challenge faded and City ended the season with a run of five games without a win to finish the season 15th. The summer brought more changes with Mike Newell leaving for Everton in a £600,000 deal which also brought Wayne Clarke to Filbert Street. Other signings included Tommy Wright. Yet still City struggled and it took the arrivals of loan signings Kevin Campbell and Paul Moran from Arsenal and Tottenham Hotspur to ensure they lifted themselves to 13th at the end of the season. The 1990-91 campaign started with a 3-2 win over Bristol Rovers and was followed by seven successive defeats. Pleat could only temporarily halt the slide and he was sacked following a 3-1 defeat at home to Blackburn Rovers in January.

BIG SIGNINGS

Mark Draper became Leicester City's first £1 million signing when he joined from East Midlands rivals Notts County in July, 1994. He cost £1.25 million and while his classy midfield promptings weren't enough to keep City in the Premier League, his value soared. Twelve months after joining, Draper left to rejoin former boss Brian Little at Aston Villa in a £3.25 million deal. Matt Elliott also proved to be a wise investment. He was brought to Filbert Street in a £1.6 million move from Oxford United in January, 1997 and went on to be a key figure in Martin O'Neill's side that clinched four successive top-ten Premier League finishes.

BIG FRANK

The signing of Frank Sinclair in August, 1998 set a new record for City's biggest transfer. He came to the club in a £2.05 million deal from Chelsea and a few own goals and some sloppy timekeeping aside, Sinclair proved to be another good recruit.

EADIE DOES IT

Darren Eadie became the club's first £3 million signing. He joined from Norwich City in December, 1999, an outlay that was equalled six months later when Peter Taylor splashed out to bring in defender Gary Rowett from Birmingham City. A month after signing Rowett, Taylor made another record signing when he brought striker Ade Akinbiyi to the club from Wolverhampton Wanderers for a £5 million fee. His debut season brought him nine goals in the Premier League as City finished the season 13th after suffering a record-breaking run of eight straight defeats. Akinbiyi made the headlines for all the wrong reasons during the 2001-2002 season. He didn't find the target in the opening nine Premier League games and finally ended the drought with the winning goal against Sunderland in November, 2001. If that didn't silence his critics, the sight of his muscular build when he stripped off his shirt to celebrate must have done. Sadly, he added only one more goal before being sold to Crystal Palace for a fee of £2.2 million.

WHAT A GAME!

Nice ground, shame about the results. Eight minutes into the second half of the 1993 Division One play-off final and a familiar story was unfolding for Leicester City's supporters. Their sixth appearance at Wembley Stadium was heading for a sixth defeat. Twelve months after Blackburn Rovers inflicted heartbreak, Brian Little's team were back to battle it out with Swindon Town for a place in the Premier League. Swindon player-boss Glenn Hoddle gave his side the lead just before half-time and then two strikes in the space of six minutes just after the interval from Craig Maskell and Shaun Taylor left City trailing 3-0. Incredibly, they wiped out that deficit with three goals in the space of 12 breathless minutes that will never be forgotten by any Leicester supporter among the crowd of 73,802. Four minutes after Taylor had put Swindon 3-0 ahead, Lee Philpott swung over a high, swirling cross, Steve Walsh smacked a powerful header against the post and Julian Joachim belted home the rebound. Walsh headed home another Philpott cross to make it 3-2 before City drew level. Mike Whitlow led the counter attack with a charging run out of defence and Steve Thompson took his pass in his stride before proving he had the coolest head in the stadium by slipping a sublime shot just inside the far post with the outside of his right boot. Cue absolute pandemonium. City fans cheered, danced and rubbed their eyes in disbelief. But there was to be no happy ending. With just seven minutes left, Swindon substitute Steve White went down after a challenge from City goalkeeper Kevin Poole and Paul Bodin tucked home the penalty that broke Leicester hearts. City had equalled the club record of seven straight wins on their way to Wembley. A 2-1 win over Birmingham City at Filbert Street on February 28th, 1993 was the first of seven consecutive wins. After the win over the Blues, City hit three goals in each of their next six games and while they ended the season with a 7-1 walloping at Newcastle United, Little's team still finished sixth to set up a two-legged play-off semi-final against Portsmouth. Redevelopment work at Filbert Street meant City had to play their home leg at Nottingham Forest's City Ground and a stunning solo goal from Julian Joachim meant they had the advantage going into the second leg. Ian Ormondroyd and Steve Thompson got the goals in a 2-2 draw at Fratton Park that was enough to send City back to Wembley.

WAS IT A GOAL?

There's never a Russian linesman around when you need one. Mike Newell will tell you all about that. While Nottingham Forest were busy conquering Europe and winning trophies under Brian Clough, City were yo-yoing between the top two divisions, battling relegation, sacking managers and casting envious looks at their flourishing neighbours a few junctions up the M1. The East Midlands rivals were a division apart when the draw for the fourth round of the League Cup in 1988-89 paired them together at Filbert Street for a game highly anticipated in Leicester. Although hardly setting Division Two alight, City fans had some cause for optimism. They had beaten the leaders of the top two divisions in the previous rounds. The Foxes followed a 4-1 walloping of Division Two table-toppers Watford with a 2-2 draw at Vicarage Road and then dumped out Norwich City. At the time, the Canaries led Division One, but goals from Newell and Paul Reid ended their interest in the League Cup. Newell and Reid were then key figures in the clash with Forest. Forest full-back Stuart Pearce was sent off for clattering Reid at Filbert Street in front of 26,764 fans while Newell was a whisker away from becoming a Leicester legend. His fierce right-foot shot crashed against the underside of the bar, bounced on the goal line and then away to safety. Or did it? Interviewed almost two decades later, Newell still claimed that the ball had crossed the line and that the goal should have been allowed. It clearly still bothered him. Anyway, the game ended goalless and City were beaten 2-1 in the replay at the City Ground after Paul Groves headed home a Leicester leveller from Newell's cross. The next meeting between the sides was also in a cup competition. It was in the Northern final of the Zenith Data Systems Cup. Until the arrival of Brian Little in the summer of 1991, City's form in cups had been poor. They had not won a game in the FA Cup for six years, so a run in the Zenith Data Systems competition got pulses racing and they quickened further when the two-legged Northern final meant a clash with Nottingham Forest. The winners would meet the Southern winners at Wembley. City drew 1-1 at Filbert Street with Colin Gordon on target to cancel out Scott Gemmill's opener and Forest won the second leg to end Leicester's hopes. Forest then went on to win the trophy like they usually did back then.

SQUEEZED IN

The 47,298 fans who squeezed into Filbert Street on February 18th, 1928 to watch Leicester City take on Tottenham Hostpur in the fifth round of the FA Cup set a record. It remains the highest attendance at a City home match and that figure does not include the hundreds of fans perched on top of the stands and the supporters who stormed the directors' entrance after the gates were shut. Those that paid to get in raised gate receipts of £4,703 10s 6d and the majority of supporters went home unhappy after City were dumped out 3-0.

THE HIGHEST EVER

The highest gate for a home Football League fixture is the 42,486 that watched the Division One fixture against Arsenal on October 2nd, 1954. City had been promoted to the top flight the previous season as champions and although the opening ten games of the 1954-55 campaign brought only two wins, the visit of Arsenal still attracted a record crowd and they got their money's worth. The sides shared six goals with Arthur Rowley netting twice – including a penalty – and Derek Hines grabbing the other goal for City.

PLENTY OF ROOM

The talents of Gary Lineker, Alan Smith and Kevin MacDonald were not enough to attract more than 6,155 fans through the Filbert Street turnstiles for the visit of Shrewsbury Town on February 22nd, 1983. That remains the lowest post-war attendance for a Leicester City home match and those that were there saw two goals from Lineker, and another from Ian Wilson, secure a 3-2 win that kick-started the Foxes' push for promotion. They put together a 15-game unbeaten run that pipped Fulham for the third promotion spot with the Foxes clinching their return to the top flight with a goalless draw against Burnley at Filbert Street on the final day of the season. There were 29,453 fans present to see a game that took place just over 11 weeks after the clash with Shrewsbury.

A LOW ATTENDANCE

The lowest attendance for a First Division fixture at Filbert Street was the 7,237 that watched City battle out a 2-2 draw with West Bromwich Albion on October 12th, 1985.

WORTH THE WAIT

Leicester City took on Sheffield United in the 1961 FA Cup semi-final at Elland Road. And, 234 minutes after the game kicked off, there was a goal! City set off on the long road to Wembley with a 3-1 win over Oxford United at Filbert Street that was followed by a 5-1 battering of Bristol City. The result set up a fifth-round clash with Birmingham City that went to a replay settled by Ken Leek's double. He was the match-winner again in the quarter-final replay against Barnsley. City were drawn against the Blades in the last four – and the teams came up with a cure for insomnia. There were no goals when they met at Leeds United's Elland Road and five days later, the sides fought out another 0-0 draw at St. Andrew's in a game that went to extra time. The wait for a goal looked set to end 11 minutes into the third meeting at the City Ground in Nottingham when City were awarded a penalty, but Ian King stubbed his foot into the ground at the moment of impact and the chance was gone. It was left to Jimmy Walsh to grab the tie's opening goal. He headed home 24 minutes into the third meeting between the sides and Leek doubled the lead just after the interval. The Blades were handed a route back into the game when they were awarded a 65th-minute penalty, but Graham Shaw pulled his effort wide and the opportunity was lost. City went on to lose the final 2-0 to Tottenham Hotspur.

SEVEN UP

During the 1974-75 season, City and Arsenal met an incredible seven times! Arsenal were 1-0 winners at Filbert Street on the opening day of the season and the sides were paired together the following month in the League Cup. City went through 2-1 in a replay after a goalless draw at Highbury and after another 0-0 scoreline in the return fixture in Division One, the draw for the fifth round of the FA Cup paired them together again after the Foxes had scraped past non-league Leatherhead. After a goalless draw at Highbury, the replay ended 1-1 after extra time and that set up a third meeting. Arsenal went through to the quarter-finals with a 1-0 win in front of their home fans.

WHAT A SIGNING!

Gerry Daly headed off down the M69 to join Leicester City from Coventry City and the Foxes were soon heading for promotion. Daly, a slender, stylish midfielder formerly at Manchester United, joined in February, 1983 and played all 17 remaining games of the season; City only lost once. He made his debut in a 1-0 win at Carlisle United and following a defeat at Grimsby Town, City put together a 15-game unbeaten run that enabled them to pip Fulham for the third automatic promotion spot. Daly, so accurate with his passing it was as though he had telescopic sights strapped to his boots, was called up by the Republic of Ireland while on loan at City and his only goal for the Foxes was a sweetly struck right-foot shot from the edge of the penalty area that completed a 5-0 drubbing of promotion rivals Wolverhampton Wanderers. There was much surprise and disappointment among Leicester supporters when Milne decided against trying to make Daly's move to Leicester permanent during the summer. Instead, he went on to join Derby County for £300,000.

GOAL-HUNGRY FRYATT

Matty Fryatt was another inspired signing. He joined from Walsall in January, 2006 and made his debut as a substitute in a 2-1 defeat at Sheffield Wednesday. That result left Robert Kelly's side just one place and one point above the drop zone in the second tier of English football, but in the space of four days, Fryatt helped fire his new team to safety. He was on target in the 3-2 win at Queens Park Rangers and followed it with the winner against Wolverhampton Wanderers at the Walkers Stadium. Fryatt ended the season with six goals and City survived.

KEV TO THE RESCUE

Leicester were one place off the bottom of Division Two in November, 1989 when boss David Pleat brought in Kevin Campbell on loan from Arsenal and the teenage striker's five goals in 11 games were crucial in securing City's survival. His strikes included a stunning long-range winner at Portsmouth on New Year's Day and Campbell was given an emotional send off at Filbert Street after his final game. He went on to win the Football League, FA Cup, League Cup and European Cup Winners' Cup with the Gunners.

LAST ORDERS

In the summer of 1930, The Turk's Head on Welford Road gained a new landlord and Leicester City lost a legend. City's board were not impressed by John Duncan's plan to combine his playing career with running the hostelry and the fall out spelled the end for him at Filbert Street after 295 games and 95 goals. Duncan was approached by several clubs, but was intent on his career in the licensed trade. He had joined City along with brother Tom from Scottish club Raith Rovers for a fee of £1,500 in the summer of 1922. Leicester boss Peter Hodge knew all about Duncan having previously been his manager at Raith and City fans soon discovered why he was so highly rated. Known as 'Tokey', Duncan netted twice on his debut at Stockport County in a 5-4 win and ended his first season at the club with 20 goals. The only game he missed was the trip to Bury on the last day of the season when a 2-0 loss cost City the chance of being promoted. Leicester went up as champions in 1924-25 and Duncan had a starring role. He netted 30 goals, including six in the 7-0 thumping of Port Vale on Christmas Day after Arthur Chandler had opened the scoring for the Foxes. Duncan went on to be a key player in the side that were runners-up behind Sheffield Wednesday in Division One in the 1928-29 season and was an ever-present with 40 appearances the following season as City finished eighth. After that, Duncan left Filbert Street and headed off to the pub. He stayed involved in football with Leicester Thursday League side Solaris, then Leicester Nomads, and in August, 1940, Duncan became a founder committee member of the City Supporters' Club.

He was named City's manager in March, 1946 following Tom Bromilow's departure and went on to lead Leicester out at Wembley in the 1949 FA Cup Final against Wolverhampton Wanderers. The game ended in defeat and a few months later Duncan left City after a bust up with the board over transfer policy and headed back to the pub. He died in Leicester in March, 1966 at the age of 70. His brother Tom made 42 appearances for City – scoring six goals – and moved on after being unable to dislodge Hughie Adcock. A third Duncan brother, Jim, played in the Scottish League with Lochgelly United, their uncle David Bain played for Heart of Midlothian and cousin Jack Bain appeared for Dunfermline and Dundee United.

CRAZY STUFF

In the early days of Leicester Fosse, there were some bizarre goings on… A match against Coalville in November, 1886 ended before the final whistle when Fosse's Leicestershire rivals were so disgusted with a decision by the umpire that they stormed off the pitch in protest and refused to return to complete the fixture! Later that month, Fosse turned up for a match at Belgrave with only 10 players and ended up plucking a supporter out of the crowd to play for them! Fosse still ran out 2-0 winners in the big Leicester derby. At the start of the 1887-88 season, the Belgrave Road Sports Ground became Fosse's home ground. The venue had been built seven years earlier by local entrepreneur Colonel Barnaby and while the impressive facilities included athletics and cycle tracks around a playing area big enough to be used as a cricket pitch, there was nowhere for the players to change. That meant they had to get changed before matches and later have their post-match wash at the White Hart Hotel that was almost a mile away from the ground. Fosse only stayed there for one season, however. The city's rugby union team, Leicester Tigers, outbid them for the use of the ground.

A FIRST

The game against Burton Swifts in November, 1897 became the first fixture when supporters had to pay an admission fee and they got their money's worth as Fosse were 3-2 winners through goals from Billy Dorrell, Willie Freebairn and Johnny McMillan. Presumably, supporters were offered a refund after Castle Donington didn't turn up for a fixture the following month. Instead, Fosse played their reserves in a practice match that ended in a 1-1 draw.

DRESSING FOR THE OCCASION

It was so cold when Fosse took on Doncaster Rovers in a Midland League fixture in November, 1893 that goalkeeper Jimmy Thraves took to the field wearing an overcoat! The snow became so bad that the game was eventually abandoned by the referee.

RED CARDS

The pantomime season came early in 1962. Oh yes it did. Leicester City took on Aston Villa at Filbert Street on December 8th, 1962 and after just 15 seconds, Len Chalmers put the ball in the net. The wrong net. Derek Dougan, who went on to play for City, launched the ball forward for his strikers to chase, Leicester defender Chalmers got there first and lobbed over goalkeeper Gordon Banks to gift Villa the lead. City fought back to grab a 3-3 draw with David Gibson netting twice and Mike Stringfellow getting the other.

IN THE FRAME

Willie Frame had the misfortune to score an own goal on his Leicester debut. Frame, signed from junior football in Glasgow, was handed his first start for Leicester at Tottenham Hotspur on October 6th, 1934 and his own goal in the last minute meant the home side escaped with a point from a 2-2 draw. Danny Liddle and Arthur Maw were on target for City at White Hart Lane.

DOUBLE CLANGER

Leicester defenders Colin Appleton and Ian King were the match winners in City's match at Burnley in September, 1961 – but for the Clarets rather than City! They both scored own goals to clinch a 2-0 win for the Clarets in the Division One fixture at Turf Moor.

ASSISTING THE BAGGIES

John Sjoberg scored two own goals against City for West Bromwich Albion at the Hawthorns on April 22nd, 1966. His blunders helped the Baggies to a 5-1 win.

CRUISING FOR THE RECORD BOOKS

Pat Kruse only made two appearances for City, in the last two games of the 1973-74 season, and went into the record books after leaving Filbert Street. He lined up for Torquay United against Cambridge United in a Division Four fixture on January 3rd, 1977 and netted the quickest own goal ever recorded in the Football League. There were just six seconds on the clock when Kruse put Cambridge ahead. Although his City career was brief, Kruse went on to make more than 300 appearances for clubs including Brentford, Northampton and Barnet.

STAYING PUT

Leicester City were crowned Division Two champions in 1956-57 and it didn't look like they were going to hang around in the top tier. The following season, City lost six of their opening seven games shrugging off the horror start to survive and go on to spend 12 successive seasons in Division One. That remains the longest spell the Foxes have spent in the top division of English football with their best finish being fourth in 1962-63 when they were on course for a league and FA Cup double until it all fell apart. City reached three FA Cup Finals during that spell and lifted the League Cup in 1964. They were relegated in 1969 three weeks after defeat in the FA Cup Final against Manchester City.

TEN AT THE TOP

City spent a decade in Division One between 1925 and 1935 and in 1928-29 achieved their highest-ever league placing when they finished second behind Sheffield Wednesday.

SEVENTH IN SEVEN

Jimmy Bloomfield put together a team that spent seven seasons in the top flight (1971-78), achieving a best finish of seventh in 1975-76.

STEADY

Martin O'Neill took City back into the Premier League in May, 1996 and the Foxes went on to enjoy six seasons in the top flight. City finished in the top ten for four successive seasons before O'Neill left for Celtic in the summer of 2000. Peter Taylor briefly took the Foxes to the top of the Premier League in October, 2000 and City were relegated at the end of the following season.

OVER ONE HUNDRED YEARS AGO...

The club's first taste of top-flight football was short lived. Leicester Fosse kicked off the 1908-09 season in Division One with a 1-1 draw against Sheffield Wednesday in front of around 16,000 fans at Filbert Street. Fosse had to wait until the fourth game of the season to register their first win at Preston North End, but a spell of 14 games without a win left them rooted to the bottom of the table and they stayed there.

WATERS DEBUT

"Oh yes for the youngster!" screamed excitable *Match of the Day* commentator Barry Davies and Joe Waters entered Leicester City folklore. Jimmy Bloomfield's City had drawn comparisons to Brazil in their 4-0 win at Luton Town in the fifth round of the FA Cup in 1974. The win set up a quarter-final tie at Queens Park Rangers where Bloomfield was without the injured Alan Birchenall and Alan Woollett for the trip to Loftus Road, so he handed a debut to Waters and the 21-year-old more than justified his selection. City were under pressure in the first half with Stan Bowles driving Rangers on but hit back to take the lead after the break through Waters. The ball ran to him 20 yards out and he sent his curving right-foot shot beyond Phil Parkes' fingertips and into the corner of the net. It would later be voted 'Goal of the Month' by Match of the Day viewers and there was more to come from Waters. He added the decisive second following a breathtaking counter attack. City belted clear from a corner, Frank Worthington broke away and squared for Waters to lift the ball over the advancing Parkes. Waters was plastered all over the newspapers and then got the chance to repeat his heroics against Liverpool in the FA Cup semi-final at Old Trafford. City, who would have preferred to draw Newcastle United or Burnley in the last four, had a lucky escape when Kevin Keegan hit the post in the closing minutes. Waters was missing from the side that lined up for the replay at Villa Park. Liverpool were 3-1 victors – Len Glover was on target for the Foxes – to go through to the final.

PEAKING TOO EARLY

Waters' reward for his performance at Rangers earned him a call up to the Republic of Ireland squad, but the chunky midfielder could not build on his astonishing start to his City career. After his debut, he went on to make only 15 more appearances and added only one more goal before leaving for Grimsby Town. He went on to be a Mariners legend in a career that spanned 357 league games which included a club-record run of 226 consecutive appearances. Waters then took on a player-coach role with Tacoma Stars in America's Major League Soccer where his team-mates included Keith Weller.

SWINDON FUN

The next time Leicester City meet Swindon Town, you really want to be there. There was the 1993 Division One play-off final when City wiped out a 3-0 deficit before being pipped in a seven-goal thriller. Five seasons earlier, Leicester had served up another unforgettable match at Filbert Street. City were heading for defeat when they trailed 2-0 with around 10 minutes left and, after Paul Ramsey and Steve Walsh had levelled the scores, the Foxes found an unlikely match winner. Mark Venus, for so long the target of terrace derision, walloped home an unstoppable left-foot volley from 25 yards into the top corner and the game was won. The following season, Swindon opened up a 3-0 lead at Filbert Street and City clawed their way back to earn a point with Gary McAllister on target twice.

GOAL FEST

City had a dramatic late escape in the first leg of their League Cup tie with Brentford in September, 1984. They produced a four-goal flurry in the last nine minutes to overturn Brentford's 2-0 lead with the goals coming from John O'Neill, Ian Banks, Steve Lynex and Gary Lineker. Two weeks later, City won the second leg 2-0 at Griffin Park to go through 6-2 on aggregate.

DUTCH TOUCH

City were heading for a third-round exit from the FA Cup in January, 2006 when Tottenham Hotspur opened up a 2-0 lead against Craig Levein's Championship strugglers in front of the Match of the Day cameras. Elvis Hammond handed City a lifeline and then Stephen Hughes slammed home the leveller before Mark De Vries rolled home the winner deep into injury time.

THREE IN THIRTEEN

Perhaps the most satisfying comeback of all came at Villa Park in February, 1995. Three months earlier, Brian Little had walked out on City to take charge of Aston Villa and his new side led Leicester 4-1 with just 13 minutes left. Iwan Roberts started the fightback by heading home a Mike Galloway cross and David Lowe pulled another back to set up a thrilling climax. The game was deep into injury time when Lowe forced home Colin Hill's header to snatch a point.

REED ALL ABOUT IT

Leicester City crashed out of the FA Cup and the nation was outraged. Referee Mike Reed's decision to award a spot-kick to Chelsea in the dying moments of extra time at the end of the FA Cup fifth-round replay in February, 1997 dominated headlines, radio phone-ins and even Prime Minister's Question Time. The injustice felt by City was shared by supporters across the country. Leicester had been incensed by comments made by Chelsea boss Ruud Gullit after the 2-2 draw at Filbert Street ten days earlier. His claim that Leicester had been lucky to force a replay – through goals from Steve Walsh and an own goal after they had trailed 2-0 – did not go down well with Martin O'Neill. City's manager didn't feel like a lucky man when he looked at his team's injury list and there was still the second leg of the Coca-Cola Cup semi-final against Wimbledon to come. To compound matters, they were drawn against the favourites for the FA Cup after reaching the last 16 with wins over Southend United and Norwich City. Early exits for Manchester United, Arsenal, Liverpool, Newcastle and Aston Villa meant Chelsea were fancied to end a spell of 27 years without a trophy by lifting the cup. City's late fightback at Filbert Street in a game televised live on the BBC denied them a place in the quarter-finals and O'Neill's team were similarly spirited in the replay at Stamford Bridge. The score was goalless after 90 minutes and stayed that way heading into the dying moments of extra time. Then it happened. Chelsea striker Erland Johnsen tried to burst through a gap between Leicester defenders Matt Elliott and Spencer Prior and took a tumble. Referee Reed pointed to the spot and City's protests were echoed by armchair fans around the country when Sky Sports replays showed no contact had been made.That night, BBC Radio Five Live's Danny Baker spoke for the nation when he opined: "It was scandalous, an absolute scandal." And, there was more to follow. Tabloid headlines screamed 'The Worst Referee In The World', a Leicester fan tried to claim damages because the stress of his side's controversial exit had affected his health and made him take time off work and Prime Minister John Major spoke in defence of his team Chelsea. Chelsea went on to win the cup and more than a decade later, The Guardian remembered the penalty award that went against Leicester as one of the worst refereeing decisions ever made.

WHAT A HERBERT

Leicester Fosse took the unusual step of handing goalkeeper Herbert Bown the job of penalty taker in the 1916-1917 season. Bown repaid the faith placed in him by netting Fosse's goal in a 2-1 defeat at Hull City in March, 1917. He was an ever-present between the posts for Fosse that season, but lost the job of penalty-taker during the following campaign. In October, 1917 he missed a spot-kick against Sheffield Wednesday at Filbert Street and that proved to be decisive as the Owls headed home with maximum points from a 2-1 win. Bown was never allowed to take another penalty for the club, but he was soon back in the headlines. Two weeks after that penalty miss against Wednesday, Bown was involved in another bizarre incident. As he was lining up to take a goal kick in the match at Bradford City, a dog ran onto the pitch unnoticed by the Fosse keeper and he booted the canine rather than the ball! Fortunately, the dog was not badly hurt. Fosse went on to lose the match 4-1. Bown had previously played for Essex as an amateur before joining Fosse in April, 1913. At the end of the season, he set off with the squad on their historic tour of Sweden and was between the posts in the five games that included a pair of wins over the Swedish national team. Bown went on to enter the club's record books in the 1919-1920 season for keeping a club-record seven successive clean sheets in league fixtures. The run started with a 2-0 win over Stockport County on February 7th in a Division Two fixture and Bown did not concede another goal until April 3rd when Bury snatched a 1-0 win. After nine years with Fosse, Bown left the club in May, 1922. He made 266 appearances for Leicester – including 112 during World War Two – and a goal from the penalty spot. He went on to join Halifax Town and got on the score-sheet for the Shaymen during two ever-present seasons with them. Bown was then put up for sale at the bargain price of £350, but no clubs expressed an interest and he ended up returning to Leicester to run a fish and poultry business. He was then brought out of retirement in January, 1925 to play four games for Hull City after they were hit by an injury crisis. Bown died in Leicester in February, 1959 at the age of 65.

CRAZY DAYS

Leicester Fosse marked their entry into the Football League with a bizarre seven-goal thriller at Grimsby Town. The clash at Grimsby's Abbey Park on September 1st, 1894 ended in a 4-3 defeat for Fosse and was followed by some revelations from the home side's goalkeeper. Whitehouse reckoned that the referee had not noticed a shot from Fosse player Priestman had crossed the line and that McArthur's legitimate goal for Fosse had been scored while the Grimsby keeper was pulling up his socks. New signing David Skea went into the record books as Fosse's first-ever goal scorer in a Football League fixture and it was an own goal by Harry Bailey that proved to be the decisive strike in the match. Fosse recorded their first win in their next fixture. McArthur opened the scoring after seven minutes against Rotherham Town and Skea added a hat-trick to complete a 4-2 win at Walnut Street. Fosse ended the season in fourth place and the reserves lifted the Wellingborough Cup and Leics & Northants League championship. William D. Clark came to Leicester Fosse in the summer of 1897 and brought with him some fairly bonkers ideas. Clark took on the secretary/manager role having previously held a similar post at both Burton Wanderers and Derby County and was always looking for ways to stir up some publicity. He helped arrange an exhibition baseball match between Crystal Palace and Derby County in August, 1897 and then came up with the idea of a series of 100-yard handicap races for footballers. Billy Dorrell, in his second spell with Fosse after rejoining from Aston Villa, was the winner and he also took part in the rather unusual pre-match entertainment before the home game against Darwen in February, 1898. Clark arranged a 440-yard challenge race between Dorrell and American half-miler C. H. Kilpatrick that the Fosse flyer won. His victory earned him £10, cemented his hero status at Leicester and did nothing to help Fosse. Dorrell must still have been out of puff when the opening whistle blew of the match with Darwen and the visitors left Filbert Street with a 1-0 win. A week later, the club's board had to clamp down on unruly behaviour by some players. They indefinitely suspended six players following alcohol-related incidents and several of them never played in the Football League again.

DREAM DEBUTS

If there's such a thing as a dream debut, then this is it… At the age of 16 years and 192 days, Dave Buchanan became City's youngest-ever player when he made his debut against Oldham Athletic at Filbert Street on January 1st, 1979. Not content with that feat, he then found the target in a 2-0 win to make him the youngest-ever goalscorer in the Foxes' history. Sadly, he never built on that tremendous start to his Leicester career and added only seven more goals.

THINGS CHANGE...

At the time, the signing of Arthur Rowley wasn't well received by Leicester City fans. They liked Jack Lee and Rowley was brought in to replace him. Rowley, a £14,000 signing from Fulham, set about winning over his public by scoring plenty of goals. His first came on his debut in August, 1950 and secured a 3-2 win at Bury.

UNLUCKY

Robert Ullathorne's Leicester City debut lasted all of 11 minutes. With City boss Martin O'Neill's squad decimated by injuries he brought in the former Norwich City stopper from Spanish club CA Osasuna in February, 1997. Ullathorne was handed his Foxes debut in the first leg of the Coca-Cola Cup semi-final against Wimbledon at Filbert Street but suffered a broken ankle after just 11 minutes of the goalless draw and didn't play for City again for 22 months.

A FLYING START

A few days after becoming Leicester City's record signing, Mike Newell showed why Bryan Hamilton had splashed out £350,000 to bring the striker to Filbert Street. Newell made his debut against Oldham Athletic in September, 1987 and his flying header sent City on their way to a 4-1 win at Filbert Street that ended a run of three straight defeats.

NOT AS GOOD AS HIS BROTHER

Newell's departure to Everton led to Wayne Clarke moving in the opposite direction. He marked his City debut with a goal at Hull City on the opening day of the 1989-90 season... but only scored one more for Leicester.

MORE DREAM DEBUTS

And here are a few more memorable debuts... Who needs Gary Lineker? Leicester City's team-sheet for the penultimate game of the 1982-83 season at Oldham Athletic was missing the 26-goal striker. In stepped teenager Robert Jones for his debut. Also ruled out at Boundary Park were Steve Lynex and Ian Wilson for a match that could make or break City's promotion hopes. Gordon Milne's team had jumped into the third promotion place in Division Two for the first time that season with a 2-2 draw at Leeds United seven days earlier and more than 5,000 Leicester fans headed up to Oldham hoping to see them stay there. Jones, who played for England Schoolboys and then won youth caps with Wales, went close with a long-range effort and then put City ahead three minutes before the break. He raced onto Kevin MacDonald's through ball and coolly squeezed his left-foot shot just inside the goalkeeper's near post. Jones was still beaming with joy when the game restarted and there was more reason to smile nine minutes into the second half when Paul Ramsey doubled Leicester's lead. Although Oldham pulled a goal back, the Foxes held on to their advantage and went on to secure promotion. The following season, Jones helped City secure their first top-flight point with a goal in a 2-2 draw against Stoke City in the seventh fixture, but made a total of just 17 appearances and scored three goals before being released.

IMMEDIATE IMPACT

Mark Yeates didn't take long to make an impact at Leicester. He arrived on loan from Tottenham Hotspur in January, 2007 and two days later, he made his debut against Luton Town in a Championship fixture at the Walkers Stadium. Six minutes after kick-off, he was celebrating a goal. Yeates was on hand to tuck home the loose ball after Iain Hume's shot had been blocked by goalkeeper Marlon Beresford. The game ended 1-1 and Yeates made only eight more appearances for City before returning to White Hart Lane and then making a permanent switch to Colchester United.

SIXTH ROUND

Then there is Joe Waters and his two-goal debut in the FA Cup quarter-final at Queens Park Rangers in 1974 that is mentioned elsewhere.

DERBY DAYS

The big local derby got underway in glorious sunshine – and it was all over 15 minutes later! That was how long it took Martin O'Neill's Leicester City to net four times at Derby County in April, 1998 in front of the Sky Sports cameras. City were ahead within two minutes with Emile Heskey powering home a header from Steve Guppy's cross and 46 seconds after the restart, the lead was doubled. Steve Claridge picked up a misplaced pass and sent Heskey racing away down the right who sent a cross into the penalty area for Muzzy Izzet to arrive at the right time to head into the roof of the net. Heskey added number three from Guppy's corner after just nine minutes and the scoring was completed with 15 minutes played. Robbie Savage swung over a cross from the right and Ian Marshall got above his marker to steer his header into the corner of the net. And that was that.

MARSHALL MATTERS

Marshall had been the hat-trick hero for City when the sides met at Filbert Street the previous season. City were without Neil Lennon, Heskey and Izzet and fell behind to an early strike from Dean Sturridge, who went on to play for Leicester. Marshall then netted three times in the space of just 21 first-half minutes to put the Foxes in charge and after Sturridge pulled a goal back, Claridge put the game beyond Derby in the 58th minute with a close-range finish.

SIX IN THIRTY

Leicester striker Iwan Roberts bagged a hat-trick in just 11 minutes in an astonishing six-goal thriller against Derby at Filbert Street in April, 1994. All the goals came in the opening half hour. Derby were 2-0 ahead in 12 minutes through former Fox Paul Kitson and a Jimmy Willis strike before Roberts' treble blast after 17, 22 and 28 minutes. A minute after Roberts had put City in front, Kitson levelled the scores.

GARY PITCHES IN

Gary Lineker also scored a hat-trick in the big East Midlands derby. His goal treble came in the 4-0 win at the Baseball Ground in October, 1983 and strike partner Alan Smith got the other.

WHITE TIGHTS

Ever the showman, Keith Weller left his audience wanting more... He took the Filbert Street stage on January 6th, 1979 resplendent in white tights and then dazzled his opponents, the crowd and a television audience of millions in an FA Cup third-round tie against Norwich City. A few weeks after that, it was all over. Weller's goalscoring swansong owed much to a hot-air pitch cover that meant City's game was one of only three fixtures to survive the big freeze and BBC TV's cameras were there to capture all the drama for the Match of the Day viewers. They saw Weller take to the pitch wearing white tights and then go on to score City's second goal in a 3-0 win. It proved to be Weller's last goal for City. Two weeks later, he played in the 1-1 draw against Blackburn Rovers at Filbert Street and never played for the club again. He had arrived at Leicester from Chelsea for a £100,000 fee as boss Jimmy Bloomfield set about putting together one of the most exciting teams in City's history. Weller made his debut for the Foxes in a goalless draw against Crystal Palace in October, 1971 and among his five top-flight goals in his first season was a stunning solo effort in a 2-1 win at East Midlands rivals Nottingham Forest. There would be many more highlights. In November, 1973 he belted home an unstoppable volley from the edge of the penalty area to secure victory over Newcastle United at Filbert Street. His sparkling midfield promptings helped carve out many of Frank Worthington's 24 goals in all competitions as City finished the season ninth in Division One and reached the semi-finals of the FA Cup where they bowed out to Liverpool after a replay. Weller's goal at Luton Town in the fifth round of the FA Cup was among his best and was voted Goal of the Season by ITV viewers. His form also earned him four England caps at the end of the season and he bagged the winner against Northern Ireland in May, 1974 with a rare header. Frustratingly, he never got the chance to add more caps and his refusal to come out for the second half of a fixture against Ipswich Town in December, 1974 showed his frustration at

City's inability to fulfill their potential. Weller went on to play in America and tragically died in the States in November, 2004 at the age of 58 after losing his battle with cancer.

ENDING THE JINX

Until May 30th, 1994, Wembley meant only one thing to Leicester City, and that was heartbreak. City's six previous games at the home of football had all ended in defeat. They had lost four FA Cup Finals and then suffered back-to-back losses in play-off finals against Blackburn Rovers and Swindon Town. Brian Little took his team back to Wembley for the third successive season in May, 1994 to face East Midlands rivals Derby County with a place in the Premier League at stake. City had finished fourth in the table after ending the season with a nine-game unbeaten run and edged out Tranmere Rovers in the play-off semi-finals. Simon Grayson's goal-line handball in the first leg at Tranmere was seen by everyone at Prenton Park apart from the officials to ensure the scoreline was blank going into the return at Filbert Street. Little stunned City's fans when he included Steve Walsh in the starting line-up. Walsh had suffered a cruciate ligament injury in a 2-0 defeat at Middlesbrough the previous September and his return to the side seven months later in a 1-1 draw at Watford proved to be short-lived. He was back for the second leg against Tranmere and despite clearly not being fully match fit, he had a hand in Ian Ormondroyd's opener. Rovers levelled and David Speedie grabbed the goal that sent City back to Wembley. He didn't get the chance to play there, however. The Scot was sent off in the dying moments following a bust up with Rovers keeper Eric Nixon and banned for the final against Derby. Iwan Roberts stepped in to replace Speedie and partner Walsh up front, but most of the early action was at the other end of the pitch and it was no surprise when Tommy Johnson fired the Rams into the lead after outpacing City's defence. Leicester were level when Gary Coatsworth walloped the ball skywards and Walsh out-jumped Rams keeper Martin Taylor to head in. The goal probably should have been ruled out for a foul on the keeper and definitely should have been cleared by Derby defender Paul Williams on the goal-line. Instead, City went into the break on level terms and then grabbed the winner, and their place in the Premier League, with four minutes left. Ian Ormondroyd met Simon Grayson's right-wing cross with a header that Taylor could not hang on to, and Walsh was on hand to tap home the loose ball and end the Foxes' Wembley jinx.

PAYING THE PENALTY

You could have cut the tension with a tub of lard. Leicester City beat Huddersfield Town and Charlton Athletic in the Simod Cup in 1987-88 to set up a third-round home date with Stoke City that attracted a crowd of just 5,161. It went all the way to a penalty shoot-out after two goalless hours and David Pleat's team fancied their chances. Between the posts they had Paul Cooper, who had saved a penalty during the match and kept out eight of ten spot-kicks he faced when playing for Ipswich Town in the 1979-80 season. But he didn't stop any in the shootout against Stoke. City went out 5-3 with Mike Newell missing the crucial spot-kick after Gary McAllister, Peter Weir and Mark Venus found the back of the net. "Someone had to miss," said Newell afterwards, "or we would have been there all night!"

UP FOR GRABS

There were priceless Premier League points at stake when Leicester and Manchester City squared up at the Walkers Stadium on April 24th, 2004. The sides were level at 1-1 when Leicester were awarded a penalty with just nine minutes left after Muzzy Izzet was felled by Tarnat. Paul Dickov, already a Manchester City legend for his last-gasp heroics in the 1999 play-off final against Gillingham, had his spot-kick saved by David James. Seven days later, Leicester's 2-2 draw at Charlton Athletic wasn't enough to keep them in the top division. Dickov was more accurate from the penalty spot when he lined up against City the following season. He got the only goal of the FA Cup quarter-final for Blackburn Rovers at Ewood Park in the 82nd minute after City defender Darren Kenton had brought down Morten Gamst Pedersen.

THE DREADED DROP

Iain Hume was another Leicester hero who missed a crucial spot-kick. He was off target in the clash with Sheffield Wednesday at the Walkers Stadium in April, 2008 that Leicester went into knowing victory would secure their survival. Hume missed the chance to level the scores at 2-2 and City went on to be beaten 3-1 by the Owls. They suffered relegation to the third tier of English football for the first time in their history eight days later.

THEY HAD 12 MEN

Leicester Fosse were up against it at Burslem Port Vale in April, 1892. They took to the pitch with only ten men after Owen missed his train and after the referee also failed to show, a spectator was plucked from the crowd to do the job. Fosse were beaten 2-0 and protested that the official had been far from impartial. The Midland League ordered the game to be replayed. Fosse had 11 men for the fixture next time and there was a neutral referee – but it didn't do them any good. They were beaten 4-0.

PLAY IT AGAIN

Fosse's 6-0 thumping of Derby Junction at Walnut Street in March, 1893 was also scrubbed from the record books. The sides had met in Leicester a few weeks earlier and while Derby had agreed to cede home advantage, neither club checked the fixture switch had the approval of the Midland League. So, the game was played again in Derby and Fosse ran out 3-1 winners.

WHAT A PICTURE!

The decision to make that 6-0 win over Derby void meant Alf Slack had his hat-trick wiped from the record books and 92 years later, the same thing happened to Leicester legend Gary Lineker. The draw for the third round of the FA Cup in 1985 handed City a trip to Burton Albion and the home side decided to stage the game at Derby County's Baseball Ground to pull in a bigger crowd. Burton sniffed an upset when David Vaughan put them ahead midway through the first half. City levelled and then came the incident that put both clubs in the headlines for the wrong reasons. Leicester and Derby fans clashed behind the goal and a missile was thrown which hit Burton goalkeeper Paul Evans on the head. He carried on after treatment, but later said he remembered nothing of the five goals that flew past him after he was struck. The FA ordered the game to be replayed – meaning Lineker's hat-trick no longer stood – and the sides met behind closed doors at Coventry City's Highfield Road. Paul Ramsey got the only goal of the game and the only cheers came from a pair of City fans who had managed to convince officials they were photographers!

THRASHINGS

Everyone knows – well, everyone reading this anyway – that Leicester City's record win is the 10-0 pasting they dished out to Portsmouth at Filbert Street in October, 1928. But the Foxes have recorded a couple of bigger victories in their history. In October, 1894, Fosse put 13 goals past Notts Olympic without reply in an FA Cup qualifying match with 'Tout' Miller and Willie McArthur grabbing four apiece. David Skea grabbed a hat-trick for Fosse and Johnny Hill netted twice.

A DELIGHTFUL DOZEN

Then there was the 12-1 thumping of Syston Wreake Valley in November, 1888 in a first round tie in the Leicestershire Association Challenge Cup. Harry Webb got six of them a month after becoming the club's first professional when he joined from Stafford Rangers.

A HAT-TRICK OF NINES

Leicester have put nine goals past their opponents three times. They were 9-1 winners over Walsall Town Swifts in January, 1895 with David Skea and Bob Gordon both grabbing two goals apiece and Gainsborough Trinity were walloped 9-1 in December, 1909. Dave Walker led the rout with four goals and Fred Shinton fired home a hat-trick. City smashed home nine goals again at Filbert Street in November, 1953. Lincoln City were on the receiving end of a 9-2 thrashing. Derek Hines netted five times for the Foxes and Arthur Rowley was on target twice – including a penalty. City's record away win came at Coventry City on the day Foxes legend Ken Keyworth completed a switch to Highfield Road. He saw his former team storm to an 8-1 win in a League Cup fifth-round tie over the Sky Blues in December, 1964 – despite being without goalkeeper Gordon Banks for a spell. An injury to Banks led to Graham Cross going between the posts and he was seldom troubled as City went on the rampage. Full-back Richie Norman was on target twice for City and they were collector's items. He scored just five times in 365 appearances for Leicester. Sky Blues skipper George Curtis added an own goal and City went on to lift the trophy with victory over Stoke City in the two-legged final.

SUPER STEVIE

Leicester City legend Steve Claridge followed the best goal of his career with the most stupid thing he has ever said! Time was running out in the Division One play-off final between Martin O'Neill's City and Crystal Palace at Wembley in May, 1996. The game was just seconds away from a penalty shoot-out when Palace failed to clear a free kick, the ball dropped to Claridge and he sent his shot into the top corner and the Foxes back into the Premier League. The final whistle blew just seconds later and then Claridge stunned the millions watching by saying on television that the winning goal had gone in off his shin! "I was just trying to make a joke," remembered Claridge, "and I wish I hadn't done it now. It was probably the most stupid thing I've ever said. I hit the ball as sweet as a nut. It was the best goal of my career." Eight weeks earlier, Claridge had kick-started City's promotion charge at Charlton Athletic after begging O'Neill not to be dropped. Claridge did not exactly set Filbert Street alight following his £1 million move from Birmingham City. His debut at Ipswich Town, which ended in a 4-2 defeat, was memorable only for the way his name was misspelt on the back of his shirt – with an extra 'r' – and he drew a blank in his first six games for City. Claridge remembers pleading with O'Neill to give him another chance at Charlton Athletic and he repaid his manager with the only goal of the game. Four days later, City were 1-0 winners at Crystal Palace and the charge into the play-offs was underway. City ended the season with four straight wins to set up a play-off semi-final against Stoke City. The sides battled out a goalless draw at Filbert Street and Garry Parker bagged the only goal in the Potteries to send Leicester through to Wembley. They fell behind to Andy Roberts' first-half strike for Palace and had to wait until the 76th minute to level. Parker kept his cool from the penalty spot after Muzzy Izzet had been felled by Marc Edworthy, who went on to play for City a decade later. Parker then had a hand in City's winner that came just seconds after O'Neill had stunned Leicester fans by replacing goalkeeper Kevin Poole with Zeljko 'Spider' Kalac in anticipation of a penalty shoot-out. Parker's free kick was nodded down by Julian Watts and Claridge's shin did the rest.

KOP THAT!

Ten minutes after coming on for his Leicester City debut at Liverpool, Graham Fenton was celebrating in front of a bunch of cranes and steel girders. Fenton's goal put the Foxes 2-0 ahead in front of the Kop in August, 1997, but rebuilding work at that end of the ground meant there were no supporters in one of the most famous stands in world football and no City fans there to see it. Matt Elliott had earlier put Leicester in front after just 72 seconds and with seven minutes left, Fenton tapped home number two after goalkeeper David James had failed to hang onto Emile Heskey's shot. Paul Ince rifled home a late goal for the Reds that came too late to prevent City starting their Premier League campaign with back-to-back wins. That was about as good as it got for Fenton, a £1.1 million signing from Blackburn Rovers. He netted only four more goals for City before leaving for Walsall.

FIRST REPLACEMENT

Paul Groves was the first City substitute to find the target after stepping off the bench. Groves, a £12,000 signing from Burton Albion where he combined playing with his job as a bricklayer, came on in the penultimate game of the 1987-88 season against Huddersfield Town. He marked the occasion by powering home a header in a 3-0 win as David Pleat's team ended the Division Two season with a flourish. Groves only scored once more for City – a header in the League Cup fourth-round replay at Nottingham Forest the following season – and went on to play for several clubs including Grimsby Town, where he also managed.

FIRST IMPRESSIONS LAST

Steve Thompson also made an immediate impact for City. A signing from Luton Town, he came on at the half-time interval of the clash at Oxford United in October, 1990. After a classy first contribution set City on the attack, Thompson went on to add City's second goal in a 2-1 win with a sparkling finish. He side-stepped a challenge on the edge of the penalty area and sent a curling right-foot shot beyond the goalkeeper's fingertips and into the corner of the net. Thompson went on to make more than 150 appearances for City before leaving for Burnley.

TOP TUNES

For some people, the top songs of 1974 included *Kung Fu Fighting, Seasons In The Sun, Waterloo* and *You Ain't Seen Nothin' Yet*. What do they know? In Leicester, the nightclubs throbbed and the young people danced away their cares to the classic *This Is The Season For Us*, sung by Leicester City's players. It is the number one track on the Filbert Street Blues CD, released by those good folk at Cherry Red Records, that brings together all your favourite City songs on one disc. That's right, all of them. All 19 of them are there for your listening pleasure.

This Is The Season For Us is the best of a bad bunch – not that that's saying much – and the chorus goes like this:

We've got the best crowd in England
They're going to back us all the way, yes!
This is the season for Leicester City
It's Leicester, Leicester all the way

Two decades later, an ever-so-slightly funkier version of the tune was released and there are plenty of other priceless gems on the CD. The FNF rap appeared at the height of Family Night Football's popularity when the club encouraged young families to attend reserve-team matches. The rap included the lines:

Filbert Fox the rapper
Looking rather dapper
City's leading clapper

All spat out by someone who wants to sound like Vanilla Ice, who had a number one hit in the 1980s and then almost got punched by former Leicester striker Stan Collymore when they were chucked together in the *Celebrity Big Brother* house on Channel Four's reality television show. Elsewhere on the CD, there's a song Oh Leicester City (calypso) by a group called The Back Five that is truly appalling, while Kev Price and the City Strikers aim straight for the heart with their non-hit Flowing Tears (Wembley 1993). If you think losing the play-off final against Swindon Town made you feel bad, wait until you hear that. The final track on the CD is *We're Back Where We Belong*, a tune that definitely belongs in the bargain bin.

DARK DAYS & DAVIES

The Jimmy Bloomfield era was followed by the Frank McLintock error. As a player, McLintock made 200 appearances for Leicester, appeared in the FA Cup Finals in 1961 and 1963 and then left for Arsenal for an £80,000 fee that was a record sum paid for a City player. It proved to be money well spent. McLintock was named Footballer of the Year in 1971 after helping the Gunners to the league and FA Cup double and he was awarded a CBE. So, he was regarded as something of a returning hero when appointed Leicester manager in the summer of 1977. Not for long he wasn't. His reaction to an early-season slump was to sell Frank Worthington and City fans watched their former idol go on to top the Division One scoring charts with Bolton Wanderers. As City headed for the drop, McLintock considered re-registering himself as a player and then wasted a club record £250,000 on former Derby County striker Roger Davies before deciding to walk the plank in April, 1978. City were relegated after netting just 26 goals – a record low for a 42-league game season until Stoke City scored 24 in 1984-85.

MATT FINISH

Matt Gillies was a rather more successful player turned manager. He made 103 appearances and scored eight goals before masterminding one of City's most successful spells in their history. In his decade in charge, City reached two FA Cup Finals, lifted the League Cup and had an unbroken spell in the top division.

NOT KELLY'S HEROES

Robert Kelly made 27 appearances for City – netting one memorable goal against Manchester United – and went on to manage the club in January, 2006. He had been assistant to Craig Levein and following his departure, Kelly steered City to Championship safety. But the Foxes were in relegation trouble again in April, 2007 when Kelly was sacked.

DOWN

Arthur Lochhead is another former player who took on the manager's job. Nine years after his playing debut, he became boss, but couldn't keep City in the First Division. Leicester finished seventh the following season and a boardroom bust-up led to Lochhead's departure early in 1936-37.

WHO NEEDS MONEY?

All the talk before the 1997 Coca Cola Cup Final at Wembley was about Middlesbrough's big-money foreign imports Juninho, Ravenelli and Emerson. Hardly a column inch was devoted to Leicester City and they were deserving of plenty. Martin O'Neill had worked wonders in taking City to their first major domestic final since the 1969 FA Cup Final defeat against Manchester City – and he masterminded the revival in quick time.Twelve months to the day before City took on Middlesbrough, Leicester were seventh in the second tier of English football after a win at Crystal Palace and clinging to the hope that a late run of good form could power them into the play-offs. They did just that and victory over Crystal Palace in the play-off final propelled the Foxes into the First Division. City were tipped for relegation and along with defying the bookies, they also claimed wins over Scarborough, York City, Manchester United, Ipswich Town and Wimbledon to get through to the Coca-Cola Cup Final against Middlesbrough and secure the chance to clinch their first piece of silverware since they lifted the League Cup in 1964. The form guide suggested the cup was heading to Teesside. Three weeks before the clash at Wembley, Middlesbrough's Brazilian schemer Juninho had inspired his side to a 3-1 win in the Premier League at Filbert Street. O'Neill, of course, was determined that there would be no repeat in the cup final – even if it meant Pontus Kaamark faced a moral dilemma. Kaamark was handed the job of man marking Juninho. A stylish player with caps for Sweden, Pontus admitted afterwards that he didn't feel that comfortable in the role of enforcer, but it didn't stop him doing a good job. Within a few minutes of the opening whistle, Juninho had felt Kaamark's boot and the shackles remained fastened until the final whistle. The sun shone on the 76,757 crowd and they saw City striker Emile Heskey and Fabrizio Ravanelli both hit the woodwork. The scoreline remained blank after 90 minutes and the deadlock was finally broken in the 95th minute when Boro's former Derby County striker Ravanelli smacked his shot past City goalkeeper Kasey Keller to put the favourites on course to lift their first major trophy. City had other ideas, of course. They piled on the pressure and with just three minutes left in extra time, there was a massive scramble in the Boro penalty area and Heskey was on hand to force the ball home to earn a replay…

BORO BASHERS

So we all headed off to Hillsborough 10 days later for the replay… In their two Premier League games played since the draw at Wembley, City had fought out a 1-1 draw at Everton and lost 2-0 at Arsenal and that form wasn't enough to make anyone change their minds about who was going to win the Coca-Cola Cup when Leicester and Middlesbrough clashed again. As with the first meeting, Boro were the favourites and darlings of the national media and as before, there wasn't much between the sides in front of a crowd of 39,428. A City defence superbly marshalled by skipper Steve Walsh denied Middlesbrough many sights of goal and Leicester didn't give Boro keeper Ben Roberts many anxious moments in a goalless 90 minutes. The final went into extra time and City made the breakthrough with 100 minutes on the clock. Garry Parker's free kick from the left picked out Walsh at the far post and he sent his header back across goal. Steve Claridge, his socks down by his ankles as always, squeezed between two 'Boro defenders and got on top of the ball to steer his right-foot shot beyond Roberts' fingertips and into the corner of the net. Middlesbrough's fans behind the goal sat in stunned silence while the blue half of Hillsborough erupted and within 60 seconds of Claridge finding the target came the moment that broke Boro hearts. Emerson was sent racing clear with just Kasey Keller to beat and City's goalkeeper raced from his line to block the Brazilian's shot. Leicester fans chanted: "USA" at ear-splitting volume in tribute and Keller admitted afterwards that he almost shed a tear when he heard that. After that, Boro's expensively assembled, cosmopolitan strikeforce seldom looked likely to grab an equaliser as Walsh marshalled Leicester's defence superbly. Claridge, the hero in the dramatic play-off final win over Crystal Palace 11 months earlier, was substituted to a standing ovation and the final whistle was blown three minutes later. Walsh was named Man of the Match and became the first City skipper for 33 years to get his hands on a major knockout trophy when he lifted the Coca-Cola Cup aloft to the acclaim of the wildly rejoicing Leicester fans. The victory also secured Leicester's first venture into European competition for more than three decades and completed an astonishing turnaround for the club under the leadership of manager Martin O'Neill. Ironically, Boro's line-up in both finals included future City boss Nigel Pearson.

TO THE RESCUE

The combined talents of Frank Worthington, Keith Weller and Steve Whitworth couldn't keep Leicester City out of the drop zone going into the closing weeks of the 1974-75 season. Foxes boss Jimmy Bloomfield issued an SOS to Chris Garland and in the space of just ten games, the flame-haired hitman became a Leicester legend. In March, Bloomfield went back to former club Chelsea to sign Garland for £95,000 and he repaid the investment with eight goals to help keep City in the top flight. After making his debut in a 2-2 draw at Coventry City, Garland helped Leicester take a point from a clash with Liverpool at Filbert Street and remembered: "That result gave players like Weller and Worthington the confidence to play at their best." Three days later, Garland was the hat-trick hero in the 3-2 win over Wolverhampton Wanderers that took the Foxes out of the bottom three. Garland went on to find the target five times in just three games to fire the Foxes to the brink of top-flight survival. Garland then grabbed five goals in just three games to help Leicester take a huge stride towards securing safety. He was on target in a 2-2 draw at Leeds United and then bagged two goals in both the 3-0 win over West Ham United on April 1st and the 4-0 demolition of Newcastle United that followed four days later to lift City up to 17th in the table. They were 15th after Worthington's goal secured a 1-0 win over Middlesbrough at Filbert Street which was enough to keep City in the top division. Leicester survived despite taking only one point from the final three games of the season and went into the 1975-76 campaign with realistic hopes of qualifying for Europe. They missed out after finishing seventh – despite ending the season with a 2-1 win over Manchester United secured by Garland's winner – and after 63 games and 19 goals for Leicester, he went on to rejoin boyhood heroes Bristol City for a fee of £110,000 in November, 1976 and lead another successful survival fight. Garland was on target four times in three games to help keep the Robins in the First Division and he shrugged off several injuries to continue playing until he had taken his career tally of goals in all competitions to 103 in the 1982-83 season. Garland was revealed to be suffering with Parkinson's disease in 1992 and in 2006, he underwent major brain surgery to help treat the condition. He has chronicled the events of his colourful football career and struggles after that in his book *A Life Of Two Halves*.

FRIENDLIES

Most of the 32,086 fans at the Walkers Stadium on August 8th, 2003 were there to see one man. Three weeks after Ronaldinho joined Barcelona in a £21 million transfer from Paris St. Germain, the Brazilian was lining up against Leicester City in a pre-season friendly. City boss Micky Adams was preparing his side for the start of the Premier League following the previous season's promotion and ten of his summer signings made an appearance – including former England international Les Ferdinand. But the game was really about Ronaldinho, a World Cup winner the previous summer and regarded as one of the best players on the planet. He had snubbed a possible move to Manchester United to join the Spanish giants and had a starring role in Barca's 1-0 win at Leicester that was watched by Gary Lineker, who played for both clubs. City made them battle hard for victory. After Leicester goalkeeper Ian Walker denied Ronaldinho an early opener, Barcelona were reduced to ten men. Phillip Cocu was given his marching orders in the 20th minute for hacking down Craig Hignett, but Barcelona led at the break through Javier Saviola's sweetly-struck goal following good work from Ronaldinho. He was given a standing ovation when he was substituted after 61 minutes.

TOP SCOTS

City celebrated their centenary with a friendly against Aberdeen at Filbert Street in August, 1984. Alex Ferguson had made Aberdeen the leading force in Scottish football – leading them to the European Cup Winners' Cup in 1982-83 – and they held Leicester to a 1-1 draw. Steve Lynex got City's goal from the penalty spot.

NOT ALWAYS

Friendlies aren't always very friendly. Five days before the centenary match against Aberdeen, Ian Wilson was sent off in City's 2-2 draw against Rangers at Ibrox.

AGAINST GERMAN FRIENDS?

David Lowe suffered a shattered cheekbone in another less than friendly pre-season warm up. He made a £200,000 move from Ipswich Town in the summer of 1992 and the striker was then ruled out of the start of the following season after being injured in the clash against German side Borussia Monchengladbach at Filbert Street. Brian Little's side were beaten 3-1.

FOREIGN LEGION

Leicester City boss Tom Mather thought Frank Soo was a Foxes player – and got a shock when he looked at Port Vale's team sheet! Soo, the first player of Chinese extraction to play in the Football League, was a high-profile signing for City when he joined in September, 1945 after 12 years at Stoke City alongside Stanley Matthews. A regular for England in Wartime and Victory fixtures, he cost City a fee of £4,600 at the start of the first post-war campaign – and his midfield skills soon made an impression before the event that led to his departure from Filbert Street. Soo played as a guest for Port Vale in a fixture on Christmas Eve, 1945 without gaining City's permission and was immediately placed on the transfer list by Foxes boss Mather.The dispute led to Soo leaving City for Luton Town at the end of the season for £3,000 after just 16 appearances for Leicester and three goals.

NICE ONE THEO

Greece stunned world football when they won the European championships in 2004 – and holding aloft the trophy at the end of it all was a former City player. Theo Zagorakis led his country to victory in Portugal four years after leaving City. He came to Filbert Street in February, 1998 for a fee of £250,000 with an impressive CV having been named Greece's Player of the Year in 1997 and helped PAOK dump Arsenal out of the UEFA Cup. Zagorakis, a stylish midfielder, made his debut as a substitute against Leeds United in February, 1998 and went on to make 68 appearances for the Foxes before returning to Greece with AEK in the summer of 2000.

PONTUS MADE HIS MARK

Pontus Kaamark had already made his mark in world football before he joined City from Swedish club IFK Gothenburg for £840,000 in September, 1995. He was a regular in the Swedish national team and had been a part of the squad that finished third in the 1994 World Cup. Kaamark didn't have the best of luck with injuries early in his Leicester career and put that behind him to become a crowd favourite. He played a key role in City's Coca-Cola Cup triumph in 1997 with his shackling of Middlesbrough's Brazilian playmaker Juninho.

MISSED THE BUS

Leicester Fosse took to the pitch for the start of the 1892-93 season without their goalkeeper! After Jimmy Thraves missed the bus to the season's opener at Mansfield Town; three goals flew past stand-in Kiddy Lowe before he got there. After Thraves arrived, Lowe went on to score Fosse's goal in a 4-1 defeat. Thraves made it in time for the start of the next match at Rotherham and was kept busy as Fosse were hammered 6-1.

LATE

In December, 1907, Fosse striker Fred Shinton turned up half an hour late for the game at Barnsley after his train was delayed. Fosse were still 3-1 winners in the Division Two clash.

TEAM ON THE RUN!

There was a mix up before Leicester City's clash at Crystal Palace in September, 1922. A London charabanc driver delivered the team to the Crystal Palace believing the team were competitors in a band festival! He managed to get them to Selhurst Park just in time for kick-off and all the upheaval didn't bother the team. They were 1-0 winners through a goal from Dennis Jones.

OH, SWEET LORD

At least the above all made it to the game. George Harrison missed his farewell match for Leicester Fosse! He missed the train to what was set to be his last game in Fosse colours at Bradford Park Avenue on October 16th, 1915. A friend of a Fosse player, named Cope, ended up playing after going along to watch and Leicester won 2-1.

THAT'S NOT THE TICKET

Billy Dorrell suffered a similar fate. He made a popular return to Leicester Fosse from Aston Villa in the 1895-96 season and marked his first appearance back with a goal in the 5-0 thumping of Burslem Port Vale. He then helped Fosse to a 2-0 win at Burton Swifts before missing his train for the home date with Rotherham Town. He must have had mixed emotions when he learned Fosse had won 8-0 without him, but he was back in the side for the next match.

WHO'S THE DADDY?

Matt Elliott had other things on his mind, but it didn't show. Elliott's wife took her place among the crowd at Wembley for the Worthington Cup Final between Leicester City and Tranmere Rovers on February 27th, 2000 despite expecting to give birth to the couple's fourth child that very day! He put that behind him to power City to victory in a historic match. Leicester's 2-1 win meant they lifted the first major trophy of the new millennium and also won the last League Cup Final to be held at the old Wembley. City had become quite used to playing at the old place – this was their seventh trip to the Twin Towers in nine years – and Elliott was the two-goal hero against a Tranmere side led by former Foxes striker David Kelly and containing the throw-in launcher David Challinor. However, it was City who took the lead from a set piece. In the 29th minute, Guppy swung over a corner that Elliott headed home while Muzzy Izzet missed the chance to double the lead when he shot wide from a good position on the hour. Tranmere were dealt a massive blow three minutes later when defender Clint Hill was red carded after clattering into City striker Emile Heskey on the edge of the penalty area. As often happens, the dismissal fired up the side reduced in numbers and Rovers were level in the 77th minute. Kelly latched on to a flick on and steered his shot into the City net. But the sides were on level terms for just three minutes.

Elliott was on target for City again with another header from a Guppy corner and, unsurprisingly, his two goals earned him the man-of-the-match award at the final whistle. He had more to celebrate a few days later when his wife gave birth. Elliott had also been on target in the semi-final victory over Aston Villa. He had been pushed into the forward line after Martin O'Neill's side were hit by injuries and came up with the only goal of the two-legged affair with City's Midlands rivals. The first leg at Villa Park ended goalless and that prompted the home side's manager John Gregory to make some ungracious comments about Leicester not crossing the halfway line. He was gleefully reminded of those remarks by City fans after Elliott's header in the second leg at Filbert Street hit the back of the net to send Leicester back to Wembley for a third League Cup Final in four years.

HANGING AROUND

Sep Smith is in Leicester City's record books for having the longest first-team career with the club. He made his debut on August 31st, 1929 and his last game came 19 years and 249 days later on April 14th, 1949. In between those dates, Smith made an astonishing 586 appearances – ranking him second in the club's list of highest appearance makers behind Graham Cross on 599 – and ensured that City fans of a certain vintage got all misty eyed when he walked onto the Filbert Street pitch after the final game there against Tottenham Hotspur in May, 2002. Smith was the seventh of seven brothers from Whitburn, County Durham – Tom also played for City – and the 1934 FA Cup semi-final against Portsmouth at St. Andrew's brought him face to face with brothers Willie and Jack. Pompey clinched a trip to Wembley with a 4-1 victory. Sep had been spotted by City's scouts while playing in a North versus South schoolboy trial match at Filbert Street in March, 1926 and Foxes boss Willie Orr soon moved to sign the promising teenager. He made his debut rather prematurely as a 17-year-old with the local press reporting that he was "unable to pull his weight" when he took his place in the forward line in the absence of the ill Arthur Lochhead in the 3-2 defeat at Huddersfield Town on the opening day of the 1929-30 season. Smith, top scorer for the reserves in 1930-31 with 19 goals, went on to blossom in a deeper, right-half role in the 1930s that was better suited to his distributive skills and it was a surprise that he was rewarded with only one cap for England – as a second-half substitute against Scotland in the Jubilee international in 1935. He won the Second Division with City in 1937 and there were those who hoped he would be called up to replace the injured Don Revie for the Foxes' first appearance in the FA Cup Final in 1949. Instead, he missed out in the reshuffle and made his final appearance for City seven days later in the 1-1 draw at Cardiff City that ensured Leicester maintained their record of never having played outside the top two divisions in English football. Smith was still at Filbert Street at the start of the following season as coach and a testimonial fund raised him £2,100. The departure of boss Johnny Duncan and arrival of Norman Bullock in December, 1949 led to Smith's departure from the club.

MILAN IS A LEICESTER FAN

Milan Mandaric completed his takeover of Leicester City in February, 2007 – and the club's fans celebrated. Mandaric had turned Portsmouth from second-tier strugglers into a Premier League force and planned a similar revolution at the Walkers Stadium. But he had to find the right man to take City to the top – and that wasn't going to be easy. Two months after Mandaric took charge, manager Robert Kelly was on his way out of the Walkers Stadium. Kelly was sacked after a 3-0 defeat at Plymouth Argyle left City hovering just above the Championship drop zone with five games left and Mandaric turned to former Norwich City boss Nigel Worthington to keep the Foxes up. He did just that thanks to back-to-back wins at Preston North End and Barnsley – and then left the club at the end of the season! Mandaric's search for a new manager took him to MK Dons and Martin Allen. He was appointed in May, 2008 and lasted just three months. During that time, he made an astonishing 16 signings, but it was his insistence that City shouldn't sign Jimmy Floyd Hasselbaink that apparently led to him leaving after just four Championship games in charge. Mandaric was reportedly keen for City to sign the former Chelsea marksman, Allen wasn't. Ironically, Allen's last game in charge brought City's best performance in a season that ended in relegation to the third tier of English football. His team handed out a 4-1 thrashing to Watford at the Walkers Stadium and four days later, Allen left the club by mutual consent. Gary Megson then became City's fourth manager in Mandaric's seven months at the helm when he took on the job in September, 2007. Megson had been out of management since leaving City's East Midlands rivals Nottingham Forest 19 months earlier – and stayed at Leicester for just 41 days! He took charge of nine games in the Championship and then left to take on the manager's job at Premier League side Bolton Wanderers, much to the dismay of Mandaric and City's supporters. Mandaric went on to appoint Ian Holloway as manager. He made the move from Plymouth Argyle and ended up going into City's history books for all the wrong reasons. Holloway was at the helm when the Foxes suffered the drop into the third tier of English football for the first time in their history following a goalless draw at Stoke City in May, 2008. Holloway was sacked and Nigel Pearson took on the manager's job…

THE LATE, LATE SHOW

If you want drama, read on… Leicester City's promotion hopes – and possibly manager Nigel Pearson's job – hung by a thread on the final day off the 2012-13 season. A poor run of form meant that a play-off place was the best City could hope for after being among the Championship's pacesetters earlier in the season and with just 90 minutes left, even that looked unlikely. To have any chance, Leicester had to win at Nottingham Forest – and they hadn't won a league match there for 31 years. Even then, if Bolton beat

Blackpool, it wouldn't be enough. Forest also had to win to have any chance of a play-off place and with the game locked at 2-2 entering injury time, both City and Forest looked set to miss out. With just seconds left on the clock, Anthony Knockaert, excitably dubbed "the French Lionel Messi of the Championship" by French television following a spectacular goal double at Huddersfield Town, polished off a City counter attack by rolling the ball into an empty net in front of the delirious travelling support to win the match and snatch sixth spot. City would meet Watford in the two-legged play-off semi-finals – and the amateur psychologists fancied Leicester to go through. Watford had missed out on automatic promotion after losing 2-1 at home to Leeds on the final day, while City's last-gasp heroics at Forest sent them into the play-offs in more buoyant mood. David Nugent's header at the King Power Stadium meant City headed down the M1 to Vicarage Road for the second leg with a 1-0 lead. That was wiped out after 15 minutes by Matej Vydra's strike, but within four minutes Nugent was on target again to restore City's aggregate lead. Vydra tied things up again after the break and with the match six minutes into injury time and surely just seconds away from extra time, Knockaert took a tumble in the area, the referee pointed to the penalty spot and Wembley was just a kick away. Knockaert sent keeper Manuel Almunia the wrong with his penalty, but somehow still blocked it, then smothered the Frenchman's attempt to force home the rebound. Watford cleared, counter attacked at a million-miles-per-hour and just 20 seconds after Knockaert's penalty was saved, Troy Deeney lashed an unstoppable shot past Kasper Schmeichel and Leicester hearts were broken. Knockaert was still agonising over his penalty miss at the other end of the pitch when the ball hit the back of the net.

SOUSA AND SVEN

"Lock up your mothers!" The cry went around Leicester in October, 2010 after the most unlikely playboy in football, Sven-Goran Eriksson, became surely the highest profile manager in the club's history. Eriksson had previously been in charge up the road at moneybags Notts County and before that, led England to the quarter-finals of the World Cup in both 2002 and 2006. If the England manager's job is the toughest job in football, being Leicester boss can't be far behind. Eriksson was the club's 15th manager in six years and his predecessor lasted just nine games. That was how long it took the club's owners to realise that if Paulo Sousa was going to take City out of the Championship it would be via the trapdoor rather than the play-offs. City turned to Sousa after Nigel Pearson's shock exit to Hull City and his job application made impressive reading. As a player, Sousa represented Portugal at the World Cup and had twice been a Champions League winner with Juventus and Borussia Dortmund. As a manager, he took Swansea City to their highest league placing for 27 years – seventh in the Championship – and that convinced the Leicester owner that Sousa was the right man for the job. He inherited a squad that Pearson had taken into the play-offs the previous season, but just 45 minutes into his reign as Leicester boss, Sousa's new team were 3-0 down at sunny Selhurst Park to Crystal Palace. Goals from Andy King and DJ Campbell pegged it back to 3-2, but the game was lost and after nine games, Leicester had just one win and were bottom of the Championship. Sousa was sacked following a 4-3 defeat at Norwich City after less than three months in charge and the tabloid tittle-tattle that followed linked Eriksson with the job. Eriksson had walked away from Notts County after discovering their backers weren't as wealthy as they had made out and set about lifting Leicester off the foot of the Championship. As David Pleat had done two decades earlier, Erikkson used his connections to bring in top-flight quality on loan – Yakubu, Kyle Naughton and Curtis Davies all joined – and took Leicester to 10th in the table. He invested heavily before the 2011-12 season kicked off – Matt Mills arrived for £5 million from Reading – but a 3-0 defeat at home to Millwall in October that left City adrift of the Championship pacesetters was his last game in charge. Who would they find to replace him...?

ANYONE ORDER PIZZA?

Chances are you had forgotten – or were trying to forget – all about Yann Kermorgant until you read his name just then. His 'Pizza Hut' moment in the play-off semi-final against Cardiff City in May, 2010 ended Leicester City's chances of reaching the Premier League and ended Nigel Pearson's quiet revolution. Pearson had found Leicester at their lowest point. He took on the manager's job in the summer of 2008 after City had been relegated to the third tier in English football for the first time in their history. Pearson left Southampton to take on the job and introduced himself to the local press as a rather monosyllabic, no-nonsense straight talker. Presumably, he is the same with his players. Whatever his methods, they work. To the amusement of City fans, Nottingham Forest had previously found it a struggle to escape League One, but Leicester made their stay more temporary. The title was wrapped up with two games to spare by a 2-0 win at Southend United and City ended the season with a 3-0 win at Crewe Alexandra that was a club record 14th away league win.

Leicester finished the season with a massive 96 points and Matty Fryatt was the club's top scorer with a mighty 32-goal haul. The Championship, of course, would be tougher, but the Foxes were beaten only once in their opening eight games. They avenged a 5-1 thumping at Forest with a 3-0 win in the return fixture and went into the end-of-season play-offs as the form team after securing a top-six spot with five straight wins. Their play-off opponents were Cardiff and they took a 1-0 lead into the second leg in Wales after a Peter Whittingham goal separated the sides at the Walkers Stadium. Leicester looked sure to miss out after Cardiff took the lead in the second leg, but goals by Fryatt, an own goal and Andy King took City into a 3-2 lead on aggregate. Cardiff bagged a second goal on the night to force extra time and after no further goals, the match went to a penalty shoot-out. At 4-3 behind, Kermorgant stepped up to take City's fifth spot kick needing to score. The French midfielder tried one of those audacious chips that when they work, make the scorer look like a genius. But it didn't work. His effort was saved one-handed by the grounded goalkeeper and City were beaten. Kermogant's penalty became the subject of YouTube tributes including a song and he left the club during the summer.

JULIAN

Firstly, the myths... Julian Joachim didn't live with Iwan Roberts in a Leicester council flat as the song had it and he was not, is not and never will be Brazilian. He was born and raised in Boston, Lincolnshire. He just played football like a Brazilian sometimes. The Brazilian myth really started in Barnsley on a chilly January night. The BBC cameras were there to see Joachim, playing for City in an FA Cup third-round replay, zig zag his way in from the touchline, then when the goal was within his range, bend a right-foot shot into the top corner. The BBC named it their goal of the month and if you look at the DVD of City's best-ever goals you will see a few more just like it. They start with Joachim receiving the ball around the halfway line, looking up, finding a gap to accelerate into, then setting off with his chest out, legs whirring before he belts an unstoppable shot past some hapless goalkeeper or other. He almost uprooted the goalposts with a thunderbolt against Millwall at Filbert Street, but perhaps his finest solo effort was against Portsmouth in the play-off semi-finals at the City Ground in 1993. He did all of the above – got the ball on the halfway line, raced away from defenders at a million-miles-per-hour – but rather than wallop home emphatically, he provided a cheeky finishing touch by poking the ball through the goalkeeper's legs. "They told me he was quick," said Portsmouth skipper Andy Awford afterwards, "but not that quick." Everyone with Leicester City in their heart feared Joachim would leave like Gary Lineker, Alan Smith and Gary McAllister before him, but he stuck around to play in the Premier League and grabbed a memorable double against Ossie Ardiles' exciting, but vulnerable Tottenham Hotspur to have the optimists dreaming of Europe. But with relegation looking more likely, Joachim followed Brian Little (boo!) to Aston Villa (hiss) and despite his lack of inches he once popped up with a header in the dying moments to deny his former club victory at Villa Park. Leicester – and its betting shops – remained in Joachim's thoughts and when he fell out of favour at Coventry he issued one of those come-and-get-me pleas via the sports pages of the *Leicester Mercury*. Nothing came of it and instead the latter part of his career was spent drifting between clubs such as Walsall, Darlington and Boston United where he formed a high-profile, but disappointing partnership with Noel Whelan.

BEATING FOREST

Years of rivalry, jealousy and loads of other unpleasant stuff was forgotten at Nottingham Forest's City Ground in September, 2008. The draw for the second round of the Carling Cup sent Leicester City to their East Midlands rivals and Forest led at the break. But the game had to be abandoned during the half-time interval after City defender Clive Clarke suffered a suspected heart attack in the changing room and was rushed to hospital. Clarke, who was on loan from Sunderland, made a full recovery, but still had to retire from football. Three weeks later, the sides met again in the rearranged fixture and Gary Megson's Leicester earned headlines across the world for their gesture of goodwill at kick-off. Megson was taking charge of just his second game following the departure of previous boss Martin Allen – and the former Forest boss decided to gift the home side the lead inside the opening 20 seconds. City allowed Forest goalkeeper Paul Smith to walk the ball into the net unopposed to hand the home side back the advantage they had held when the first game had to be called off. Both sets of supporters applauded the gesture and Megson said: "We just thought it was the right thing to do. The first game ended in tragic circumstances with Clive's heart attack, but the rules say that Forest would have been perfectly entitled to play out the game." Alan Sheehan cancelled out Forest's early opener with a free kick, but Forest went back in front and looked to be heading through to the third round with just two minutes left. Richard Stearman scrambled home an equaliser for City and with just seconds left on the clock, Mark De Vries laid the ball off for Foxes captain Stephen Clemence to curl home a dramatic last-gasp winner that capped a memorable night. City fans celebrated their first win at Forest for 36 years, but it was the team's sporting gesture that made all the headlines. Paul Grant of BBC Nottingham wrote: "Football and its administrators, coaches and players can still be galvanised in the face of adversity and follow the path of decency. That both clubs were, at different times, willing to jeopardise the promise of money, prestige and local bragging rights in favour of common courtesy and camaraderie on the field speaks volumes about the value of sportsmanship in a sport which many see as having suffered a moral degeneration in recent years." Leicester and Forest still don't like each other much, though.

SUPER STAN

Stan Collymore stuck up three fingers at the Filbert Street press box. He was really sticking up two fingers at them. Collymore was already a tabloid target for his outspoken comments and tumultuous relationships before he joined Leicester City in February, 2000 and the reporters from the red tops were soon writing about him again. Collymore, who had become Britain's most expensive footballer when he joined Liverpool from Nottingham Forest for £8.5 million in the summer of 1995, made his City debut in a 1-1 draw at

Watford and then headed off to La Manga with the rest of his new team-mates for a four-day break that didn't last four days. City were booted out after a bar-room rumpus that included the new star striker setting off a fire extinguisher. Collymore's rather daft prank was seized upon by the tabloids and splashed all over the front pages, so it was a fired-up Stan that made his home debut for City against Sunderland. City paraded the Worthington Cup won seven days earlier before the game and then Collymore paraded his talents. He opened the scoring with a thumping right-foot shot after latching onto Emile Heskey's header and then Heskey doubled the lead after taking Neil Lennon's pass in his stride and bursting through two defenders to net. Kevin Phillips halved the lead just after the break and Collymore made it 3-1 with a perfectly-directed header from Lennon's cross. Sunderland were back in it through Niall Quinn's goal, but the destiny of the points was settled when Stef Oakes sent Heskey racing away down the right flank and his cross was tapped home by the unmarked Collymore. Collymore held three fingers aloft to all four corners of the ground – and made sure the Press Box got the message. Oakes added a fifth in the dying moments. City fans thought their team had one of the best front pairings in the Premier League and they had – but only for five days. The Collymore-Heskey partnership was broken when Heskey joined Liverpool for £11 million. Collymore suffered a broken leg at Derby County the following month and by the start of the 2000-01 season, he thought he had recovered. New boss Peter Taylor disagreed and there followed a transfer request, a fine for missing training and a bust-up with team-mate Trevor Benjamin during the half-time interval of a reserve-team game against Charlton Athletic.After just 12 appearances and five goals, Collymore was on his way to Bradford City, then Spain and then retirement.

IS THERE ANYBODY THERE?

The smallest crowd ever recorded at a Football League match were there to watch Leicester City. All 13 of them! That was the attendance recorded for City's match at Stockport County on May 7, 1921, but the figure is misleading. Stockport's Edgeley Park ground had been closed by the FA and that meant the final game of the season had to be hastily switched to be played at Old Trafford as part of a double header. The game kicked off at 6.30pm after the Division One match between Manchester United and Derby County and the figure of 13 represents the number of supporters who went through the turnstiles after the United game and before City's match kicked off and so did not take the opportunity to watch both games. It is estimated there were between 1,000 and 2,000 supporters there when Leicester and already-relegated Stockport battled out a goalless draw five days after the sides drew 0-0 at Filbert Street. Ironically, during the same season, City set a new record for their highest attendance at Filbert Street. A crowd of 29,149 squeezed into the ground to watch Leicester take on Burnley in the first round of the FA Cup – bettering the previous highest mark of 23,109 set when Manchester City were the visitors in the FA Cup. Burnley were the biggest draw in English football when they were paired with City. They were top of Division One and were in the middle of a record-breaking 30-game unbeaten run that helped take them to the championship. Burnley had too much firepower for City and stormed to a 7-3 win. Tom Smith, John Roxburgh and Jock Paterson were on target for the outgunned Foxes. The biggest crowd ever to attend Filbert Street was a staggering 47,298. That was the attendance for the FA Cup fifth-round tie with Tottenham Hotspurs in February, 1928 that ended in a 3-0 defeat for City. The capacity had been increased earlier that season when the Double Decker was built and the attendance figure for the Spurs match does not include the hundreds who forced their way into the ground via the directors' entrance and those who sat on the roof of the Filbert Street stand!

FA CUP AGONIES

Mention Harlow Town to Leicester City supporters of a certain age and they won't thank you for it. The draw for the third round of the FA Cup in 1979-80 handed Jock Wallace's team a home date with the Isthmian League underdogs and City, fourth in Division Two and heading for promotion to the top flight, were straight onto the attack at the opening whistle. They had to wait until the 27th minute for Martin Henderson to open the scoring – slamming home from 12 yards – but the expected goal glut did not materialise. Leicester had a penalty appeal turned down, Alan Young went close with a couple of headers and more chances were missed before the non-leaguers punished City for their waywardness in front of goal by converting their only opening of a one-sided match. Neil Prosser was on target in injury time to send the game to a replay at the tiny Hammerskjold Stadium in Essex and on an utterly forgettable night for the Foxes, accountant John Mackenzie got the only goal of the game for Harlow. The following season, City were on the wrong end of another FA Cup humbling. After a 3-0 win over Cardiff City at Filbert Street in the third round, City were handed a home date with Exeter City from the third tier. Wallace's top-flight team were held to a 1-1 draw – Martin Henderson on target for City – and then crashed out on a murky night at St James Park. Tony Kellow put the Grecians ahead and Jim Melrose ensured the scores were level at the break by following up to score after Kevin MacDonald's shot was blocked. Exeter went back in front through Kellow's spot kick that was awarded following a foul by City defender Larry May that looked to have been committed outside the penalty area. Kellow completed the scoring – and his hat trick – to put City ahead. Leicester's response to that defeat at Exeter was impressive. Three days after defeat at Exeter, they were 2-1 winners at Liverpool to end the Reds' 85-match unbeaten run in front of their home supporters. City's FA Cup fortunes improved as well. They reached the semi-finals the following season before bowing out to Tottenham Hotspurs.

WHAT A MATCH

The FA Cup tie between Leicester Fosse and Tottenham Hotspur at Filbert Street on January 10, 1914 brought together two sides battling against the drop. Fosse were in trouble at the muddy end of Division Two following a run of four straight defeats during which they scored only once, while Spurs were trying to claw themselves away from the bottom of the top flight. So the FA Cup clash gave them the chance to forget about all that. They forget to defend as well – not that any of the crowd of 9,454 were complaining at the final whistle. The game went ahead in muddy conditions and the sides shared four goals in a breathless opening 21 minutes. Within a minute, Fosse had struck the woodwork and Fred Mortimer put them ahead with seven minutes gone. Claude Stoodley capitalised on a slip by Bobby Steel to double the lead on 12 minutes and the visitors delighted the several hundred fans who had followed their team by levelling. Fanny Walden followed up to net after Fosse goalkeeper Herbert Bown blocked his penalty and the scores were level when Jimmy Cantrell found the target. Incredibly, Spurs then went ahead 3-2 through a goal from Bert Bliss, but Stoodley ensured the scores were level at the break by netting after a mistake by the visitors' goalkeeper Arthur King. Stoodley completed his hat-trick six minutes after the break to put Fosse 4-3 ahead and he looked to have put the game beyond Spurs when he added another with just ten minutes remaining. An injury to Teddy King was a devastating blow to Fosse, however, and proved to be the final turning point. In the closing minutes of the game, Spurs threw everything into a late onslaught on Fosse's goal and went on to level the scores at 5-5 and force a replay. Billy Minter trimmed the gap on 82 minutes before the leveller came from Bliss in the dying moments. Fosse's hopes of reaching the quarter-finals were gone. They were beaten 2-0 in the replay and they then lost a couple of their most influential players. Spurs were so impressed by the performances of Tommy Clay and Harry Sparrow in the two games that they signed both players. Fosse continued their battle against the drop without them and avoided the embarrassment of having to apply for re-election. But only just. They finished out of the bottom two on goal difference with a 2-0 win over relegation rivals Lincoln City proving crucial.

LOCAL HERO

1966 was all about Geoff Hurst, a Russian linesman and some people on the pitch who thought it was all over. David Nish had a pretty good year as well. He was called up by England youth, helped Leicestershire win the FA County Youth Cup and got his hands on the County Cup with Measham Social Welfare. On top of all that, he also made his breakthrough with Leicester City in their top-flight campaign. All this and he was still only 18 years old. Nish marked his first-team debut with a goal in a 4-2 thumping of Stoke City at Filbert Street in December, 1966 and his opportunity for City may have come even sooner had he not decided to complete his studies at Ashby Grammar. When he did get his chance, Nish proved to be a versatile player. Nish was a creative midfielder, then a defensive wing back and finally an attacking left back. Wherever he played, he showed a coolness that made him an inspiration to others and Nish became the youngest-ever captain of an FA Cup Final team when he led the team out at Wembley in 1969. That ended in a 1-0 defeat against Manchester City and that was followed by the blow of relegation. Although City missed out on an instant return to the top flight – finishing third behind Huddersfield Town and Blackpool – Nish's displays still earned him caps for England under-23s and Football League honours. Nish led the Foxes to the Second Division championship in 1970-71 and was an ever present the following season. He made 42 appearances as City marked their return to the top flight by finishing 12th and among the teams above them were champions Derby County. They had obviously admired Nish's performances for City and after just four games of the 1972-73 season, the Rams made Leicester an offer they couldn't refuse. Derby boss Brian Clough bid a then British record fee of £225,000 and so after 272 mostly faultless appearances for Leicester and 31 goals, Nish went and spoiled it all by joining City's arch rivals. It was a good move for him. Nish went on to win five full England caps – playing alongside Leicester players Frank Worthington and Keith Weller in games against Northern Ireland and Scotland in 1974 – and helped the Rams win the First Division championship in 1974-75. He suffered a knee injury that led to his retirement following a spell in America and Nish went on to rejoin City's Academy as a coach.

REMEMBER FNF?

These days, reserve-team games are watched by a handful of managers, scouts and obsessive supporters with way too much time on their hands. But there was a time when Leicester City reserve team matches were all about screaming kids, face painting and dancing girls. The visits of Manchester United and Liverpool reserves would often attract bumper crowds and the introduction of 'Family Night Football' in 1994 led to Filbert Street being the only place in Leicester to be on a Monday night. 'FNF' was designed to attract families with other attractions outside the ground and at pitch side including jugglers, clowns and dancing girls – and it was a huge success for City. Average crowds were between 5,000 and 6,000 and amid all this razzmatazz, there was some entertaining football to watch on the pitch as well. Robbie Fowler made a shock return from injury at Filbert Street and the Liverpool and England striker was on target from the penalty spot and Lawrie Dudfield inspired City reserves to a thrilling win over a star-studded West Ham United line up that included several internationals. Dudfield was among a crop of players tipped for big things by Family Night Football regulars who never quite made the grade at Filbert Street and another was Guy Branston, an uncompromising centre half with an eye for goal who grew up in Braunstone. Both went on to have Football League careers away from Filbert Street and Dudfield is remembered as something of a hero by Boston United fans for his last-gasp winner in the big Lincolnshire derby against Lincoln City. Talent spotters at 'FNF' would have spotted the early potential of Matt Piper among others, but nobody in the crowd saw the real half-time entertainment when City reserves and Charlton Athletic reserves clashed in October, 2000. Stan Collymore, on the road to recovery after suffering a broken leg in a defeat at Derby County in the Premier League six months earlier, came to blows with team-mate Trevor Benjamin after a row that apparently centred on effort or lack thereof. The story was splashed all over the front page of the following day's *Leicester Mercury* and a few days later, Collymore was on his way out of Filbert Street. After the move to the Walkers Stadium in the summer of 2002, City took their reserve team matches away from Leicester to places such as Kettering Town, Rushden & Diamonds and Hinckley United to protect the pitch and that effectively spelled the end for 'Family Night Football'.

BANKS OF ENGLAND

Geoff Hurst got the hat-trick, the Russian linesman got the blame from the defeated Germans and then there is Leicester City's link to the greatest day in English football. Gordon Banks was between the posts during England's 4-2 win over West Germany in the World Cup Final on July 30, 1966 at Wembley having kept clean sheets all the way to the semi-finals when it took Eusebio's late penalty for Portugal to finally beat him. 'Banks of England' won 37 of his 73 caps for his country while playing for Leicester. Banks played for City in the FA Cup finals in 1961 and 1963 and also played in the League Cup finals in 1964 and 1965 during Leicester's golden era to more than repay the £7,000 that was paid to Chesterfield for his services in March, 1959 after just 23 senior appearances for the Spireites. Ten months after getting his hands on the Jules Rimet trophy, Banks was on his way out of Filbert Street having made 356 appearances for the Foxes following the emergence of England's next goalkeeping legend. Peter Shilton went on to be City's and England's No 1, while Banks had further success at Stoke City and went on to pull off arguably the greatest save ever seen in the 1970 World Cup in Mexico. Brazilian legend Pele was so convinced his header was going to find its way into England's net that he shouted: "Goal!" Banks had other ideas –scrambling across his goal line to somehow claw the ball over the crossbar to the astonishment of Pele and the watching millions. Two years later, Banks won the League Cup with Stoke City after victory over Chelsea at Wembley. His save from Geoff Hurst's penalty in the semi-final against West Ham United had helped the Potters through and a few months later, his career was over at the age of 34 following a car crash that left him blind in his right eye. Banks has proved to be popular on the after-dinner circuit – particularly in Leicester – and admits he owes his success to missing a bus! He remembered: I couldn't find a team after I left school and I spent my Saturday afternoons going to watch Sheffield United and Sheffield Wednesday. "I missed my bus one week and went over to the local rec to watch the game. I was approached and asked if I wanted a game because one of the team's goalkeepers hadn't turned up. That's how it all started."

WHO IZZET?

Muzzy who? Muzzy Izzet wasn't even a household name in his own household when Leicester City boss Martin O'Neill plucked him from Chelsea reserves in March, 1996. Izzet, who used to clean Dennis Wise's boots at Stamford Bridge, went on to make himself a City legend and play in the semi-finals of the World Cup. His Leicester career got off to the worst possible start, however. Izzet came off the bench in the 2-0 defeat at home to Sheffield United that left City ninth in the table and sparked protests from a section of disgruntled fans. That loss proved to be the turning point and Izzet starred as Leicester won their last four games to reach the play-offs. His header at Watford on the final day wrapped up a fifth place finish and Izzet also had a key role in the dramatic play-off final victory over Crystal Palace. He was upended for the penalty that allowed Garry Parker to level the scores before Steve Claridge netted the winner. That took City back into the Premier League and Izzet and Neil Lennon formed one of the best midfields in the top flight – and the stats back that up. Lennon and Izzet occupied the top two spots in the list of top tacklers in the Premier League put together by those studious fellows at Carling Opta. There was more to Izzet than tackling, though. In more than eight years with City, he was also the creative spark and there were times during the 2003-04 Premier League season under Micky Adams that it seemed Leicester's survival chances depended on Izzet's fitness. Izzet could create a chance and a goal out of nothing and among his 37 goals for City are the thumping volley against Tottenham Hotspur in October, 1998 that helped convince Martin O'Neill to stay at Filbert Street. Better than that was the spectacular bicycle kick at Grimsby Town in November, 2002 that secured maximum points for ten-man City at a rain-lashed Blundell Park. Izzet's form in his Premier League pomp wasn't enough to earn an England call up, so instead he took the chance to represent Turkey. Muzzy qualified through having a Turkish Cypriot father and was a 74th-minute substitute in the 2002 World Cup semi-final defeat against Brazil. Izzet turned down a move to Middlesbrough before leaving City for Birmingham City in the summer of 2004 following relegation from the top flight, but his career was cut short by injury and he retired two years later.

PENALTY KINGS

Martin O'Neill's Leicester City were kings of the penalty shoot-out in 1999-2000. They came out on top in three nerve-jangling shoot-outs in the space of five weeks – and French goalkeeper Pegguy Arpehexad was twice the hero. City met Leeds United in the fourth round of the Worthington Cup in December, 1999 and after two hours, the scoreline was blank and the game went to a shoot-out. Tim Flowers was between the posts for Leicester, but wasn't needed. Leeds sent two penalty attempts wide and City went through 4-2. Their reward was a home draw against Fulham in the last eight and City were on their way out when they trailed 2-0 after 84 minutes. Ian Marshall netted twice and Steve Walsh also scored as the game ended 3-3 after extra time and Pegguy Arphexad was City's hero in the shoot-out. He kept out two penalties and City won 3-0. Seven days later, City were at it again. They faced Arsenal in an FA Cup fourth-round replay at Filbert Street after a goalless draw at Highbury. Tim Flowers denied the Gunners when the sides met again before being replaced by Arphexad and the scoreline remained blank at the end of extra time. The penalty shoot-out lasted an incredible 14 kicks and City went through 6-5 after Arphexad kept out Gilles Grimaldi's penalty. Leicester bowed out in the last 16 at Chelsea after a controversial penalty award in extra time. In the 1991-92 Division One play-off final, Carl Muggleton became one of only a handful of goalkeepers to save a penalty at Wembley. City's keeper was beaten by Mike Newell's first-half spot kick for Blackburn Rovers, but then saved another penalty from the former Leicester striker. Muggleton conceded the penalty by bringing down Mark Atkins and got down to his left to push Newell's shot onto the post. Mark Bunn was the penalty hero when City set a new club record in 2008-09. Bunn, making his second appearance after joining on loan from Blackburn Rovers, saved a penalty from Bristol Rovers striker Craig Disley and City went on to win 1-0 to make it 20 league games unbeaten and break the record set 38 years earlier.

LEICESTER ARE BACK

So often had Leicester City yo-yoed between the top two divisions, there was talk that a picture of The Duke of York would be added to the club badge. That reputation was lost in the decade that followed relegation from the Premier League in 2004. This time City didn't bounce back. They hung around in the Championship and, worse still, even spent a season outside the top two divisions for the first time in the club's history. Nigel Pearson led them out of League One at the first attempt in 2008-09 – winning the division with a whopping 96 points – and the following season, when realistically the best that could be hoped for was consolidation, he took City to the Championship play-offs. City's hopes of a tenth trip to Wembley were ended by Yann Kermorgant's ill-advised penalty at Cardiff City and in the summer, Pearson left for Hull City, claiming the Leicester board didn't show they wanted to keep him. Then he came back after Paulo Sousa and Sven-Goran Eriksson undid much of his good work. Early in the 2012-13 season, Pearson appeared to be under pressure. Newspapers reported his job was on the line and that 'Arry Redknapp was on his way to the King Power Stadium. But you shouldn't believe everything you read in the papers. City stuck with Pearson and they snatched a play-off place again with that tell-your-grandkids win at Nottingham Forest on the last day, only to have their hearts broken at Watford in the semi-finals. In 2013-2014, there would be no need for the play-offs. Records tumbled as, after a decade away, Leicester returned to the Premier League as champions. They set club records for most wins in a season (31), along with most home wins (17), most away wins (14) and most consecutive wins (9). The nine-game winning run started at Loftus Road four days before Christmas when Jamie Vardy's sweetly-struck goal ensured City became the first side to beat table-toppers Queens Park Rangers in front of their home crowd during the season. The run came to an end the following February when Watford managed to escape from Leicester with a draw, but the team's unbeaten run went on. City were unbeaten for 21 games – a club record for the second tier – until Brighton powered to a 4-1 win at the King Power Stadium. Promotion back to the Premier League had been confirmed three days earlier and the title was secured by Lloyd Dyer's long-range screamer at Bolton Wanderers.

LONG IN THE TOOTH

At an age when most footballers have long since hung up their boots, Chris Powell was making his debut for Leicester City. On August 27, 2008, Powell became City's oldest-ever debutant at the age of 38 years 354 days in a League Cup tie at Premier League Fulham that ended in a 3-2 defeat. Six days later, the former England international lined up in a defence at Hartlepool United that also included Luke O'Neill. He was making his City debut at the age of 17 years and 13 days and the Foxes won the Johnstone's Paint Trophy fixture 3-0. Powell's appearance at Fulham makes him the third oldest player to have appeared for City behind goalkeeper Joe Calvert (40 years and 313 days) and Arthur Chandler (39 years and 114 days). Calvert's final appearance came in a 3-1 defeat at Southampton in Division Two on December 13, 1947. He also set a club goalkeeping record by failing to finish five first team and three reserve-team fixtures through injury. Calvert went on to join Watford – and was stretchered off on his debut! Chandler finished his record-breaking Leicester career that spanned more than 15 years in the 2-2 draw against Grimsby Town in a Division One fixture at Filbert Street on April 22, 1935. Unsurprisingly, Chandler is the oldest goalscorer in City's history. He was 39 years and 32 days old when he was on target against Wolverhampton Wanderers on December 29, 1934 in the 3-1 defeat at Filbert Street in a Division One fixture. Tony Cottee is second in the list of the club's oldest goalscorers. He was 34 years and 300 days old when he netted in the 3-0 win over Bradford City in the Premier League at Filbert Street on May 6, 2000. Cottee was a goalscoring legend in two spells with boyhood heroes West Ham United – netting 116 times – and he also played for Everton. But the pint-sized goal poacher had to wait until he joined City from Selangor in Malaysia in August, 1997 to score his first goal at Old Trafford and claim the only winner's medal of an 18-year career. His first goal for the club handed Martin O'Neill's team maximum points against Manchester United and Cottee's five goals helped the Foxes reach the Worthington Cup Final in 1999. Although they were beaten by Tottenham Hotspur, Leicester were back at Wembley for the following season's final and Tony finally picked up a winner's medal after a 2-1 win over Tranmere Rovers.